The Autobiography
of Margot Asquith

The Autobiography
of Margot Asquith

EDITED WITH AN INTRODUCTION
BY MARK BONHAM CARTER

Weidenfeld & Nicolson
LONDON

This edition published in Great Britain in 1995 by
Weidenfeld & Nicolson

The Orion Publishing Group Ltd
Orion House,
5 Upper Saint Martin's Lane,
London WC2H 9EA

THE AUTOBIOGRAPHY OF MARGOT ASQUITH was originally
published in two volumes, Volume I in 1920 and Volume II in 1922. This
one-volume edition, edited and introduced by Mark Bonham Carter, was
published by Eyre and Spottiswoode in 1962.

A catalogue reference is available from the British Library

ISBN 0 297 81602 0

Printed and bound in Great Britain by
Butler & Tanner Ltd, Frome and London

I DEDICATE THIS BOOK TO MY HUSBAND

Contents

WHAT? HAVE YOU NOT RECEIVED POWERS, TO
THE LIMITS OF WHICH YOU WILL BEAR ALL THAT
BEFALLS? HAVE YOU NOT RECEIVED MAGNAN-
IMITY? HAVE YOU NOT RECEIVED COURAGE?
HAVE YOU NOT RECEIVED ENDURANCE?

EPICTETUS

Introduction

by Mark Bonham Carter

The first volume of this autobiography was published in 1920. Margot Asquith was then fifty-eight years old, the wife of the former Prime Minister, H. H. Asquith, and a famous, not to say notorious, figure in her own right. The second volume was published two years later, and appears in this book as Part II. It was succeeded by other volumes of reminiscences which contain memorable passages but which lack the distinction of the Autobiography proper. When it was published the Autobiography caused some embarrassment to her family and friends, and received shocked and critical comment in the press. None the less it won an immediate and widespread success which has been ascribed chiefly to its characteristic indiscretion and to its revelations of high life in society and politics. But this is greatly to underestimate the merits of the book. Written with a rare candour which was certainly spontaneous, it discusses a world of extreme artificiality that has quite disappeared. The prose is vigorous, simple, and yet highly individual, carrying to those who remember her Margot's emphatic tone of voice and giving to those who do not some hint of her personality. More than forty years have passed since it was written, and though what it describes belongs to an age that seems infinitely remote the book itself has improved with the passage of time

This edition is abridged from the original two volumes, and in all I have cut about one-third of the text. In general I have followed the principle that cuts should be large rather than small: only occasionally have sentences been deleted, but where it seemed necessary for reasons of space or relevance I have omitted single incidents as well as whole chapters.

Though she spent the greater part of her life in a world preoccupied with politics, Margot never became a good or perceptive judge of the political scene. It happened to be that in which she found herself, but it was people rather than ideas or issues which engaged her attention. Had fate involved her in the world of the theatre or of art she would have thrown herself into it with equal enthusiasm and perhaps with more discrimination, for she was a woman of great natural taste. But she was absorbed by the conflict of great men, and by the simple issues of victory and defeat which the politics of that time seemed to offer. Because political judgment was not her strongest suit, the bulk of the cuts have been made where Margot is describing the political scene and occur mainly in the second volume. She writes best about events where she was at the centre. I have therefore omitted altogether her account of the Lansdowne Letter, the Maurice Debate and the Epilogue to Volume II which deals with the consequences of the Peace Treaty. What remains is, I hope, a vivid portrait of a most remarkable woman, a unique yet true reflection of her age, which may seem to many who read this book as remote as that of Mme de Sevigné. The life she describes and the assumptions that she makes are separated from our own by a gulf. Yet her book provides a bridge and though it was first published in 1920 Margot lived on in all her vitality until 1945. Her life spanned the gulf, and being a woman her intimate experience of the great world, which was her chosen stage, was far longer than that of any male contemporary. A woman bursts on the world in the glory of youth while men of talent clamber more laboriously up the ladder of fame. A young, attractive, intelligent woman who likes fun and gives it, is welcome in any society, not least English society towards the end of the last century. Nor has the English aristocracy ever been pernickety about absorbing the rich into its system.

Margot liked great men and she wanted those whom she liked to be great. Her memories seem brightly coloured for drabness was something to be avoided at almost any cost. The men she describes are nearly always brilliant and successful – the word failure hardly occurs in the whole chronicle – and the women are beautiful and dashing. No one who knew Margot would claim that she was an accurate witness or pretend that the events she wrote down happened in precisely the way in which she recorded them. Her imagination enlarged the world which she describes, endowing it with some of her own vitality. Her glorious youth, as she calls it, seems triumphant, as it was, and the reader quickly accepts a world largely populated by future Prime Ministers, dukes, peers, god-like figures from the hunting field and magnificent women with rich husbands, supported by a chorus of housekeepers, butlers, footmen, and maids. The two nations of Disraeli still exist in her book. Every parent including her father, Charles Tennant, expects a pretty daughter to marry a rich man and fears that she may marry a groom. Though Margot was not without a social conscience, the poor, who were numerous, remain objects of charity to be elevated by religious instruction, imparted if necessary by their youngers and betters,[1] weaned from drunkenness and generally assisted by philanthropic exercises such as those described in Chapter III, 'Whitechapel and Society'. They talk in funny accents, solemnly transcribed into funny spelling, and follow very closely the stereotypes depicted in the pages of *Punch*. They make only occasional incursions into a story that is mainly concerned with Society.

This, it must be remembered, was a serious expression. Society existed. Margot and her sisters became part of it, and she, together with her fellow Souls, may have given the last thirty years of its life a slight shift of emphasis. The first world war destroyed Society as well as the old Liberal Party. After the war 'Café Society', with which Margot was quite capable of making terms, took over. It spread from America to England where it found in the Duff Coopers its most distinguished members and in Cecil Beaton its most successful publicist. Since the second world war the social life of the rich has become even more incoherent and even less capable of classification. They no longer comprehend within their circle the educated, the civilized or the significant and the Society which might have been influenced by a group like the Souls has totally disappeared in the maelstrom of events. It has been replaced by a series of cliques, having little in common with each other, which are international

---

[1] See Chapter II, the Sunday classes conducted by Margot's sister, Laura, aged sixteen, in the housekeeper's room at Glen for the benefit of the housekeeper, butler and maids.

in character and lacking both the power or the will to influence events.

*   *   *

Margot was the sixth daughter of Sir Charles Tennant and she used to convey the impression that he was an entirely self-made man, somewhat lacking in refinement, who had risen by his own efforts from rags to riches. This was very far from the truth. Margot's great-grandfather founded the family firm and his son, John Tennant, left no less than £1,000,000 when he died in 1878. Though Charles Tennant was doubtless brought up austerely he can never have been in much danger of starvation. Indeed, the rise of the Tennant family, if somewhat spectacular, is typical of many industrial revolution families in Scotland. They came from Ayrshire where they had lived for as long as the records go back. In England they would have been called yeoman farmers, in Scotland bonnet lairds, and their first claim to fame is a close association with Robert Burns. An early John Tennant of Glenconner witnessed Burns' baptismal register and he is celebrated in the couplet

> *My heart-warm love to guid auld Glen,*
> *The ace an' wale of honest men,*

which comes from the *Epistle to James Tennant of Glenconner*, Burns' particular friend. 'Guid auld Glen' may be regarded as the founder of the family. He married three times and fathered no less than sixteen children, a feat equalled among his descendants only by Margot's father. Of these Charles, known as Wabster Charlie, was born in 1768, and was his fourth son by his second wife. Charles was apprenticed as a weaver, but soon started a bleachfield in Paisley which happened to be within sight of the house of a certain Mr Wilson, a prominent citizen of Glasgow, whose daughter Charles wisely married. Bleaching was in those days a laborious process: cloth was stretched out in a field, watered regularly and exposed to the sun and wind. Charles Tennant produced a solution of chloride of lime which was an effective bleaching agent and he subsequently discovered a means of making bleaching powder. He formed a partnership to commercialise this invaluable commodity and in 1797 the works was moved to St

Rollox in Glasgow. Among his colleagues in this venture were his father-in-law, Mr Wilson, and Charles Mackintosh, F.R.S., of Dunchattan, the inventor of the waterproof which has been so useful to his compatriots north and south of the border ever since, not least to the citizens of Glasgow. By 1800 Charles Tennant had gained control of the St Rollox works and it was this enterprise that his son John, Margot's grandfather, inherited and greatly expanded. Charles Tennant was a close friend of George Stephenson, the engineer, and was largely responsible for the first railway in Scotland. Appropriately enough the Glasgow railway station was at St Rollox.

Like his father before him John Tennant took an active part in public life: in politics he was a strong Liberal, supported the Reform Bill of 1832 and took a leading role in the agitation for the repeal of the Corn Laws. All this and more can be learned from the memoir of Sir Charles Tennant, written by his son H. J. Tennant and printed for private circulation in 1932, on which I have drawn extensively. But of his private life much less is known. In the genealogical table attached to that volume he is granted three children, but he is not provided with a wife. According to Margot the explanation is simple. John Tennant's wife was the girl who took the shaving water round the St Rollox works and bore the beautiful and romantic name of Robina Arroll. Her portrait, now in the possession of Lord Glenconner, is included in this book as an illustration. They were married, also according to Margot, in the Scottish fashion whereby it is only necessary to declare yourself married in front of two witnesses or put up a brass plate, suitably inscribed, on your front door which is what they did.

I could find no record of Robina Arroll's death, but three children is a small family by Victorian standards and we must presume that she died young. All sorts of unsubstantiated stories have been told about her, but it is not unreasonable to suppose that some of the characteristics of her son Charles and of his children were inherited from her: irrepressible vitality, great generosity, curly hair, and among her female descendants particularly, remarkable physical attraction. These perhaps are some of the qualities which Robina Arroll herself possessed. Certainly her son Charles Tennant, generally known as the Bart, was an extraordinary man. As his photograph shows, he was small and neat, and Margot clearly got her looks and her temperament from him. Like her, he had enormous vitality; unlike her he had a flair for business: but they shared an unusual eye for beautiful objects and an unusual capacity for enjoyment. 'My father', she writes in a characteristic passage, 'was a man whose vitality, irritability, energy and impressionability amounted to genius.'

Though it is untrue to say that he was in the normal sense a self-made man, he certainly came up the hard way and came up very quick. He was sent to Ayr Academy at the age of seven and from there he went to Liverpool where 'he learned French from a Swiss, Mr Brunner, father of Sir John, of Brunner Mond & Co.' At fourteen he had finished his formal education and was working in the office of Mr Nevett, a Liverpool merchant, who long remained his friend. Though he started like every tycoon as an office boy, his ability was quickly noticed and he soon became 'the youngest and best judge of indigo and madder dyes, which he went to inspect on their arrival at the docks. No doubt Mr Nevett had a great opinion of him, for he wished to take him into partnership, but his father would not consent as he wished to take him into the St Rollox business.'[1] Margot's account of these years was naturally more dramatic. According to her, at the age of nineteen Charles made a corner in cochineal and a profit of £70,000. His father was so shocked by this transaction – for Charles could not have covered himself had it failed – that he sent a telegram to Mr Nevett asking him to dismiss his son. The reply came back: 'Have made him a partner.'

Whatever the truth of this story (and we know he was not made a partner), it was not long before Charles was making money on a very large scale, something which he did with apparent ease for the rest of his life.

No introduction to Margot's autobiography can avoid a look at her father's extraordinary financial success. This was the base from which she and her sisters operated. Their personal qualities made them attractive; the fortune amassed by their father made them highly respectable as well. It also released them from the solid,

[1] *Sir Charles Tennant: His Forbears and Descendants* by H. J. Tennant. Privately Printed; 1932.

provincial world of Glasgow business into the wider worlds of politics and culture which in those days were not so far apart. It was the Bart who opened these doors because of his financial genius, his tastes and his 'impressionability'.

Shortly after his apprenticeship in Liverpool, Charles Tennant moved down to London where he worked in Tennants, Knox & Co. which traded in chemicals, copper, steel and other commodities, acting at the same time as agent for the parent firm at St Rollox. It was from here that he made his first accredited coup. He approached Gurney's bank and obtained a very large loan on the understanding that the securities he purchased would be lodged with them. How rich he was at the time it is impossible to discover. All we know is that his father gave him an allowance of £400 per annum and had provided him with a capital sum of £2,000, which, if Margot's story is true, he had considerably increased. But in any case the loan in question was of many thousands and it is doubtful if he would have obtained it but for his father's reputation. It was invested in the Midland Railways at some date between 1843 and 1850 and he made a considerable sum. In 1848 he followed this up by an investment in an Australian land company from which he secured a profit of £80,000. He was still only twenty-five. Then and later, like many men who have proved to themselves that they can make money (and unlike so many others who inherit it), the Bart was never afraid to spend it either on himself or others. He was justly famous for his generosity and there was nothing which gave him more pleasure than the exercise of this most attractive of virtues, which was inherited by Margot to the full. Any and every begging letter would receive a favourable response and his propensity to give sometimes alarmed his family who found it hard to reconcile with his reputation as a shrewd and hard-headed businessman.

In 1852 he brought Glen Estate in Peeblesshire of about 4,000 acres and proceeded to build the house 'designed in the tradition of Glamis and Castle Fraser, in what is called the Scottish baronial style', which Margot describes so vividly in the second chapter of this book. Whatever we may think of the Scottish baronial style nowadays, Glen stands in the most beautiful situation and was described by Lord Rosebery in a letter to Mr Gladstone as 'the most perfect of all modern houses, architecturally speaking'. The house was completed in 1858 and the tower added twenty years later. It was designed on a generous scale, twenty-nine bedrooms and six reception rooms, with gardens and greenhouses to match. Though Charles Tennant had become a partner in the St Rollox business in 1850 his father was so surprised by this display of affluence that he felt constrained to ask his son how much money he had. '£90,000' was the reply, and probably an understatement. 'The devil you have', said old John Tennant, who had built his fortune on rather more conservative lines. Undeterred, the Bart continued to spend large sums of money on the embellishment of Glen, filling it with beautiful and expensive pictures, mezzotints, furniture and fine books which he bought wisely and well. His taste in pictures may have been conventional – Hoppners, Reynolds, Romneys, and Raeburns for the most part – but he rarely bought anything ugly and the pleasure his acquisitions gave him was very real. The description of his visit to the library of his house in Grosvenor Square, late at night and armed with a candle, to inspect his pictures, while Margot and Peter Flower, that wonderfully romantic hero to whom she was then engaged, concealed themselves in the shadows of the sofa, is a touching example of how much his possessions meant to him.

But it was in mining that his genius as an investor was most generously rewarded. And his courage, flair and dash in these operations take one's breath away – as well as the rewards he won. In the 1860's, in collaboration with others, he bought the Tharsis Copper Mine, near Huelva in Spain. As the moving spirit and the largest investor, he conducted the final negotiations with the French proprietors in person. Acting on the assumption that his partners would see him safe, and in order to complete the deal, he made out a cheque for £100,000 in his own name, which he subsequently related was every penny that he then possessed. Since on this occasion (as on others) he was acting without the approval of his father, this may well be true. In its early days the company ran into difficulties and there were complaints from some of the shareholders. The Bart took this in his stride. 'If any shareholders who are dissatisfied with their investment will come to me after the meeting,' he announced, 'I am prepared to give them par value for their holding.' A few accepted his offer and no doubt regretted it, for over the first ten years the dividend of this company averaged 19 per cent (the highest was 40 per cent) and the amount distributed was over one and a half million pounds. In the 'eighties he developed the great gold reefs of Mysore, Champion Reef and Nundyroog Mines, and I transcribe the results:

MYSORE GOLD MINING COMPANY

	Dividend (%)
1889	75
1890	75
1896–1905 always over	100
The highest was	150

CHAMPION REEF

1896	67½
1897–1905 always over	100
The highest was	165

To modern eyes these figures may be astonishing and to some perhaps shocking. But in those days there was a derisory income tax, no surtax, and the pursuit of capital gains and the evasion of taxation were not the rich man's chief preoccupation. Those who possessed the gift made money without any pangs of conscience and spent it, if they were like Charles Tennant, on themselves and their families, on politics and pictures, on pleasure and on charity, confident that there was always more to be made. Moreover, the Bart held the view that high dividends were the just reward for those who put money into investments which were necessarily highly speculative. Such bold spirits deserved their reward in the present, and the future, if it was at all like the present, which all assumed it must be, could look after itself.

Charles Tennant was the first of the Tennants to marry over the border, and Emma Winsloe, whom he married in 1849, was no Robina Arroll. She was an Englishwoman of ascertainable origins and she came, writes Margot, 'of quite a different class from my father'. Her father was a west country parson and her mother Catherine Walter, daughter of the founder of *The Times*. In temperament they could not have been more different, for 'she was as timid as he was bold, as controlled as he was spontaneous, and as refined, courteous and unassuming as he was vibrant, sheer and adventurous.' Nonetheless, their marriage appears to have been happy and successful and their union produced a brood of twelve children, six boys and six girls, of whom Margot was the eleventh.

Thus it was that in 1879, aged fifty-five, one year after the death of his father, Charles Tennant felt able to enter the political world in person. He had proved immensely successful in business, he was the head of a large and growing family firm, he had provided himself with a suitable country estate in addition to the large family mansion in George Street, Glasgow, and he was the father of a Victorian family among whom three daughters glittered like diamonds (not cairngorms). Charty (Charlotte) was twenty-one and had already married Lord Ribblesdale, a great *parti*, whose splendid appearance is preserved for our eyes in Sargent's magnificent portrait at the Tate Gallery. Laura was eighteen and Margot sixteen. In the following year Charles Tennant abandoned his safe seat in Glasgow, to which he had been elected without contest, and stood for the combined counties of Peebles and Selkirk. His Tory opponent, Sir Graham Montgomery, had held the seat for twenty-eight years without ever making a speech in the House of Commons, nor was it his habit to make more than two from the hustings in the course of a General Election. Tennant won by a very small margin, and his victory was a blow to the county establishment which was neither soon forgotten nor forgiven. It was a typically dashing act and it is worth noting that at this time his life and that of his family were still firmly based on Scotland, though his sons were already being sent to Eton and Cambridge for their education. The process of anglicization had begun.

This then was the platform from which Margot was launched, more like a rocket than a ship. But it cannot be pretended that her appearance on the hunting field or in London society was unheralded. She had been preceded by her two sisters, and if Charty was the more beautiful in the formal sense, there is no question that Laura was the more remarkable. The legend of Laura Tennant, who died in childbirth at the age of twenty-three in 1886, is one which it is difficult today to recreate or even fully to understand. A reputation such as hers is only possible in a small, tightly-knit society in which everyone knows a good deal about everyone else. Yet the more one reads about her the more the evidence accumulates, and accumulates in favour of the legend. No one would be easier to debunk than her. One paragraph from Lytton Strachey's pen would have reduced her to a handful of dust. To make matters worse she married Alfred Lyttelton, England cricketer and cabinet minister, the prototype of the Edwardian hero, the golden boy of his age. Nothing is more true than that today's hero (or heroine) is tomorrow's caricature, and both Laura and Margot suffer from this automatic depreciation. Laura was immediately attractive to most men: she was a cool but inveterate flirt; yet she also possessed the ability to make friends of all ages, both male and female, and to leave them with the impression of someone *sui generis*, lovable, warm, irreplaceable and almost saintly, in her essential goodness. She had, it was said, '*le don fatal de familiarité* and she always made straight for the heart of her friends'. Lady Horner[1] was a woman of great beauty, perception, intelligence and, when I knew her, experience. Until the end of her long life Laura remained a heroine, never to be forgotten, though she had died so many years ago. But quite apart from the impact Laura made on those who knew her as friends, from Mr Gladstone to Godfrey Webb, and from Frances Horner to Tennyson, there is also for our purpose the more important fact of her relationship with Margot.

Margot is widely regarded as an egoist, to use a word which was frequently on her lips, nor does her Autobiography do much to dispel this view. Yet her relationship with Laura was entirely free from egotism. It is quite apparent, I think, to anyone who reads what she wrote of Laura that she not only loved her in an entirely selfless fashion, but that in addition she admired her as one who possessed her own qualities, yet to a superior degree. Her feeling for Laura

[1] Lady Horner, née Frances Graham, of Mells Manor, Somerset. B. 1858, d. 1940. Friend of Burne Jones and Ruskin: author of *Time Remembered*, her autobiography. Her daughter Katherine married Raymond Asquith.

was probably the deepest, the most completely unselfish and the most important in her life.

Much of Margot's book is devoted to describing her triumphant youth before she married Mr Asquith at the age of thirty in 1894, and it is not my intention to cover the same ground. But in reading her story one cannot but suspect that her greatest qualities, and those which contributed most to her success, were her vitality, courage and spontaneity. She welcomed life with an everlasting yea: on the hunting field riding horses far too strong for her to control, or in Dresden, in the drawing-rooms of London, or dancing in front of Dr Jowett after tea at Gosford. She injected an element of the unexpected into the rich routine of late Victorian society. *Dodo*, E. F. Benson's indifferent novel[1], which is a totally misleading and exceedingly malicious study of Margot's character (it is doubtful if he ever met her), is enlightening in one respect. The chronic ailment of society in the 1880's and 1890's was boredom; most of its members had plenty of money, a great deal of leisure and few duties to perform beyond the empty ritual of exchanging one gun for another. The circle was tiny and within it the standard of wealth without precedent. The future seemed completely secure. *Dodo* brings home the monotony of social life in those days when throughout the summer splendid young men occupied their mornings hanging around the Row in Hyde Park, their afternoons gossiping with ladies over tea in their drawing-rooms, and their evenings at dinner-parties and balls. The year was rigorously governed by semi-compulsory activities designed to fill in time. Outside politics and the army excitement had to be carefully cultivated and sought out. Lord Desborough, the champion punter of all time, twice swam the rapids below the Niagara Falls; Cole devised elaborate practical jokes; Lord Ripon shot one thousand birds to his own gun in one day; Peter Flower, when neither hunting nor boxing nor escaping his creditors, jumped on to mantelpieces over blazing fires or over areas into library windows in London. The arrival of Margot in such a world was bound to cause more than a ripple of excitement, for here was someone new, unpredictable and totally without precedent. Women like her or Frances Horner were able to disregard conventions which men

[1] Published 1892.

accepted as laws of nature, to break down the barriers that separated the various social groups, and being, as they were, more flexible and therefore more adventurous than their male contemporaries they introduced new ideas, new books, new activities and even new and rather pretentious pencil games after dinner — above all they provided an infusion of new life and new blood.

The sensation can well be imagined when in 1894 it was rumoured that Margot was engaged to H. H. Asquith, the young Home Secretary 'with his great and solemn career before him'. The difference in age was not great; she was thirty; he, eleven years older. But he had been married before, his first wife having died three years previously, and he was the father of five young children. No one, least of all Margot herself, could see her as step-mother to this brood, and while his friends felt her frivolity would wreck his career, hers thought that the difference in their tastes was too wide to be bridged. It seemed unlikely that a woman who had fallen in love with Peter Flower would find happiness as the wife of H. H. Asquith. Frances Horner who knew both parties, put *Dodo* by his bed as a warning, when he went to stay at Mells (he threw it out of the window into the garden), Lord Rosebery and Lord Randolph Churchill expressed the gravest doubts. Meanwhile Margot's friends pointed out 'that he did not care for hunting, out-of-door games, or the good-humoured, ill-educated people with whom I spent my winters'. All of which was absolutely true. Mr Asquith was no Alfred Lyttelton, and out-of-door games played a small part in his life. When, shortly after their marriage, Margot urged him to run to catch a train, he replied, temperately: 'I don't run much.' This was an understatement, he didn't run at all. He played a little indifferent golf with great pleasure and when he first visited Balmoral as Prime Minister he was sent out stalking. He shot two stags with two shots and on subsequent visits wisely refused all suggestions that he should attempt to repeat this admirably economical performance. But all this, wrote Margot, 'did not make as much difference to my decision as my friends supposed, but I feared that my inadequacy might cool his great love'. Her decision to marry Mr Asquith must be accounted an example of her courage. The event was so public and the warnings she received so numerous that even her worst enemies, who regarded her as totally insensitive, could not pretend that she was unaware of the task which she had undertaken. Nor can it be supposed that she was swept off her feet by a grand passion, for at the time they first met she was very unhappy because of her attachment to Peter Flower. In so far as Margot ever made a considered decision, this must have been one of them.

Mr Asquith on the other hand, is generally supposed – probably wrongly – to have been a man who only made up his mind after weighing the evidence with judicial detachment. There can be little doubt that in matters of the heart and in the case of both his marriages this was not so. He fell in love with Helen Melland, his first wife, at the age of eighteen and married her seven years later, when he was still a poor and struggling barrister. It is not easy to improve on Margot's description of her, which is not included in the Autobiography:

'When later I met his wife – Helen – she was so different from me that I had a longing for her approval. She was gentle, pretty and unambitious, and spoke to me of her home and children with love and interest that seemed to exclude her from a life of political aggrandizement, which was from early days the life that captivated my imagination. I was anxious that she should care for me and know my friends, but after a weekend spent at Taplow with Lord and Lady Desborough, where everyone liked her, she told me that though she had enjoyed her visit she did not think she would ever care for the sort of society that I loved, and was happier in the circle of her home and family.

'When I said that she had married a man who was certain to attain the highest political distinction, she replied that that was not what she coveted for him. Driving back from Hampstead where we had been alone together I wondered if my ambition for the success of her husband, and other men was wrong.'[1]

It was Helen Melland's five children that Margot married as well as their father. The youngest, always known as Cys, was only four at the time; the eldest, Raymond, was just fifteen, and old enough to be fully aware of what was happening. The Asquiths as a breed re-

[1] p. 98 *Life of Lord Oxford and Asquith* (Spender & Asquith) Vol. I. Hutchinson, 1932.

mained for Margot a constant source of perplexity, irritation, and wonder. She used to describe them as 'skeletons with brains' and thought, possibly rightly, that they over-valued intellect. But above all they lacked 'temperament', a characteristic which she regarded as essential and which included all those qualities which she and Laura and the Bart so conspicuously possessed. The Asquith children neither cried nor quarrelled, and they practised an extreme reserve which was probably reinforced by her demands for more frequent and complete emotional intercourse. They were, in fact, as she frequently pointed out, quite unlike the Tennants. Certainly they would never have greeted her as she and her family greeted the Bart's second wife, Marguerite Miles, who was luckily of an equable nature, and whom he married at the age of seventy-five (she subsequently bore him four daughters). On being introduced to her at Glen the whole Tennant clan, the youngest of whom was well over thirty, simply sat round her chair and sobbed. But if the Asquiths' lack of temperament amazed and shocked Margot, the Asquith children were doubtless equally surprised, in their reserved way, to be suddenly transferred from an austere villa near Redhill to a magnificent house in Cavendish Square presided over by a bird of paradise. 'She filled us', one of them has since broadcast 'with admiration, amazement, amusement, affection, sometimes even (as children) with a vague sense of uneasiness as to what she might, or might not, do next'[1] — and this, I suspect, is putting it mildly.

A whole anthology could be compiled of Margot's comments on the Asquiths. 'They rarely looked at you,' she writes, 'and never got up when anyone came into the room.' In addition they slept deplorably well. To sleep lightly was for Margot right, to sleep badly a virtue. 'All Asquiths', she wrote in her diary, 'sleep like hogs.' Margot's diary was never a very secret document and this particular passage became public property. Mr Asquith was delighted to discover that, struck by contrition, she had tried to amend 'hogs' to 'logs'. The deep black of the original 'h' proved ineradicable and clearly legible through the pale blue of the afterthought. She was also critical of her husband's sleeping habits, 'I like', she said, 'heat without weight, Henry likes weight without heat. I sleep under a couple

[1] Lady Violet Bonham Carter on the B.B.C.

of Shetland shawls, Henry would be happy stark naked under a grand piano.'

Given that Margot and her step-children 'were so opposite in temper, temperament and outlook', it says much for both sides that she succeeded in eliciting so strongly not only their admiration, but also their affections. They, like so many others, could not resist her candour and her courage, her spontaneity and her endless ability to make fun. 'She was never in the least like a mother, nor was she like a step-mother, wicked or otherwise',[1] but she was by nature at her ease with children, the irresponsibility and the vitality of childhood never left her altogether and she spoke to them as equals. The tragedy of Margot's life was that three of her five children died at birth, nor is it possible to do more than guess how much this meant to her. 'No true woman ever gets over the loss of a child,' she writes of her own mother in the Autobiography, four of whose children also died. 'She suffered many sorrows . . . and I do not think I made enough allowances for them.'

Such, very broadly, is the background to Margot and her book. She had never received a systematic education (she always counted on her fingers), but throughout her life she associated with highly educated companions; she read eagerly; and she had considerable natural talent, as she did not hesitate to explain, as an amateur musician, draftsman and dancer. Writing, however, was something in which she was not altogether an amateur. Unlike many good talkers, talk did not exhaust her powers of self-expression. She always wrote – letters, notes, diaries – and everything she wrote bears the stamp of her style quite apart from being written in her own very beautiful, quite individual and unmistakable hand-writing. All through her life she kept a diary and she used it as well as her memory and her imagination as the source for this book. In 1892 she had privately printed and circulated to her friends a small volume entitled *A Little Journey and a Week in Glasgow*. This is an account of a voyage she took with her mother and father to Rome, Cairo, and the Sudan, and of the campaign fought by one of her brothers in Glasgow during the General Election of 1892. I do not know what would be thought today of a young woman who issued so frank, uninhibited

[1] Lady Violet Bonham Carter on the B.B.C.

and at the same time lively an account of herself, her family and her friends. But it does not seem to have caused any particular sensation and in connection with the present volume it merely confirms that Margot had a naturally easy style, an unusual gift of phrase and the ability to make characters and situations come alive for the reader. This is not to say she did not take trouble; she drafted, re-drafted and revised assiduously. She wrote well by nature, but she improved on nature by industry.

In the preface to the Autobiography, which is not included in this edition, she explains that she never showed it to her husband before publication. 'When I began this book, I feared that its merit would depend upon how faithfully I could record my own impressions of people and events; when I had finished it, I was certain of it. Had it been any other kind of book the judgment of those nearest me would have been invaluable; but being what it is, it had to be entirely my own, since whoever writes as he speaks must take the whole responsibility; and to ask "Do you think I may say this?" or "write that?" is to shift a little of that responsibility on to someone else. This I could not bear to do, above all in the case of my husband, who sees this book now for the first time.' It was bought outright for a considerable sum by the publishers, Thornton Butterworth, and was serialized in the United Kingdom by the *Sunday Times* and in the U.S.A. by *The Metropolitan*.

It was widely and promptly reviewed. The treatment it received in *The Times*, then still owned by Lord Northcliffe, deserves some other term. A leader and four full columns starting on the turnover position were devoted to it. The headlines read:

MRS ASQUITH'S BOOK

CRITICAL ANALYSIS

A REVELATION OF CHARACTER

VANITY AND SELF-LOVE

The text below goes on in much the same style, a laborious and savage personal attack, designed presumably to destroy the author's reputation, studded with innuendo and written in the manner of one whose delicate moral susceptibilities have been seriously wounded and probably permanently damaged. The book is 'a scandal which cannot be justified or excused', which would sell, not on its merits 'but because it is a scandal'. After these general statements of dis-approval it gets down to the character, life and motives of the author. Margot's mother had lived 'until her daughter had done enough to shock most people'; having read the book many might wonder whether the writer 'knows right from wrong in the domain of con-ventional manners'; there is a strong suggestion that she lived an immoral life; she is 'as insensible to received standards of conduct as a blind man is to colour'; and the book itself could only have been prompted by 'a reckless desire for money or an inordinate craving for notoriety'. It would do great mischief not only by acting as an example to 'silly and underbred young women' but it would also be 'cited by domestic Bolshevists'. The *coup de grâce* repeats the head-line: 'It has its roots in vanity and self-love.'

The leader reinforcing this piece was written in a style which *The Times* has never been able entirely to escape when it decides that a high moral tone is the best way to attain a thoroughly unworthy purpose:

'We say elsewhere what we think of Mrs Asquith's book. Remark-able as it is and exceptional as Mrs Asquith's opportunities have been for writing it, it is not the only specimen of its kind at the present time. Indeed, to judge by what is published, self-revelation, in one form or another, is now the fashion, and autobiography, once a stately and instructive form of literary composition, when undertaken by elderly persons of eminence with careers behind them, has be-come, under the modern treatment, merely a form of self-advertise-ment.'

The peroration of this truly splendid piece by one of Lord Northcliffe's hacks referred to the responsibility which is borne by those who write for publication.

The other reviews, including that in *The Times Literary Supplement* which showed a creditable independence, were less obviously inspired by personal and political malice. It was reviewed by Mr Winston Churchill in the *Daily Mail* and by Desmond MacCarthy in the *New Statesman*, and there were long unsigned articles in the *Spectator* and *The Nation* (the latter probably from the pen of Middle-ton Murry). The book's reception was in the main critical; it could hardly have failed to surprise contemporaries by its candour about the writer herself and other living persons. The reporting of private conversations, the revelations of who had and who had not proposed to her, the unqualified assessments of the character, ability and integrity of her friends and of her husband's colleagues and rivals, quite apart from the lime-lit role in which Margot quite rightly cast herself – all this coming from the wife of an ex-Prime Minister – was bound to produce a disapproving reaction from English readers. '*Etonnes-moi, Jean*' was Diaghilev's instruction to Cocteau, and he could not have asked more than Margot provided. The shock she produced obscured to some extent the more permanent merits of the book which today we are better able to appreciate. The *Spectator's* critic probably summed up the general reaction when he wrote that publication could only be justified had the book been by a dead woman about dead men and women. He finished by quoting Samuel Rogers' comment on Michael Angelo's statue of Lorenzo de Medici: 'It fascinates but is intolerable.'

What was both fascinating and intolerable was the uninhibited way in which Margot wrote about living persons. As *The Times Literary Supplement* pointed out, she had the curious habit of referring to her friends in the past tense as though they were dead. It is not impossible that when writing about them she thought of them as dead, for she had a great taste for writing obituaries and rarely missed an opportunity of doing so. This was not prompted by any morbid interest in death but rather by her permanent interest in people and the pleasure she found in writing about them. Once, when she was staying with Arthur Balfour, he was surprised to find written in Margot's hand on a sheet of paper an unfinished opening: 'So Arthur Balfour is dead. . . . ' Her preface provides a further explanation of her frankness about her friends when she says that she wrote as she spoke. And it is certainly true that there is nothing in the Autobiography which she would have hesitated to say to the person in question or which she would have minded their reading. That 'dangerous, graceless, disconcerting, invigorating, merciless, shameless, lovable candour', as Desmond MacCarthy put it, was part of the Margot which anyone who knew her had to accept and get used to and even enjoy. She always told people exactly what she thought, not only because she was unable to believe that they would mind, but also – and this is not unimportant – because she felt that it might do them good: they should not be allowed to walk like camels, deal cards in a slovenly manner, or even paint bad pictures. She felt it her duty to tell people the truth, particularly about themselves – and she was constantly surprised by the way they reacted. 'Can I be your skin doctor?' she wrote in one of her midnight notes to a young man staying at The Wharf, her country house, for the first time. Her candour knew no bounds. On one occasion Margot unwisely agreed to present at Court a lady of doubtful reputation. The application was refused and Margot received a furious letter of protest from her aquaintance. Her reply was in her best vein: 'I am sure that what you say is perfectly true and that many people just as, if not even more, immoral than yourself have been presented at Court. . . .'

In this respect and in many others the Autobiography was no more than a reflection of the person who wrote it, and of this Mr Churchill and Desmond MacCarthy who knew her well, must have been aware. Not that Margot and Mr Churchill were exactly made for each other: both were talkers rather than listeners, both believed in pouring in, rather than drawing out. Moreover, Margot belonged to the generation which saw Winston Churchill as the brilliant Lord Randolph's somewhat bumptious son who was so transparently determined to get on. None the less, Mr Churchill's review in the *Daily Mail* is a very just appraisal. Having expressed some reservations about the book's taste and historical accuracy he writes: 'The story is told with art, and, what is better with unconscious art. . . . These memoirs, apart from their controversial touches, might well find a place in the bibliography of the Victorian era.' There is also a splendid passage in which he points out that Margot's assessment of her own position was in no way exaggerated: 'Few there were in the gay, hard-riding crowd which frequented Melton Mowbray or followed the Duke of Beaufort's hounds in the 'nineties able to surpass this feather-weight daredevil, mounted upon enormous horses, who with fault-less nerve and thrust and inexhaustible energy, spurred by love of chase and desire to excel, came sometimes to grief but always to the fore.'

It is not my purpose to argue whether or not the publication of this book in 1920 was a breach of taste. It can only be said that those who suffered from its revelations were for the most part people who knew Margot well – very largely her friends – and they can have been surprised less by what it said in print (which she never hesitated to say in person) than by the sheer merit of the book. She was able to translate the flavour of her conversation into the written word and though something is lost, something is also gained. Her descriptions of hunting are among the best I know. They convey, even to those without experience in the field, the excitement, the beauty, almost the exaltation which hunting arouses. Her encounter with General Booth of the Salvation Army and her affair with Peter Flower must excite the envy of many novelists and the dialogue with which the book is interspersed, generally so unsatisfactory in works of this nature, is here used to increase the sense of drama and throw light on the characters concerned.

The central accusation is that the book reveals the author as very pleased with herself, 'very interested in herself' as Mr Churchill put it in his review. Of course, Margot was interested in herself; how pleased is another and far more complicated question. But her egoism was of a very simple, spontaneous and unselfconscious kind, which she extended to all those connected with her, most intensely to her daughter Elizabeth and her son Anthony (known to his family as Puffin). 'Forty boys in poor Puff's bedroom', she said with shocked surprise when she went to Winchester and saw the dormitories in College where he would sleep. Interest in one's self is closely connected with interest in other people. The word egoism, after all, was invented to describe Montaigne whose self-analysis was intended to reveal the characters of others. Not the least remarkable virtue of this book is the shrewdness and the insight with which Margot judged her contemporaries. Like Sir Winston Churchill, her apparent self-absorption was superficial; as she was pouring in, so at the same time she was drawing out, absorbing, tasting, listening to the echoes which her drumfire produced and composing in the process a remarkably accurate picture of the person who was being subjected to this bombardment.

But the whole Margot, to be enjoyed and loved, had to be seen and known in the flesh. When I first remember her she was already over sixty, her book had been published and my grandfather, Mr

Asquith, was out of office. As a child I saw her through her physical appearance: small, neat, angular. Her gestures were sharp yet free, her hands bony and claw-like with long blood-red nails and big rings. I was fascinated by her nose which she explained had been broken hunting and her short, almost misshapen, upper lip. Her voice was as low as a man's and vehement.

We used to stay at The Wharf regularly for the holidays at Christmas and in the summer. It was an unattractive house in Sutton Courtenay, near Abingdon, and did not escape the vulgarity which hangs about the Thames valley. The garden led down to the river opposite a thundering weir and the house itself, red-brick with leaded windows, had been made by knocking together a public house and a cottage. It could digest an almost incredible number of people in small poky rooms, the largest being the kitchen. The drawing-room, where life went on, was divided into two parts connected by a doorway and a serving hatch, having been in its earlier incarnation the public and private bar. The part beyond the hatch was given over to bridge, the rest was dominated in my memory by a round table on which stood two huge glass jars, such as are to be seen in sweet shops, one full of bull's-eyes, the other of acid-drops. Beside these was a box of Turkish Delight and a solitaire board. I cannot eat Turkish Delight to this day or see those opaque pink cubes powdered with icing-sugar in their exotic wooden box without being reminded of that room at The Wharf. This room was dark and smelled of Turkish cigarettes, cigars and grown-ups.

Across the lawn from this room and beyond a delightful mulberry tree stood a timbered building called The Barn, where Margot slept. You entered it by a latched door leading into a large drawing-room with a piano, on the writing table lay the skull given to her by the shepherd's son at Glen to which she refers in her book A slippery wooden staircase led up into her bedroom where once more one was met by the smell of Turkish cigarettes: she smoked in bed and dropped the butts into a glass of Malvern water by her side. Here after breakfast I sometimes used to see her sitting in bed, swathed in Shetland shawls, which she regarded as vital to her health, looking very like the wolf about to eat Little Red Riding Hood She was surrounded by sheets of white vellum writing paper on which she scribbled notes to the various people who were staying at The Wharf and these were delivered to their bedrooms by a footman. These notes, written and sent at all hours of the day and night, were a feature of life with Margot and contained all manner of advice and unwelcome home truths. More urgent messages were sometimes delivered by word of mouth. One morning a footman was rung for at 4 a.m. with orders to tell Hugh Godley to stop hooting like an owl (it was an owl). At the time I am remembering the butler was Clouder, a man of great charm and distinction, all of whose teeth had been taken out on Margot's instructions. She regarded a full mouth as a sign of insanity, an act of culpable negligence which would lead to an early death. Any footman at The Wharf was under constant pressure to follow her advice on this and other matters connected with his health.

The children all stayed in the Mill House just across the village street. It was a delightful house, lit by oil-lamps with a charming walled garden full of hollyhocks and roses, a private bridge over a branch of the Thames and a pair of resident kingfishers. After lunch we would be led across to The Wharf to say 'how do you do' to the grown-ups. We would find them, packed into the dining-room and we would walk round the table being introduced to each and kissed by all too many. My clearest recollection of my grandfather is connected with this alarming and noisy ritual. He sat at the head of the table at the far end of the room and his chair was to that extent a haven, which marked the conclusion of one's itinerary. I remember a pink face, bright blue eyes, white hair and a halo of cigar smoke. When I arrived he would take the ring of his cigar which he had kept and recite with apparent pleasure and absolute regularity 'The Owl and the Pussycat', placing the cigar ring on my finger as he reached 'Said the Piggy I will'. After this we were sometimes compelled to recite to the assembled grown-ups and I could rarely do better than:

> 'Pease pudding hot
> Pease pudding cold
> Pease pudding in the pot
> Five days old.'

When this ordeal was over we could go into the drawing-room, take a sweet from one of the jars, and go into the garden.

The Wharf was always packed with people at weekends, and others made the journey from Oxford for lunch. The dining-room was small and filled with a sound like the parrot house at the zoo. Indeed the noise was so great that as we walked across the village street from the Mill House we could hear the roar of conversation, and attempts were made to deaden the sound in the dining-room itself by stretching wires across the ceiling. There was a great deal of shouting and this was only temporarily interrupted by the entrance of the children or by Margot banging the table and demanding 'General Conversation!' People were discouraged from talking to their neighbours, she preferred conversation and interruption to be conducted 'generally', in all directions, across, and along, the table, and like a bishop's move from corner to corner. This, together with the penetrating voices possessed by Asquiths, accounted for the noise.

This is how Desmond MacCarthy describes it:[1] 'I am back in the narrow white dining-room of The Wharf, with its two garden windows. Sunday luncheon is in progress; and, as is often the case in that room, there are more guests than you might think it could accommodate, and more talk in the air than you would think even so many to produce. The atmospherics are terrific. . . . The conversation resembles rather a wild game of pool in which everyone is playing his or her stroke at the same time. One is trying to send a remark into the top corner pocket furthest from her, where at the same moment another player is attempting a close-up shot at his own end: while anecdotes and comments whizz backwards and forwards, cannoning and clashing as they cross the table. Sometimes a remark leaps right off it at somebody helping himself at the sideboard, who with back still turned, raises his voice to reply. And not only are half a dozen different discussions taking place simultaneously, but his guests are at different stages of the meal. Some have already reached coffee, others are not yet near the sweet, for everyone gets up and helps himself as he finishes a course.'

Margot was a brave hostess: she mixed the most incongruous people without thought or hesitation, but she was always kind to the young and took trouble to see that weak swimmers were not totally

[1] *Portraits* by Desmond MacCarthy. London 1931.

submerged. Her own contribution was a hit or miss affair. A succession of bull's-eyes might be succeeded by a complete miss: a brilliantly told anecdote by a totally mistaken or even irrelevant judgment. She was that rare combination, both witty and funny, and at her best she was truly incomparable. Everyone who knew Margot and many who did not, have their Margot stories which range from her comment on Lloyd George, 'He couldn't see a belt without hitting below it' (though, she added, he had political sex appeal), to the kind of lunatic remark in which she sometimes indulged: 'My dear old friend King George V always told me he would never have died but for that vile doctor, Lord Dawson of Penn.' She talked to everyone in exactly the same way, and was quite incapable of modifying her conversation to suit her audience; 'Free trade is my religion' were her first words to a new and astounded Swiss governess. On the other hand, there was no category of person with whom she might not strike up an intimate relationship – and for 'oddities', as she called them, she had a self-confessed weakness.

As children she used to terrify and enthral us with stories about ghosts, lunatics, murderers and a particularly unsuitable one about a baby farmer she visited in prison 'with a face like Lady Randolph Churchill'. She loved fun and made it; charades, hunt the thimble, murder, the simplest game of cards – all gave her real pleasure. But above all she was an inspired and spontaneous clown. At Christmas she would dress up in the butler's clothes (looking exactly like photographs of the Bart), which were far too big for her, and say with apparent surprise, 'Look how loose these clothes are. I would swear I was twice Clouder's size.' Margot was about five feet two. Once at Downing Street the German governess came rushing into the room saying: *'Veilchen, Veilchen, Kom schnell! Die Mama tanzt in ihren Beinkleider vor dem neuen Sekretar!'*[1]

And she was always on the children's side. She wanted us to be adventurous, to climb walls and trees, to go on expeditions by day or night, nor was she surprised if it ended in tears. When I was very

---

[1] 'Violet, Violet, come quickly! Mama is dancing in front of the new secretary in her combinations!'

small – about two – I fell into the Thames at the end of The Wharf garden while fishing with a leaf on the end of a stick, and disappeared from sight beneath the muddy water. My sisters, who were not much older, screamed for Margot who had organized this lethal game. She could not swim a stroke nor had she any idea how deep the water was, but without a moment's hesitation she jumped in and dredging about the bottom found me and hauled me out. In a crisis Margot could be very practical and cool.

After my grandfather's death in 1928 The Wharf and the Mill House were sold, though Margot kept her house in Bedford Square. It was large and beautifully arranged in Margot's style; the drawing-room was her favourite skull colour and every object and picture was in the right place. It was the same with her clothes, which though *chic* were rarely fashionable; they were outside fashion. She had an exquisite carriage, with narrow hips and a somewhat hollow back. By day her dresses came down to her ankles, and her shoes were long and pointed, their toes stuffed with cotton wool. In the country she used to wear spats, and keep up her stockings with safety pins attached to combinations. She adored bridge and ruthlessly dragged the best partners to their doom, and played golf keenly on the courses round North Berwick. A 'North Berwick swing' she regarded as an essential part of one's social equipment. Her own was extremely exaggerated, and a very good drive by Margot from the ladies' tee rarely went more than twenty-five yards. You could never be certain how she would react. When a car-load of people drove into North Berwick harbour and were drowned, we all expressed appropriate sorrow. The tragedy, however, made Margot 'rock with laughter – that harbour full of bones'. A few days later an hysterical man tried and failed to commit suicide with a small penknife on his mother's grave. It was our turn to laugh and Margot's to be shocked. My sister and cousin were sent with flowers to the hospital where he was recovering from his scratch.

No book and no introduction can fully evoke her personality, and her book and the legend fail to bring out the intensely human qualities, and the very admirable and endearing virtues which she so conspicuously possessed: a simple but deep religious faith: complete physical and social courage: a surprising clear-sightedness about herself and others: generosity, zest and vitality to an unusual degree: candour and honesty to a supreme degree: and a warmth of heart which included all those close to her or connected with her and the young in particular.

The last years of her life were darkened by the war and by the death of her daughter Elizabeth in Rumania in 1943. She stayed in London, not at Bedford Square, but at the Savoy Hotel, and owing to the times we all saw far too little of her. Yet she continued to make and enjoy new friends up to the end of her life. She died in 1945.

PART I

I · *The Tennant Family*

———◦❦◦———

I was born in the country of Hogg and Scott between the Yarrow and the Tweed, in the year 1864.

I am one of twelve children, but I only knew eight, as the others died when I was young. My eldest sister Pauline – or Posie, as we called her – was born in 1855 and married on my tenth birthday one of the best of men, Thomas Gordon Duff.[1] She died of tuberculosis, the cruel disease by which my family have all been pursued. We were too different in age and temperament to be really intimate, but her goodness, patience and courage made a deep impression on me.

My second sister, Charlotte, was born in 1858 and married, when I was thirteen, the present Lord Ribblesdale,[2] in 1877. She was the only member of the family – except my brother Edward[3] – who was tall. My mother attributed this – and her good looks – to her wet-nurse, Janet Mercer, a mill-girl at Innerleithen, noted for her height and beauty. Charty – as we called her – was in some ways the most capable of us all, but she had not Laura's genius, Lucy's talents, nor my understanding. She had wonderful grace and less vanity than anyone that ever lived; and her social courage was a perpetual joy. I heard her say to the late Lord Rothschild, one night at a dinner party:

'And do you still believe the Messiah is coming, Lord Natty?'

On one occasion when her husband was to make a political speech in the country, she telegraphed to him:

'Mind you hit below the belt!'

[1] Thomas Gordon Duff, of Drummuir Castle, Keith.
[2] Lord Ribblesdale, of Gisburne.
[3] Lord Glenconner, of Glen, Innerleithen.

She was full of nature and impulse, free, enterprising and un-concerned. She rode as well as I did, but was not so quick to hounds nor so conscious of what was going on all round her.

One day when the Rifle Brigade was quartered at Winchester, Ribblesdale sent Charty out hunting with old Tubb, the famous horse-dealer, from whom he had hired a mount for her. On their return he asked how her ladyship had got on; the old rascal – want-ing to sell his horse – raised his eyes to heaven and gasped:

'Hornamental palings! my lord!!'

It was difficult to find a better-looking couple than Charty and Ribblesdale; I often observed people following them in picture-galleries; and their photographs appeared in many of the London shop-windows.

My next sister, Lucy,[1] was the most talented and the best educated of the family. She fell between two stools in her youth, because Charty and Posie were of an age to be companions and Laura and I; consequently she did not enjoy the happy childhood that we did and was mishandled by the authorities both in the nursery and the schoolroom. Our real intimacy only began after her marriage, which took place when I was fourteen. She was my mother's favourite child – which none of us resented – and, although like my father in hospitality, courage and generous giving, she had my mother's stubborn modesty and delicacy of mind. Her fear of hurting the feelings of others was so great that she did not tell people what she was thinking; she was truthful but not candid. Her drawings – both in pastel and water-colour – her portraits, landscapes and interiors were further removed from amateur work than Laura's piano-playing, or my dancing, and, had she put her wares into the market, as we wanted her to do years ago, she would have been a rich woman; but like all saints she was uninfluenceable. I owe her too much to write about her; tormented by pain and crippled by arthritis, she has shown a heroism and gaiety which command the love and respect of all who meet her.

Of my other sister, Laura, I will write later.

The boys of the family were different from the girls, though they all had charm and an excellent sense of humour. My mother said

[1] Mrs Graham Smith, of Easton Grey, Malmesbury.

the difference between her boys and girls came from circulation and would add, 'The Winsloes always had cold feet'; but I think it lay in temper. They would have been less apprehensive and more serene if they had been brought up to some settled profession; and they were clever enough to do most things well.

My brother Jack[1] was petted and mismanaged in his youth. He had good health, but his nerves were strained by his being allowed, when he was a little fellow, to walk twelve to fifteen miles a day with the shooters; and, however tired he might be, he was taken out of bed to play billiards after dinner. Leather footstools were placed one on the top of the other by a proud papa and the company made to watch this lovely little boy score big breaks; excited and exhausted, he would return to bed long after midnight, with praises singing in his ears.

'You are more like lions than sisters!' he said one day in the nursery when we snubbed him.

In making him his Parliamentary Secretary, my husband gave him his first political chance; and in spite of his early training and teasing he has turned his life to good account.

In the terrible years 1914, 1915 and 1916, he distinguished himself as Under-Secretary for War to the late Lord Kitchener and was finally made Secretary for Scotland, with a seat in the Cabinet. Like every Tennant, he had powers of emotion and showed much generosity to his family. He was a fine sportsman with an exceptionally good eye for games.

My brother Frank[2] was the artist among the boys. He was born with a perfect ear for music and eye for colour and could distinguish what was beautiful in everything he saw. He had the sweetest temper of any of us and the most humility.

In his youth he had a horrible tutor who showed him a great deal of cruelty; and this retarded his development. One day at Glen, I saw this man knock Frank down. Furious and indignant, I said, 'You brute!' and hit him over the head with both my fists. After he had boxed my ears, Laura protested, saying she would tell my father, whereupon he toppled her over on the floor and left the room.

When I think of our violent teachers – both tutors and governesses

[1] The Right Hon. H. J. Tennant.   [2] Francis Tennant, of Innes.

– and what the brothers learnt at Eton, I am surprised that we knew as much as we did and my parents' helplessness bewilders me.

My eldest brother, Eddy, though very different from me in temperament and outlook, was the one with whom I got on best. We were both devoured by impatience and punctuality and loved being alone in the country. He hated visiting, I enjoyed it; he detested society and I delighted in it. My mother was not strong enough to take me to balls; and, as she was sixty-three the year I came out, Eddy was by way of chaperoning me, but I can never remember him bringing me back from a single party. We each had our latch-keys and I went home either by myself or with a partner.

We shared a secret and passionate love for our home, Glen, and knew every clump of heather and every birch and burn in the place. Herbert Gladstone told me that, one day in India, when he and Eddy after a long day's shooting were resting in silence on the ground, he said to him:

'What are you thinking about, Eddy?'

To which he answered:

'Oh, always the same . . . Glen! . . .'

In all the nine years during which he and I lived there together, in spite of our mutual irascibility of temper and uneven spirits, we never had a quarrel. Whether we joined each other on the moor at the far shepherd's cottage, or waited for grouse on the hill; whether we lunched on the Quair, or fished on the Tweed, we have a thousand common memories to keep our hearts together.

My father[1] was a man whose vitality, irritability, energy and impressionability amounted to genius.

When he died, 6th June 1906, I wrote this in my diary:

I was sitting in Elizabeth's[2] schoolroom at Littlestone yesterday – Whit-Monday – after hearing her recite *Tartuffe* at 7 p.m., when James gave me a telegram; it was from my stepmother:

'Your father passed away peacefully at five this afternoon.'

I covered my face with my hands and went to find my husband. My father had been ill for some time, but, having had a letter from him that morning, the news gave me a shock.

Poor little Elizabeth was terribly upset at my unhappiness; and

[1] Sir Charles Tennant, 1823-1906.   [2] My daughter Elizabeth Bibesco.

I was moved to the heart by her saying with tear-filled eyes and a white face:

'Darling mother, he had a *very* happy life and is very happy now . . . he will *always* be happy.'

This was true. . . . He had been and always will be happy, because my father's nature turned out no waste product: he had none of that useless stuff in him that lies in heaps near factories. He took his own happiness with him and was self-centred and self-sufficing: for a sociable being, the most self-sufficing I have ever known; I can think of no one of such vitality who was so independent of other people; he could golf alone, play billiards alone, walk alone, shoot alone, fish alone, do everything alone; and yet he was dependent on both my mother and my stepmother and on all occasions loved simple playfellows . . . someone to carry his clubs, or to wander round the garden with, would make him perfectly happy. It was at these times, I think, that my father was at his sweetest; calm as a sky after showers, he appeared to be unupsettable; he had eternal youth and was unaffected by a financial world which had been spinning round him all day.

The striking thing about him was his freedom from suspicion. Thrown from his earliest days among common, shrewd men of singularly unspiritual ideals – most of them not only on the make but, I might almost say, on the pounce – he advanced on his own lines rapidly and courageously, not at all secretively, almost confidingly; yet he was rarely taken in.

He had great character, minute observation, a fine memory and all his instincts charged with almost superhuman vitality, but no one could argue with him. Had the foundation of his character been as unreasonable and unreliable as his temperament, he would have made neither friends nor money; but he was fundamentally sound, ultimately serene and high-minded in the truest sense of the word. He was a man of intellect, but not an intellectual man; he did not really know anything about the great writers or thinkers, although he had read odds and ends. He was essentially a man of action and a man of will; this is why I call him a man of intellect. He made up his mind in a flash, partly from instinct and partly from will.

He had the courage for life and the enterprise to spend his fortune on it. He was kind and impulsively generous, but too hasty for disease to accost or death to delay. For him they were interruptions, not abiding sorrows.

He knew nothing of rancour, remorse, regret; they conveyed much the same to him as if he had been told to walk backwards and received neither sympathy nor courtesy from him. He hated presents, but he liked praise and was easily flattered; he was too busy even for *much* of that, but he could stand more than most of us. If it is a little simple, it is also rather generous to believe in the nicest things people can say to you; and I think I would rather accept too much than repudiate and refuse: it is warmer and more enriching. He was an artist with the gift of admiration. He had a good eye and could not buy an ugly or even moderately beautiful thing; but he was no discoverer in art. Here I will add to make myself clear that I am thinking of men like Frances Horner's father, old Mr Graham,[1] who discovered and promoted Burne-Jones and Frederick Walker; or Lord Battersea, who was the first to patronise Cecil Lawson; or my sister, Lucy Graham Smith, who was a fine judge of every picture and recognized and appreciated all schools of painting. My father's judgment was warped by constantly comparing his own things with other people's.

He was fond of a few people – Mark Napier,[2] Ribblesdale, Lord Haldane, Mr Heseltine, Lord Rosebery and Arthur Balfour – and had a friendly feeling for everybody, but he did not *love* many people. When we were girls he told us we ought to make worldly marriages, but in the end he let us choose the men we loved and gave us the material help in money which enabled us to marry them. I find exactly the opposite plan adopted by most parents: they sacrifice their children to loveless marriages as long as they know there is enough money for no demand ever to be made upon themselves.

I think I understood my father better than the others did. I guessed his mood in a moment and in consequence could push further and say more to him when he was in a good humour. I lived with him, my mother and Eddy alone for nine years (after my sister

[1] Mr William Graham, father of Lady Horner, of Mells, Frome.
[2] The Hon. Mark Napier, of Ettrick.

Laura married) and therefore had a closer personal experience of him. He liked my adventurous nature. Ribblesdale's courtesy and sweetness delighted him and they were genuinely fond of each other. He said once to me of him:

'Tommy is one of the few people in the world that has shown me gratitude.'

* * *

I cannot pass my brother-in-law's name here in my diary without some reference to the effect which he produced on us when he first came to Glen.

He was the finest-looking man that I ever saw, except old Lord Wemyss,[1] the late Lord Pembroke,[2] Mr Wilfrid Blunt[3] and Lord D'Abernon. He had been introduced to my sister Charty at a ball in London, when he was twenty-one and she eighteen. A brother-officer of his in the Rifle Brigade, seeing them waltzing together, asked him if she was his sister, to which he answered:

'No, thank God!'

I was twelve when he first came to Glen as Thomas Lister: his fine manners, sense of humour and picturesque appearance captivated everyone; and, whether you agreed with him or not, he had a perfectly original point of view and was always interested and suggestive. He never misunderstood but thoroughly appreciated my father.

Writing now, fourteen years later, I do not think that I can add much to this.

Although my father was a business man, he had a wide understanding and considerable elasticity. My father and grandfather were brought up among City people and I am proud of it; but it is folly to suppose that starting and developing a great business is the same as initiating and conducting a great policy, or running a big Government Department.

It has been and will remain a puzzle over which intellectual men are perpetually if not permanently groping:

'How comes it that Mr Smith or Mr Brown made such a vast fortune?'

[1] The Earl of Wemyss and March, father of the present Earl.
[2] George, Earl of Pembroke, the present Earl's uncle.
[3] Mr Wilfrid Blunt, of Newbuildings Place, Sussex.

The answer is not easy. Making money requires *flair*, instinct, insight or whatever you like to call it, but the qualities that go to make a business man are grotesquely unlike those which make a statesman; and, when you have pretensions to both, the result is the present comedy and confusion.

I write as the daughter of a business man and the wife of a politician and I know what I am talking about, but, in case any believer in the 'business man' should honour me by reading these pages and still cling to his illusions on the subject, I refer him to the figures published in the Government White Book of 1919.

When my father gambled in the city, he took risks with his own rather than other people's money. I heard him say to a South African millionaire:

'You did not make your money out of mines, but out of mugs like me, my dear fellow!'

Born a little quicker, more punctual and more alive than other people, he suffered fools not at all. He could not modify himself in any way; he was the same man in his nursery, his school and his office, the same man in church, club, city or suburbs, and was as violent when he was dying as when he was living.

*   *   *

My mother[1] was more unlike my father than can easily be imagined. She was as timid as he was bold, as controlled as he was spontaneous, and as refined, courteous and unassuming as he was vibrant, sheer and adventurous.

Fond as we were of each other and intimate over all my love-affairs, my mother never really understood me; my vitality, indepen-

---

[1] My mother, Emma Winsloe, came of quite a different class from my father. His ancestor of earliest memory was factor to Lord Bute and a friend and companion of Robert Burns. His grandson was my grandfather Tennant of St Rollox Chemical Works, Glasgow. My mother's family were of gentle blood. Richard Winsloe (1770-1842) was rector of Minster-Forrabury in Cornwall and of Ruishton, near Taunton. He married Catherine Walter, daughter of the founder of the *Times*. Their son, Richard Winsloe, was sent to Oxford to study for the Church. He ran away with Charlotte Monkton, aged 17. They were caught at Evesham and brought back to be married next day at Taunton, where Admiral Monkton was living. They had two children: Emma, our mother, and Richard, my uncle.

dent happiness and physical energies filled her with fatigue. She never enjoyed her prosperity and suffered from all the apprehension, fussiness and love of economy that should by rights belong to the poor, but by a curious perversion almost always blight the rich.

Her preachings on economy were a constant source of amusement to my father. I made up my mind at an early age, after listening to his chaff, that money was the most overrated of all anxieties; and not only has nothing occurred in my long experience to make me alter this opinion but everything has tended to confirm it.

In discussing matrimony my father would say:

'I'm sure I hope, girls, you'll not marry penniless men; men should not marry at all unless they can keep their wives,' etc.

To this my mother would retort:

'Do not listen to your father, children! Marrying for money has never yet made anyone happy; it is not blessed.'

Mama had no illusions about her children nor about anything else and her mild criticisms balanced my father's obsessions. When Charty's looks were praised, she would answer with a fine smile: '*Tant soit peu mouton!*'

She thought us all very plain. When someone suggested that we should be painted it was almost more than my mother could bear. The poorness of the subject and the richness of the price shocked her profoundly. Luckily my father – who had begun to buy fine pictures – entirely agreed with her, though not for the same reasons:

'I am sure I don't know where I could hang the girls, even if I were fool enough to have them painted!' he would say.

I cannot ever remember kissing my mother without her tapping me on the back and saying, 'Hold yourself up!' or kissing my father without his saying, 'Don't frown!' And I shall never cease being grateful for this, as *à l'heure qu'il est* I have not a line in my forehead and my figure has not changed since my marriage.

My mother's indifference to – I might almost say suspicion of – other people always amused me:

'I am sure I don't know why they should come here, unless it is to see the garden! I cannot help wondering what was at the back of her mind.'

When I suggested that perhaps the lady she referred to had no mind, my mother would say, 'I don't like people with *arrière-pensées*'; and ended most of her criticisms by saying, 'It looks to me as if she had a poor circulation.'

My mother's sense of humour was excellent; and it might have been said of her what Doll Liddell[1] said of my sister Lucy: 'She has a touch of mild genius.'

People thought her a calm, serene person, satisfied with pinching green flies off plants and incapable of deep feeling, but my mother's heart had been broken by the death of her first four children and she dreaded emotion. Any attempt on my part to discuss old days or her own sensations was resolutely discouraged. There was a lot of fun and affection but a tepid intimacy between us, except about my flirtations; and over these we saw eye to eye.

My mother, who had been a great flirt herself, thoroughly enjoyed all love-affairs and was absolutely unshockable. Little words of wisdom would drop from her mouth:

MY MOTHER: 'Men don't like being run after . . .'

MARGOT: 'Oh, don't you believe it, mama!'

MY MOTHER: 'You can do what you like in life if you can hold your tongue, but the world is relentless to people who are found out.'

She told my father that if he interfered with my love-affairs I should very likely marry a groom.

She did me a good turn here, for, though I would not have married a groom, I might have married the wrong man, and, in any case, interference would have been cramping to me.

[1] The late A. G. C. Liddell.

II · *Glen and Laura*

My home, Glen, is on the border of Peeblesshire and Selkirkshire, sixteen miles from Abbotsford and thirty from Edinburgh. It was designed on the lines of Glamis and Castle Fraser, in what is called Scottish baronial style. I well remember the first shock I had when someone said:

'I hate turrets and tin men on the top of them!'

It unsettled me for days. I had never imagined that anything could be more beautiful than Glen. The classical style of Whittingehame – and other fine places of the sort – appeared to me better suited for municipal buildings; the beams and flint in Cheshire reminded me of Earls Court; and such castles as I had seen looked like the pictures of the Rhine on my blotting-book. I was quite ignorant and 'Scottish baronial' thrilled me.

What made Glen really unique was not its architecture but its situation. The road by which you approached it was a cul-de-sac and led to nothing but moors. This – and the fact of its being many miles from a railway station – gave it security in its wildness. Great stretches of heather swept down to the garden-walls; and, however many heights you climbed, moor upon moor rose again in front of you.

Someone said when I was young that my hair was biography: as it is my only claim to beauty, I would like to think that this is true, but the hills at Glen are my real biography.

Nature inoculates its lovers from its own culture; sea, downs and moors produce a different type of person. Shepherds, fishermen and poachers are a little like what they contemplate and, were it possible to ask the towns to tell us whom they find most untamable, I have not a doubt that they would say, those who are born on the moors. I am glad that Emerson wrote 'human nature . . . is everywhere the same, but the wilder it is, the more virtuous.'

I married late and spent all my early life at Glen: I was a child of the heather. After my sister Laura Lyttelton died, my brother Eddy and I lived alone with my parents for nine years at Glen.

When he was abroad shooting big game, I spent long days out of doors, seldom coming in for lunch. Both my pony and my hack were saddled from 7 a.m., ready for me to ride, every day of my life. I wore the shortest of tweed skirts, knickerbockers of the same stuff, top-boots, a covert-coat and a coloured scarf round my head. I was equipped with a book, pencils, cigarettes and food. Every shepherd and poacher knew me; and I have often shared my 'piece' with them, sitting in the heather near the red burns, or sheltered from rain in the cuts and quarries of the open road.

After my first great sorrow – the death of my sister Laura – I was suffocated in the house and felt I had to be out of doors from morning till night.

One day I saw an old shepherd called Gowanlock coming up to me, holding my pony by the rein. I had never noticed that it had strayed away and, after thanking him, I observed him looking at me quietly – he knew something of the rage and anguish that Laura's death had brought into my heart – and putting his hand on my shoulder, he said:

'My child, there's no contending. . . . Ay . . . ay . . .' shaking his beautiful old head, '*that is so*, there's no contending. . . .'

Another day, when it came on to rain, I saw a tramp crouching under the dyke, holding an umbrella over his head and eating his lunch. I went and sat down beside him and we fell into desultory conversation. He had a grand, wild face and I felt some curiosity about him; but he was taciturn and all he told me was that he was walking to the Gordon Arms, on his way to St Mary's Loch. I asked him every sort of question – as to where he had come from, where he was going to and what he wanted to do – but he refused to answer, so I gave him one of my cigarettes and a light and we sat on peacefully smoking in silence together. When the rain cleared, I turned to him and said:

'You seem to walk all day and go nowhere; when you wake up in the morning, how do you shape your course?'

To which he answered:

'I always turn my back to the wind.'

Border people are more intelligent than those born in the South; and the people of my birthplace are a hundred years in advance of the Southern English even now.

When I was fourteen, I met a shepherd-boy reading a French book. It was called *Le Secret de Delphine*. I asked him how he came to know French and he told me it was the extra subject that he had been allowed to choose for studying in his holidays; he walked eighteen miles a day to school – nine there and nine back – taking his chance of a lift from a passing vehicle. I begged him to read out loud to me, but he was shy of his accent and would not do it. The Lowland Scotch were a wonderful people in my day.

*   *   *

I remember nothing unhappy of my glorious youth except the violence of our family quarrels. Reckless waves of high and low spirits, added to quick tempers, obliged my mother to separate us for some time and forbid us to sleep in the same bedroom. We raged and ragged till the small hours of the morning, which kept us thin and the household awake.

My mother told me two stories of myself as a little child:

'When you were sent for to come downstairs, Margot, the nurse opened the door and you walked in – generally alone – saying, "Here's me! . . ." '

This rather sanguine opening does not seem to have been sufficiently checked. She went on to say:

'I was dreadfully afraid you would be upset and ill when I took you one day to the Deaf and Dumb Asylum in Glasgow, as you felt things with passionate intensity. Before starting I lifted you on to my knee and said, "You know, darling, I am going to take you to see some poor people who cannot speak." At which you put your arms round my neck and said, with consoling emphasis, "*I* will soon make them speak!" '

The earliest event I can remember was the arrival of the new baby, my brother Jack, when I was two years old. Dr Cox was spoiling my mother's good-night visit while I was being dried after my bath. My pink flannel dressing-gown, with white buttonhole stitching, was hanging over the fender: and he was discussing some earnest subject in a low tone. He got up and, pinching my chin said:

'She will be very angry, but we will give her a baby of her own,' or words to that effect.

The next day a huge doll obliterated from my mind the new baby which had arrived that morning.

We were very much alone in our nursery, as my mother travelled from pillar to post, hunting for health for her child Pauline. Our nurse, Mrs Hills – called 'Missuls' for short – went away on my tenth birthday to become my sister's lady's maid; and this removed our first and last restriction.

We were wild children and, left to ourselves, had the time of our lives. I rode my pony up the front stairs and tried to teach my father's high-stepping barouche-horses to jump – crashing their knees into the hurdles in the field – and climbed our dangerous roof, sitting on the sweep's ladder by moonlight in my night-gown. I had scrambled up every tree, walked on every wall and knew every turret at Glen. I ran along the narrow ledges of the slates in rubber shoes at terrific heights; this alarmed other people so much that my father sent for me one day to see him in his 'business room' and made me swear before God that I would give up walking on the roof; and give it up I did, with many tears.

Laura and I were fond of acting and dressing up. We played at being found in dangerous and adventurous circumstances in the garden. One day the boys were rabbit-shooting and we were acting with the doctor's daughter. I had spoilt the game by running round the kitchen garden-wall instead of being discovered – as I was meant to be – in a Turkish turban, smoking on the banks of the Bosphorus. Seeing that things were going badly and that the others had disappeared, I took a wild jump into the radishes. On landing I observed a strange gentleman coming up the path. He looked at my torn gingham frock, naked legs, tennis shoes and dishevelled curls under an orange turban; and I stood still and gazed at him.

'This is a wonderful place,' he said; to which I replied:

'You like it?' ....

HE: 'I would like to see the house. I hear there are beautiful things in it.'

MARGOT: 'I think the drawing-rooms are all shut up.'

HE: 'How do you know? Surely you could manage to get hold of a servant or someone who would take me round. Do you know any of them?'

I asked him if he meant the family or the servants.

'The family,' he said.

MARGOT: 'I know them very well, but I don't know you.'

'I am an artist,' said the stranger; 'my name is Peter Graham. Who are you?'

'I am an artist too!' I said. 'My name is Margot Tennant. I suppose you thought I was the gardener's daughter, didn't you?'

He gave a circulating smile, finishing on my turban, and said:

'To tell you the honest truth, I had no idea what you were!'

We had a dancing-class at the minister's and an arithmetic-class in our schoolroom. I was as good at the Manse as I was bad at my sums; and poor Mr Menzies, the Traquair schoolmaster, had eventually to beg my mother to withdraw me from the class, as I kept them all back. To my delight I was withdrawn; and from that day to this I have never added a single row of figures.

I showed a remarkable proficiency in dancing and could lift both my feet to the level of my eyebrows with disconcerting ease. Mrs Wallace, the minister's wife, was shocked and said:

'Look at Margot with her Frenchified airs!'

I pondered often and long over this, the first remark about myself that I can ever remember. Someone said to me:

'Does your hair curl naturally?'

To which I replied:

'I don't know, but I will ask.'

I was unaware of myself and had not the slightest idea what 'curling naturally' meant.

We had two best dresses: one made in London, which we only wore on great occasions; the other made by my nurse, in which we went down to dessert. These dresses gave me my first impression of civilised life. Just as the Speaker, before clearing the House, spies strangers, so, when I saw my black velvet skirt and pink Garibaldi put out on the bed, I knew that something was up! The nursery confection was of white alpaca, piped with pink, and did not inspire the same excitement and confidence.

We saw little of our mother in our youth and I asked Laura one day if she thought she said her prayers; I would not have remembered this had it not been that Laura was profoundly shocked. The question was quite uncalled for and had no ulterior motive, but I never remembered my mother or anyone else talking to us about the Bible or hearing us say our prayers. Nevertheless we were all deeply religious, by which no one need infer that we were good. There was one service a week, held on Sundays, in Traquair Kirk, which everyone went to; and the shepherds' dogs kept close to their masters' plaids, hung over the high box-pews, all the way down the aisle. I have heard many fine sermons in Scotland, but our minister was not a good preacher; and we were often dissolved in laughter, sitting in the square family pew in the gallery. My father closed his eyes tightly all through the sermon, leaning his head on his hand.

The Scottish Sabbath still held its own in my youth; and, when I heard that Ribblesdale and Charty played lawn-tennis on Sundays, I felt very unhappy. We had a few Sabbath amusements, but they were not as entertaining as those described in Miss Fowler's book, in which the men who were heathens went into one corner of the room and the women who were Christians into the other and at the beating of a gong, conversion was accomplished by a close embrace. Our Scottish Sabbaths were very different and I thought them more than dreary. Although I love church music and architecture and can listen to almost any sermon at any time and even read sermons to myself, going to church in the country remains a sacrifice to me. The custom in the Church of England of reading indistinctly and in an assumed voice has alienated simple people in every parish. In my country you can still hear a good sermon. When staying with Lord Haldane's mother – the best-looking, most humorous and saintly of old ladies – I heard an excellent sermon at Auchterarder on this very subject, the dullness of Sundays. The minister said that, however brightly the sun shone on stained-glass windows, no one could guess what they were really like from outside; it was only from the inside that you should judge of them.

Another time I heard a man end his sermon by saying:

'And now, my friends, do your duty and don't look upon the world with eyes jaundiced by religion.'

My mother hardly ever mentioned religion to us and, when the subject was brought up by other people, she confined her remarks to saying in a weary voice and with a resigned sigh that God's ways were mysterious. She had suffered many sorrows and, in estimating her lack of temperament, I do not think I made enough allowance for them. No true woman ever gets over the loss of a child; and her three eldest had died before I was born.

I was the most vital of the family and what the nurses described as 'a venturesome child'. Our coachman's wife called me 'a little Turk'. Self-willed, excessively passionate, disconcertingly truthful, bold as well as fearless and always against convention, I was, no doubt, extremely difficult to bring up.

My mother was not lucky with her governesses – we had two at a time, and of every nationality, French, German, Swiss, Italian and Greek – but, whether through my fault or our governesses', I never succeeded in making one of them really love me. Mary Morison,[1] who kept a high school for young ladies at Innerleithen, was the first person who influenced me and my sister Laura. She is alive now and a woman of rare intellect and character. She was fonder of Laura than of me, but so were most people.

Here I would like to say something about my sister and Alfred Lyttelton, whom she married in 1885.

A great deal of nonsense has been written and talked about Laura. There are two printed accounts of her that are true: one has been written by the present Mrs Alfred Lyttelton, in generous and tender passages in the life of her husband, and the other by A. G. C. Liddell:[2] but even these do not quite give the brilliant, witty Laura of my heart.

I will quote what my dear friend, Doll Liddell, wrote of her:

'My acquaintance with Miss Tennant, which led to a close intimacy with herself, and afterwards with her family, was an event of such importance in my life that I feel I ought to attempt some description

[1] Miss Morison, a cousin of Mr William Archer.
[2] *Notes from the Life of an Ordinary Mortal*, by A. G. C. Liddell. John Murray, 1911.

of her. This is not an easy task, as a more indescribable person never existed, for no one could form a correct idea of what she was like who had not had opportunities of feeling her personal charm. Her looks were certainly not striking at first sight, though to most persons who had known her some weeks she would often seem almost beautiful. To describe her features would give no idea of the brightness and vivacity of her expression, or of that mixture of innocence and mischief, as of a half-child, half-Kelpie, which distinguished her. Her figure was very small but well made, and she was always prettily and daintily dressed. If the outward woman is difficult to describe, what can be said of her character?

'To begin with her lighter side, she had reduced fascination to a fine art in a style entirely her own. I have never known her meet any man, and hardly any woman, whom she could not subjugate in a few days. It is as difficult to give any idea of her methods as to describe a dance when the music is unheard. Perhaps one may say that her special characteristic was the way in which she combined the gaiety of a child with the tact and aplomb of a grown woman. . . . Her victims, after their period of enchantment, generally became her devoted friends.

'This trifling was, however, only the ripple on the surface. In the deeper parts of her nature was a fund of earnestness and a sympathy which enabled her to throw herself into the lives of other people in a quite unusual way, and was one of the great secrets of the general affection she inspired. It was not, however, as is sometimes the case with such feelings, merely emotional, but impelled her to many kindnesses and to constant, though perhaps somewhat impulsive, efforts to help her fellows of all sorts and conditions.

'On her mental side she certainly gave the impression, from the originality of her letters and sayings, and her appreciation of what was best in literature, that her gifts were of a high order. In addition, she had a subtle humour and readiness, which made her repartees often delightful and produced phrases and fancies of characteristic daintiness. But there was something more than all this, an extra dose of life, which caused a kind of electricity to flash about her wherever she went, lighting up all with whom she came in contact. I am aware that this description will seem exaggerated, and will be put down to the writer having dwelt in her "Ægæan isle." but I think that if it should meet the eyes of any who knew her in her short life, they will understand what it attempts to convey'.

This is good, but his poem is even better; and there is a prophetic touch in the line 'Shadowed with something of the future years.'

> *A face upturned towards the midnight sky,*
> *Pale in the glimmer of the pale starlight,*
> *And all around the black and boundless night,*
> *And voices of the winds which bode and cry.*
> *A childish face, but grave with curves that lie*
> *Ready to breathe in laughter or in tears,*
> *Shadowed with something of the future years*
> *That makes one sorrowful, I know not why.*
> *O still, small face, like a white petal torn*
> *From a wild rose by autumn winds and flung*
> *On some dark stream the hurrying waves among:*
> *By what strange fates and whither art thou borne?*

Laura had many poems written to her from many lovers. My daughter Elizabeth Bibesco's godfather, Godfrey Webb – a conspicuous member of the Souls, not long since dead – wrote this of her:

HALF CHILD, HALF WOMAN
Tennyson's description of Laura in 1883

> *"Half child, half woman" – wholly to be loved*
> *By either name she found an easy way*
> *Into my heart, whose sentinels all proved*
> *Unfaithful to their trust, the luckless day*
> *She entered there. "Prudence and reason both!*
> *Did you not question her? How was it pray*
> *She so persuaded you?" "Nor sleep nor sloth,"*
> *They cried, "o'ercame us, a child at play*
> *Went smiling past us, and then turning round*
> *Too late your heart to save, a woman's face we found."*

Laura was not a plaster saint; she was a generous, claimative, combative little creature of genius, full of humour, imagination, temperament and impulse.

Someone reading this memoir will perhaps say:

'I wonder what Laura and Margot were really like, what the differences and what the resemblances between them were.'

The men who could answer this question best would be Lord Gladstone, Mr Arthur Balfour, Lord Midleton, Sir Rennell Rodd, or Lord Curzon of Kedleston. I can only say what I think the differences and resemblances were.

Strictly speaking, before I broke my nose I was better-looking than Laura, but she had rarer and more beautiful eyes. Brains are such a small part of people that I cannot judge of them as between her and me; and, at the age of twenty-three, when she died, few of us are at the height of our powers; but Laura made and left a deeper impression on the world in her short life than anyone that I have ever known. What she really had to a greater degree than other people was true spirituality, a feeling of intimacy with the other world and a sense of the love and wisdom of God and His plan of life. Her mind was informed by true religion; and her heart was fixed. This did not prevent her from being a very great flirt. The first time that a man came to Glen and liked me better than Laura, she was immensely surprised – not more so than I was – and had it not been for the passionate love which we cherished for each other, there must inevitably have been much jealousy between us.

On several occasions the same man proposed to both of us and had to find out from each other what our intentions were.

Laura was gentler than I was and her goodness resolved itself into greater activity.

She and I belonged to a reading-class. I read more than she did and at greater speed, but we were all readers and profited by a climate which kept us indoors and a fine library. The class obliged us to read an hour a day, which could not be called excessive, but the real test was doing the same thing at the same time. I would have preferred three or four hours' reading on wet days and none on fine, but not so our Edinburgh tutor.

Laura started the Girls' Friendly Society in the village, which was at that time famous for its drunkenness and immorality. We drove ourselves to the meetings in a high two-wheeled dog-cart behind a fast trotter, coming back late in pitch darkness along icy roads. These drives to Innerleithen and our moonlight talks are among my most precious recollections.

At the meetings – after reading aloud to the girls while they sewed and knitted – Laura would address them. She gave a sort of lesson, moral, social and religious, and they all adored her. More remarkable at her age than speaking to mill-girls were her Sunday classes at Glen, in the housekeeper's room. I do not know any girl now of any age – Laura was only sixteen – who could talk on religious subjects with profit to the butler, housekeeper and maids, or to grown-up people, on a Sunday afternoon.

Compared with what the young men have written and published during this war, Laura's literary promise was not great; both her prose and her poetry were less remarkable than her conversation.

She was not so good a judge of character as I was and took many a goose for a swan, but, in consequence of this, she made people of both sexes – and even all ages – twice as good, clever and delightful as they would otherwise have been.

I have never succeeded in making anyone the least different from what they are and, in my efforts to do so, have lost most of my female friends. This was the true difference between us. I have never influenced anybody but my own two children, Elizabeth and Anthony; but Laura had such an amazing effect upon men and women that for years after she died they told me that she had both changed and made their lives.

This is a tremendous saying. When I die, people may turn up and try and make the world believe that I have influenced them and women may come forward whom I adored and who have quarrelled with me and pretend that they always loved me, but I wish to put it on record that they did not, or, if they did, their love is not my kind of love and I have no use for it.

The fact is that I am not touchy or impenitent myself and forget that others may be and I tell people the truth about themselves, while Laura made them feel it. I do not think I should mind hearing from anyone the naked truth about myself; and, on the few occasions when it has happened to me, I have not been in the least offended. My chief complaint is that so few love one enough, as one grows older, to say what they really think; nevertheless I have often wished that I had been born with Laura's skill and tact in dealing with men and women. In her short life she influenced more people than I have done in over twice as many years. I have never influenced people even enough to make them change their stockings and I have never succeeded in persuading any young persons under my charge – except my own two children – to say that they were wrong or sorry, nor at this time of life do I expect to do so.

There was another difference between Laura and me: she felt sad when she refused the men who proposed to her; I pitied no man who loved me. I told Laura that both her lovers and mine had a very good chance of getting over it, as they invariably declared themselves too soon. We were neither of us *au fond* very susceptible. It was the custom of the house that men should be in love with us, but I can truly say that we gave quite as much as we received.

I said to Rowley Leigh[1] – a friend of my brother Eddy's and one of the first gentlemen that ever came to Glen – when he begged me to go for a walk with him:

'Certainly, if you won't ask me to marry you.'

To which he replied:

'I never thought of it!'

'That's all right!' said I, putting my arm confidingly and gratefully through his.

He told me afterwards that he had been making up his mind and changing it for days as to how he should propose.

Sir David Tennant, a former Speaker at Cape Town and the most distant of cousins, came to stay at Glen with his son, a youth of twenty. After a few days, the young man took me into one of the conservatories and asked me to marry him. I pointed out that I hardly knew him by sight, and that 'he was running hares'. He took it extremely well and, much elated, I returned to the house to tell Laura. I found her in tears: she told me Sir David Tennant had asked her to marry him and she had been obliged to refuse. I cheered her up by pointing out that it would have been awkward had we both accepted, for, while remaining my sister, she would have become my mother-in-law and my husband's stepmother.

We were not popular in Peeblesshire, partly because we had no

[1] The Hon. Rowland Leigh, of Stoneleigh Abbey.

county connection, but chiefly because we were Liberals. My father had turned out the sitting Tory, Sir Graham Montgomery, of Stobo, and was member for the two counties Peeblesshire and Selkirkshire. As Sir Graham had represented the counties for thirty years, this was resented by the Montgomery family, who proceeded to cut us. Laura was much worried over this, but I was amused. I said the love of the Maxwell Stuarts, Maxwell Scotts, Wolfe Murrays and Sir Thomas – now Lord – Carmichael was quite enough for me; as a matter of fact, neither Sir Graham nor his sons disliked us. I met Basil Montgomery at Traquair House many years after my papa's election, where we were entertained by Herbert Maxwell, the owner of one of the most romantic houses in Scotland and our courteous and affectionate neighbour. Not knowing who he was, I was indignant when he told me he thought Peeblesshire was dull; I said where we lived it was far from dull and asked him if he knew many people in the county. To which he answered:

'Chiefly the Stobo lot.'

At this I showed him the most lively sympathy and invited him to come to Glen. In consequence of his visit he told me years afterwards his fortune had been made. My father took a fancy to him and at my request employed him on the Stock Exchange.

Laura and I shared the night nursery together till she married; and, in spite of mixed proposals, we were devoted friends. We read late in bed, sometimes till three in the morning, and said our prayers out loud to each other every evening. We were discussing imagination one night and were comparing Hawthorne, De Quincey, Poe and others, in consequence of a dispute arising out of one of our pencil-games; and we argued till the housemaid came in with the hot water at eight in the morning.

I will digress here to explain our after-dinner games. There were several; one was called 'Styles', another 'Epigrams', a third 'Clumps' – which was a development of 'Twenty Questions' – and the most dangerous of all 'Character Sketches'. We were given no time-limit, but sat feverishly silent in different corners of the room, writing as hard as we could. When it was agreed that we had all written enough, the manuscripts were given to our umpire, who read them out loud. Votes were then taken as to the authorship, which led to general conversation on books, people and manner of writing. We had many interesting umpires, beginning with Bret Harte and Laurence Oliphant and going on to Arthur Balfour, George Curzon, George Wyndham, Lionel Tennyson,[1] Harry Cust and Doll Liddell: all good writers themselves.

Some of our guests preferred making caricatures to competing in the more ambitious line of literature. I made this drawing of the Dowager Marchioness of Aylesbury, better known as 'Lady A.';

I drew this of (Maria) Lady Aylesbury at Althorp March 1891.

Colonel Saunderson – a famous Orangeman – did the sketch of Gladstone for me; while Alma Tadema gave me the portrait of Queen Victoria, done in four lines.

These games were good for our tempers and a fine training; any loose vanity, jealousy, or over-competitiveness were certain to be shown up; and those who took the buttons off the foils in the duel of argument – of which I have seen a good deal in my life – were instantly found out.

[1] Brother of the present Lord Tennyson.

I never saw a playing-card at Glen till after I married, though – when we were obliged to dine downstairs to prevent the company being thirteen at dinner – I vaguely remember a view of my grandfather's back playing whist.

*   *   *

Laura was a year and a half older than I and came out in 1881, while I was in Dresden. The first party that she and I went to together was a political crush given by Sir William and Lady Harcourt,

where I was introduced to Spencer Lyttelton and shortly after this Laura met his brother Alfred.

One day, as she and I were leaving St Paul's Cathedral, she pointed out a young man to me and said:

'Go and ask Alfred Lyttelton to come to Glen any time this autumn,' which I promptly did.

The advent of Alfred into our family coincided with that of several new men, the Charterises, Balfours, George Curzon, George Wyndham, Harry Cust, the Crawleys, Jack Pease, 'Harry' Paulton,

Portrait of The Queen.
in four lines by Mr.
Alma Tadema R.A.
1890 -

Lord Houghton, Mark Napier, Doll Liddell and others. High hopes
had been entertained by my father that some of these young men
might marry us, but after the reception we gave Lord Lymington –
who, to do him justice, never proposed to any of us except in the
paternal imagination – his nerve was shattered and we were left to
ourselves.

Some weeks before Alfred's arrival, Laura had been disturbed by
hearing that we were considered 'fast'; she told me that receiving
company in our bedroom shocked people and that we ought, perhaps,
to give it up. I listened closely to what she had to say and at the end
remarked that it appeared to me to be quite absurd. Godfrey Webb
agreed with me and said that people who were easily shocked were

like women who sell stale pastry in cathedral towns and he advised
us to take no notice whatever of what anyone said. We hardly
knew the meaning of the word 'fast', and, as my mother went to bed
punctually at eleven, it was unthinkable that men and women friends
who wanted to sit up should not be allowed to join us. Our bedroom had been converted out of the night nursery into a sitting-
room. The shutters were removed and bookshelves put in their
place. The Morris carpet and chintzes I had discovered for myself
and chosen in London and my walls were ornamented with curious
objects, varying from caricatures and crucifixes to prints of prize-
fights, fox-hunts, Virgins and Wagner. In one of the turrets I hung
my clothes; in the other I put an altar on which I kept my books of
prayer and a skull which was given to me by the shepherd's son
and which is on my bookshelf now; we wore charming dressing-
jackets and sat up in bed with coloured cushions behind our backs,
while the brothers and friends sat on the floor or in comfortable
chairs round the room. On these occasions the gas was turned low,
a brilliant fire made up and either a guest or one of us would read
by the light of a single candle, tell ghost-stories or discuss current
affairs: politics, people and books. Not only the young but the old
came to our gatherings. I remember Jowett reading aloud to us
Thomas Hill Green's lay sermons; and, when he had finished, I
asked him how much he had loved Green, to which he replied:

'I did not love him at all.'

That these midnight meetings should shock anyone appeared
fantastic; and as most people in the house agreed with me, they were
continued.

It was not this alone that disturbed Laura; she wanted to marry a
serious, manly fellow, but, as she was a great flirt, other types of a
more brilliant kind obscured this vision and she had become profoundly undecided over her own love-affairs; they had worked so
much upon her nerves that when Mr Lyttelton came to Glen she
was in bed with acute neuralgia and unable to see him.

My father welcomed Alfred warmly, for, apart from his charming
personality, he was Gladstone's nephew and had been brought up in
the Liberal creed.

On the evening of his arrival, we all went out after dinner. There

had been a terrific gale which had destroyed half a wood on a hill
in front of the library windows and we wanted to see the roots of
the trees blown up by dynamite. It was a moonlight night, but the
moon is always brighter in novels than in life and it was pitch dark.
Alfred and I, walking arm in arm, talked gaily to each other as we
stumbled over the broken brushwood by the side of the Quair burn.
As we approached the wood a white birch lay across the water at a
slanting angle and I could not resist leaving my companion's side to
walk across it. It was, however, too slippery for me and I fell.
Alfred plunged into the burn and scrambled me out. I landed on
my feet and, except for sopping stockings, no harm was done. Our
party had scattered in the dark, and as it was past midnight, we
walked back to the house alone. When we returned, we found everybody had gone to their rooms and Alfred suggested carrying me up
to mine. As I weighed under eight stone he lifted me up like a toy
and deposited me on my bed. Kneeling down, he kissed my hand
and said good-night to me.

Two days after this my brother Eddy and I travelled North for
the Highland meeting. Laura, who had been gradually recovering,
was well enough to leave her room that day; and I need hardly say
this had the immediate effect of prolonging Alfred's visit. On my
return to Glen ten days later, she told me she had made up her mind
to marry Alfred Lyttelton.

*   *   *

After what Mrs Lyttelton has written of her husband, there is
little to add, but I must say one word of my brother-in-law as he
appeared to me in those early days.

Alfred Lyttelton was a vital, splendid young man of fervent
nature, even more spoilt than we were. He was as cool and as
fundamentally unsusceptible as he was responsive and emotional.
Everyone adored him; he combined the prowess at games of a
Greek athlete with moral right-mindedness of a high order. He was
neither a gambler nor an artist. He respected discipline but loathed
asceticism.

What interested me most in him was not his mind – which lacked
elasticity – but his religion, his unquestioning obedience to the

will of God and his perfect freedom from cant. His mentality was brittle and he was as quick-tempered in argument as he was sunny and serene in games. There are people who thought Alfred was a man of strong physical passions, wrestling with temptation till he had achieved complete self-mastery, but nothing was farther from the truth. In him you found combined an ardent nature, a cool temperament and a peppery intellectual temper. Alfred would have been justified in taking out a patent in himself as an Englishman, warranted like a dye never to lose colour. To him most foreigners were 'frogs'. In Edward Lyttelton's admirable monograph of his brother you will read that one day, when Alfred was in the train, sucking an orange, 'a small, grubby Italian, leaning on his walking-stick, smoking a cheroot, at the station,' was looked upon, not only by Alfred but by his biographer, as an 'irresistible challenge to fling the juicy, but substantial fragment full at the unsuspecting foreigner's cheek.' At this we are told that 'Alfred collapsed into noble convulsions of laughter.' I quote this incident, as it illustrates the difference between the Tennant and the Lyttelton sense of fun. Their laughter was a tornado or convulsion to which they succumbed; and even the Hagley ragging, though, according to Edward Lyttelton's book, it was only done with napkins, sounds formidable enough. Laura and Alfred enjoyed many things together – books, music and going to church – but they did not laugh at the same things. I remember her once saying to me:

'Wouldn't you have thought that, laughing as loud as the Lyttel-tons do, they would have loved Lear? Alfred says none of them think him a bit funny and was quite testy when I said his was the only family in the world that didn't.'

It was his manliness, spirituality and freedom from pettiness that attracted Laura to Alfred; he also had infinite charm. It might have been said of him what the Dowager Lady Grey wrote of her husband to Henry when thanking him for his sympathy:

'He lit so many fires in cold rooms.'

After Alfred's death, my husband said this of him in the House of Commons:

'It would not, I think, be doing justice to the feelings which are uppermost in many of our hearts, if we passed to the business of the day without taking notice of the fresh gap which has been made in our ranks by the untimely death of Mr Alfred Lyttelton. It is a loss of which I hardly trust myself to speak; for, apart from ties of relationship, there had subsisted between us for thirty-three years a close friendship and affection which no political differences were ever allowed to loosen, or even to affect. Nor could I better describe it than by saying that he, perhaps, of all men of this generation, came nearest to the mould and ideal of manhood which every English father would like to see his son aspire to and, if possible, to attain. The bounty of nature, enriched and developed not only by early training, but by constant self-discipline through life, blended in him gifts and graces which, taken alone, are rare and in such attractive union are rarer still. Body, mind and character, the schoolroom, the cricket-field, the Bar, the House of Commons – each made its separate contribution to the faculty and the experience of a many-sided and harmonious whole. But what he was he gave – gave with such ease and exuberance that I think it may be said without exaggeration that wherever he moved he seemed to radiate vitality and charm. He was, as we here know, a strenuous fighter. He has left behind him no resentments and no enmity; nothing but a gracious memory of a manly and winning personality, the memory of one who served with an unstinted measure of devotion his generation and country. He has been snatched away in what we thought was the full tide of buoyant life, still full of promise and of hope. What more can we say? We can only bow once again before the decrees of the Supreme Wisdom. Those who loved him – and they are many, in all schools of opinion, in all ranks and walks of life – when they think of him, will say to themselves:

This is the happy warrior, this is he
Who every man in arms should wish to be.'

I will quote from my diary the account of Alfred's second visit to Glen in December of that year:

Laura came into my bedroom in her peignoir and asked me what she should wear for dinner. I said:

'Your white muslin and hurry up. Mr Lyttelton is strumming in the Doo'cot and you had better go and entertain him, poor fellow, as he is leaving for London tonight.'

She tied a blue ribbon in her hair, hastily thrust her diamond brooch into her fichu and then, with her eyes very big and her hair low and straight upon her forehead, she went into our sitting-room (we called it the Doo'cot, because we all quarrelled there). Feeling rather small, but half-shy, half-bold, she shut the door and, leaning against it, watched Alfred strumming. He turned and gazed at the little figure so near him, so delicate in her white dress.

The silence was broken by Alfred asking her if any man ever left Glen without telling her that he loved her; but suddenly all talk stopped and she was in his arms, hiding her little face against his hard coat. There was no one to record what followed; only the night rising with passionate eyes: 'The hiding, receiving night that talks not.'

They were married on 10th May 1885.

In April of 1886 Laura's baby was expected any day and my mother was anxious that I should not be near her when the event took place. The Lytteltons lived in Upper Brook Street; and, Grosvenor Square being near, it was thought that any suffering on her part might make a lasting and painful impression on me, so I was sent down to Easton Grey to stay with Lucy and hunt in the Badminton country. Before going away, I went round to say goodbye to Laura and found her in a strange humour.

'I am sure I shall die with my baby,' she said.

MARGOT: 'How can you talk such nonsense? Everyone thinks that. Look at mama! She had twelve children without a pang!'

LAURA: 'I know she did; but I am sure I shall die.'

MARGOT: 'I am just as likely to be killed out hunting as you are to die darling! It makes me miserable to hear you talk like this.'

LAURA: 'If I die, Margot, I want you to read my will to the relations and people that will be in my bedroom. It is in that drawer. Promise me you will not forget.'

MARGOT: 'All right, darling, I will; but let us kneel down and pray that, whether it is me or you who die first, if it is God's will, one of us may come to the other down here and tell us the truth about the next world and console us as much as possible in this!'

We knelt and prayed and, though I was more removed from the world and in the humour both to see and to hear what was not material, in my grief over Laura's death, which took place ten days later, I have never heard from her or of her from that day to this.

Mrs Lyttelton has told the story of her husband's first marriage with so much perfection that I hesitate to go over the same ground again, but, as my sister Laura's death had more effect on me than any event in my life, except my own marriage and the birth of my children, I must copy a short account of it which I wrote at the time:

On Saturday, 17th April 1886, I was riding down a green slope in Gloucestershire while the Beaufort hounds were scattered below vainly trying to pick up the scent; they were on a stale line and the result had been general confusion. It was a hot day and the woods were full of children and primroses.

The air was humming with birds and insects, nature wore an expectant look and all the hedgerows sparkled with the spangles of the spring. There was a prickly gap under a tree which divided me from my companions. I rode down to jump it, but, whether from breeding, laziness or temper, my horse turned round and refused to move. I took my foot out of the stirrup and gave him a slight kick. I remember nothing after that till I woke up in a cottage with a tremendous headache. They said that the branch was too low, or the horse jumped too big and a withered bough had caught me in the face. In consequence I had concussion of the brain; and my nose and upper lip were badly torn. I was picked up by my early fiancé. He tied my lip to my hair – as it was reposing on my chin – and took me home in a cart. The doctor was sent for but there was no time to chloroform me. I sat very still from vanity while three stitches were put through the most sensitive part of my nose. When it was all over, I looked at myself in the looking glass and burst into tears. I had never been pretty ('worse than that,' as the Marquis de Soveral[1] said), but I had a straight nose and a look of intelligence; and now my face, like a German student's, would be marked for life.

The next day a telegram arrived saying:

'Laura confined – a boy – both doing well.'

We sent back a message:

'Hurrah and blessings!'

On Sunday we received a letter from Charty saying Laura was ill

[1] At that time Portuguese Minister.

and another on Monday telling us to go to London. I was in a state of acute anxiety and said to the doctor, I must go and see Laura immediately, but he would not hear of it:

'Impossible! You'll get erysipelas and die. Most dangerous to move with a face like that,' he said.

On the occasion of his next visit, I was dressed and walking up and down the room in a fume of nervous excitement, for go I *would*. Laura was dying (I did not really think she was, but I wanted to be near her). I insisted upon his taking the stitches out of my face and ultimately he had to give in. At 6 p.m. I was in the train for London, watching the telegraph-posts flying past me.

My mind was going over every possibility. I was sitting near her bed with the baby on my arm, chattering over plans, arranging tea-gowns, laughing at the nurse's anecdotes, talking and whispering over the thousand feminine things that I knew she would be longing to hear. . . . Or perhaps she was dying . . . asking for me and wondering why I did not come . . . thinking I was hunting instead of being with her. Oh, how often the train stopped! Did anyone really live at these stations? No one got out; they did not look like real places; why should the train stop? Should I tell them Laura was dying? . . . We had prayed so often to die the same day. . . . Surely she was not going to die . . . it could not be . . . her vitality was too splendid, her youth too great. . . . God would not allow this thing. . . . How stiff my face felt with its bandages; and if I cried they would come off!

At Swindon I had to change. I got out and sat in the vast eating-room, with its atmosphere of soup and gas. A crowd of people were talking of a hunting accident: this was mine. Then a woman came in and put her bag down. A clergyman shook hands with her; he said someone had died. I moved away.

'*World! Trewth! The Globe!* Paper miss? Paper? . . .'

'No thank you.'

'London train!' was shouted and I got in. I knew by the loud galloping sound that we were going between high houses and at each gallop the wheels seemed to say, 'Too late! Too late!' After a succession of hoarse screams we dashed into Paddington.

It was midnight. I saw a pale, grave face and recognised Evan

Charteris, who had come in Lady Wemyss' brougham to meet me.
I said:

'Is she dead?'

To which he answered:

'No, but very, very ill.'

We drove in silence to 4 Upper Brook Street. Papa, Jack and
Godfrey Webb stood in the hall. They stopped me as I passed and
said, 'She is no worse': but I could not listen. I saw Arthur Balfour
and Spencer Lyttelton standing near the door of Alfred's room.
They said:

'You look ill. Have you had a fall?'

I explained the plaster on my swollen face and asked if I might
go upstairs to see Laura; and they said they thought I might. When
I got to the top landing, I stood in the open doorway of the boudoir.
A man was sitting in an armchair by a table with a candle on it. It
was Alfred and I passed on. I saw the silhouette of a woman through
the open door of Laura's room; this was Charty. We held each other
close to our hearts . . . her face felt hot and her eyes were heavy.

'Don't look at her tonight, sweet; she is unconscious,' she said.

I did not take this in and asked to be allowed to say one word to
her. I said:

'I know she'd like to see me, darling, if only just to nod to, and
I promise I will go away quickly. Indeed, indeed I would not tire
her! I want to tell her the train was late and the doctor would not
let me come up yesterday. Only one second, *please*, Charty! . . .'

'But, my darling heart, she's unconscious. She has never been
conscious all day. She would not know you!'

I sank stunned upon the stair. Someone touched my shoulder:

'You had better go to bed, it is past one. No, you can't sleep
here: there's no bed. You must lie down; a sofa won't do, you are too
ill. Very well, then, you are *not* ill, but you will be tomorrow if you
don't go to bed.'

I found myself in the street, Arthur Balfour holding one of my
arms and Spencer Lyttelton the other. They took me to 40 Grosvenor
Square. I went to bed and early next morning I went across to
Upper Brook Street. The servant looked happy:

'She's better, miss, and she's conscious.'

I flew upstairs and Charty met me in her dressing-gown. She was calm and capable as always, but a new look, less questioning and more intense, had come into her face. She said:

'You can go in now.'

I felt a rushing of my soul and an over-eagerness that half-stopped me as I opened the door and stood at the foot of the wooden bed and gazed at what was left of Laura.

Her face had shrunk to the size of a child's; her lashes lay a black wall on the whitest of cheeks; her hair was hanging dragged up from her square brow in heavy folds upon the pillow. Her mouth was tightly shut and a dark blood-stain marked her chin. After a long silence, she moved and muttered and opened her eyes She fixed them on me, and my heart stopped. I stretched my hands out towards her, and said, 'Laura!' . . . But the sound died; she did not know me. I knew after that she could not live.

People went away for the Easter Holidays: Papa to North Berwick, Arthur Balfour to Westward Ho! and every day Godfrey Webb rode a patient cob up to the front door, to hear that she was no better. I sat on the stairs listening to the roar of London and the clock in the library. The doctor – Matthews Duncan – patted my head whenever he passed me on the stair and said, in his gentle Scotch accent:

'Poor little girl! Poor, poor little girl!'

I was glad he did not say that 'while there was life there was hope', or any of the medical platitudes, or I would have replied that he *lied*. There was no hope – none! . . .

One afternoon I went with Lucy to St George's, Hanover Square. The old man was sweeping out the church; and we knelt and prayed. Laura and I have often knelt side by side at that altar and I never feel alone when I am in front of the mysterious Christ-picture, with its bars of violet and bunches of grapes.

On my return I went upstairs and lay on the floor of Laura's bedroom, watching Alfred kneeling by her side with his arms over his head. Charty sat with her hands clasped; a single candle behind her head transfigured her lovely hair into a halo. Suddenly Laura opened her eyes and, turning them slowly on Charty, said:

'You are *heavenly*! . . .'

37

A long pause; and then, while we were all three drawing near her bed, we heard her say:

'I think God has forgotten me.'

The fire was weaving patterns on the ceiling; every shadow seemed to be looking with pity on the silence of that room, the long silence that has never been broken.

*   *   *

I did not go home that night, but slept at Alfred's house. Lucy had gone to the early Communion, but I had not accompanied her, as I was tired of praying. I must have fallen into a heavy sleep, when suddenly I felt someone touching my bed. I woke with a start and saw nurse standing beside me. She said in a calm voice:

'My dear, you must come. Don't look like that; you won't be able to walk.'

Able to walk! Of course I was! I was in my dressing-gown and downstairs in a flash and on to the bed. The room was full of people. I lay with my arm under Laura, as I did in the old Glen days, when after our quarrels we crept into each other's beds to 'make it up'. Alfred was holding one of her hands against his forehead; and Charty was kneeling at her feet.

She looked much the same, but a deeper shadow ran under her brow and her mouth seemed to be harder shut. I put my cheek against her shoulder and felt the sharpness of her spine. For a minute we lay close to each other, while the sun, fresh from the dawn, played upon the window-blinds. . . . Then her breathing stopped; she gave a shiver and died. . . . The silence was so great that I heard the flight of Death and the morning salute her soul.

I went downstairs and took her will out of the drawer where she had put it and told Alfred what she had asked me to do. The room was dark with people; and a tall man, gaunt and fervid, was standing up saying a prayer. When he had finished I read the will through.

Out of the many letters Alfred received, this is the one we liked best:

'HAWARDEN CASTLE,
'APRIL 27TH, 1886

'My Dear Alfred,

'It is a daring and perhaps a selfish thing to speak to you at a moment when your mind and heart are a sanctuary in which God is speaking to you in tones even more than usually penetrating and solemn. Certainly it pertains to few to be chosen to receive such lessons as are being taught you. If the wonderful trials of Apostles, Saints and Martyrs have all meant a love in like proportion wonderful, then, at this early period of your life, your lot has something in common with theirs, and you will bear upon you life-long marks of a great and peculiar dispensation which may and should lift you very high. Certainly you two who are still one were the persons whom in all the vast circuit of London life those near you would have pointed to as exhibiting more than any others the promise and the profit of *both* worlds. The call upon you for thanksgiving seemed greater than on anyone – you will not deem it lessened now. How eminently true it is of her that in living a short she fulfilled a long time. If Life is measured by intensity, hers was a very long life – and yet with that rich development of mental gifts, purity and singleness made her one of the little children of whom and of whose like is the Kingdom of Heaven. Bold would it indeed be to say such a being died prematurely. All through your life, however it be prolonged, what a precious possession to you she will be. But in giving her to your bodily eye and in taking her away the Almighty has specially set His seal upon you. To Peace and to God's gracious mercy let us heartily, yes, cheerfully, commend her. Will you let Sir Charles and Lady Tennant and all her people know how we feel with and for them?

'Ever your affec.

'W. E. GLADSTONE.'

Matthew Arnold sent me this poem because Jowett told him I said it might have been written for Laura:

REQUIESCAT

Strew on her roses, roses,
    And never a spray of yew!
In quiet she reposes;
    Ah, would that I did too!

Her mirth the world required;
    She bathed it in smiles of glee.
But her heart was, tired, tired,
    And now they let her be.

Her life was turning, turning,
    In mazes of heat and sound,
But for peace her soul was yearning,
    And now peace laps her round.

Her cabin'd, ample spirit,
    It flutter'd and fail'd for breath.
Tonight it doth inherit
    The vasty hall of death.

III · *Whitechapel and Society*

After Laura's death I spent much of my time in the East End of London. One day, when I was walking in the slums of Whitechapel, I saw a large factory and girls of all ages pouring in and out of it. Seeing the name 'Cliffords' on the door, I walked in and asked a workman to show me his employer's private room. He indicated with his finger where it was and I knocked and went in. Mr Cliffords, the owner of the factory, had a large red face and was sitting in a bare, squalid room, on a hard chair, in front of his writing-table. He glanced at me as I shut the door, but did not stop writing. I asked him if I might visit his factory once or twice a week and talk to the work-girls. At this he put his pen down and said:

'Now miss, what good do you suppose you will do here with my girls?'

MARGOT: 'It is not exactly *that*. I am not sure I can do anyone any good, but do you think I could do your girls any harm?'

CLIFFORDS: 'Most certainly you could and, what is more, you *will*.'

MARGOT: 'How?'

CLIFFORDS: 'Why, bless my soul! You'll keep them all jawing and make them late for their work! As it is, they don't do overmuch. Do you think my girls are wicked and that you are going to make them good and happy and save them and all that kind of thing?'

MARGOT: 'Not at all; I was not thinking of them. *I* am so very unhappy myself.'

CLIFFORDS (*rather moved and looking at me with curiosity*): 'Oh, that's quite another matter! If you've come here to ask me a favour, I might consider it.'

MARGOT (*humbly*): 'That is just what I have come for. I swear I would only be with your girls in the dinner interval, but if by accident I arrive at the wrong time I will see that they do not stop their work. It is far more likely that they won't listen to me at all than that they will stop working to hear what I have to say.'

CLIFFORDS: 'Maybe!'

So it was fixed up. He shook me by the hand, never asked my name and I visited his factory three days a week for eight years when I was in London (till I married, in 1894).

The East End of London was not a new experience to me. Laura and I had started a crèche at Wapping the year I came out; and in following up the cases of deserving beggars I had come across a variety of slums. I have derived as much interest and more benefit from visiting the poor than the rich and I get on better with them. What was new to me in Whitechapel was the head of the factory.

Mr Cliffords was what the servants describe as 'a man who keeps himself to himself', gruff, harsh, straight and clever. He hated all his girls and no one would have supposed, had they seen us together, that he liked me; but, after I had observed him blocking the light in the doorway of the room when I was speaking, I knew that I should get on with him.

The first day I went into the barn where the boxes were made, I was greeted by a smell of glue and perspiration and a roar of wheels on the cobble-stones in the yard outside. Forty or fifty women, varying in age from sixteen to sixty, were measuring, cutting and glueing cardboard and paper together and not one of them looked up from her work as I came in.

I climbed upon a hoarding and, kneeling down, pinned a photograph of Laura on a space of the wall. This attracted the attention of an elderly woman who turned to her companions and said:

'Come and have a look at this, girls! Why, it's to the life!'

Seeing some of the girls leave their work and remembering my promise to Cliffords, I jumped up and told them that in ten minutes' time they would be having their dinners and then I would like to speak to them, but that until then they must not stop their work. I was much relieved to see them obey me. Some of them kept sandwiches in dirty paper bags which they placed on the floor with their hats, but when the ten minutes were over I was disappointed to see nearly all of them disappear. I asked where they had gone to and was told that they either joined the men packers or went to the public-house round the corner.

The girls who brought sandwiches and stayed behind liked my visits and gradually became my friends. One of them – Phoebe Whitman by name – was beautiful and had more charm for me than the others; I asked her one day if she would take me with her to the public-house where she always lunched, as I had brought my food with me in a bag and did not suppose the public-house people would mind my eating it there with a glass of beer. This request of mine distressed the girls who were my friends. They thought it a terrible idea that I should go among drunkards, but I told them I had brought a book with me which they could look at and read out loud to each other while I was away – at which they nodded gravely – and I went off with my beautiful cockney.

The 'Peggy Bedford' was in the lowest quarter of Whitechapel and crowded daily with sullen and sad-looking people. It was hot, smelly and draughty. When we went in I observed that Phoebe was a favourite; she waved her hand gaily here and there and ordered herself a glass of bitter. The men who had been hanging about outside and in different corners of the room joined up to the counter on her arrival and I heard a lot of chaff going on while she tossed her pretty head and picked at potted shrimps. The room was too crowded for anyone to notice me; and I sat quietly in a corner eating my sandwiches and smoking my cigarette. The frosted-glass double doors swung to and fro and shrill voices of children asking for drinks and carrying them away in mugs made me feel profoundly unhappy. I followed one little girl through the doors out into the street and saw her give the mug to a cabman and run off delighted with his tip. When I returned I was deafened by a babel of voices; there was a row going on: one of the men, drunk but good-tempered, was trying to take the flower out of Phoebe's hat. Provoked by this, a younger man began jostling him, at which all the others pressed forward; the barman shouted ineffectually to them to stop; they merely cursed him and said that they were backing Phoebe. A woman, more drunk than the others, swore at being disturbed and said that Phoebe was a blasted something that I could not understand.

Suddenly I saw her hitting out like a prize-fighter; and the men formed a ring round them. I jumped up, seized an underfed, bleareyed being who was nearest to me and flung him out of my way. Rage and disgust inspired me with great physical strength; but I was prevented from breaking through the ring by a man seizing my arm and saying:

'Let be, or her man will give you a damned thrashing!'

Not knowing which of the women he was alluding to, I dipped down and, dodging the crowd, broke through the ring and flung myself upon Phoebe; my one fear was that she would be too late for her work and that the promise I had made to Cliffords would be broken.

Women fight very awkwardly and I was battered about between the two. I turned and cursed the men standing round for laughing and doing nothing and, before I could separate the combatants, I had given and received heavy blows; but unexpected help came from a Cliffords' packer who happened to look in. We extricated ourselves as well as we could and ran back to the factory. I made Phoebe apologize to the chief for being late and, feeling stiff all over, returned home to Grosvenor Square.

Cliffords, who was an expert boxer, invited me into his room on my next visit to tell him the whole story and my shares went up.

By the end of July all the girls – about fifty-two – stayed with me after their work and none of them went to the 'Peggy Bedford'.

The Whitechapel murders took place close to the factory about that time; and the girls and I visited what journalists call 'the scene of the tragedy'. It was strange watching crowds of people collected daily to see nothing but an archway.

I took my girls for an annual treat to the country every summer, starting at eight in the morning and getting back to London at midnight. We drove in three large wagonettes behind four horses, accompanied by a brass band. On one occasion I was asked if the day could be spent at Caterham, because there were barracks there. I thought it a dreary place and strayed away by myself, but Phoebe and her friends enjoyed glueing their noses to the rails and watching the soldiers drilling. I do not know how the controversy arose, but when I joined them I heard Phoebe shout through the railings that someone was 'a bloody fish!' I warned her that I should leave Cliffords for ever, if she went on provoking rows and using such violent language, and this threat upset her; for a short time she was on her best behaviour, but I confess I find the poor just as uninfluenceable and ungrateful as the rich and I often wonder what became of Phoebe Whitman.

At the end of July I told the girls that I had to leave them, as I was going back to my home in Scotland.

PHOEBE: 'You don't know, lady, how much we all feels for you having to live in the country. Why, when you pointed out to us on the picnic-day that kind of a tower-place, with them walls and dark trees, and said it reminded you of your home, we just looked at each other! "Well, I never!" sez I; and we all shuddered!'

None of the girls knew what my name was or where I lived till they read about me in the picture-papers, eight years later, at the time of my marriage.

*   *   *

When I was not in the East End of London, I wandered about looking at the shop-windows in the West. One day I was admiring a photograph of my sister Charty in the window of Macmichael's, when a footman touched his hat and asked me if I would speak to 'her Grace' in the carriage. I turned round and saw the Duchess of Manchester;[1] as I had never spoken to her in my life, I wondered what she could possibly want me for. After shaking hands she said:

'Jump in, dear child! I can't bear to see you look so sad. Jump in and I'll take you for a drive and you can come back to tea with me.'

I got into the carriage and we drove round Hyde Park, after which I followed her upstairs to her boudoir in Great Stanhope Street. In the middle of tea Queen Alexandra – then Princess of Wales – came in to see the Duchess. She ran in unannounced and kissed her hostess.

My heart beat when I looked at her. She had more real beauty, both of line and expression, and more dignity than anyone I had ever seen; and I can never forget that first meeting.

[1] Afterwards the Duchess of Devonshire.

Those were the days of the great beauties. London worshipped beauty like the Greeks. Photographs of the Princess of Wales, Mrs Langtry, Mrs Cornwallis West, Mrs Wheeler and Lady Dudley[1] collected crowds in front of the shop windows. I have seen great and conventional ladies like old Lady Cadogan and others standing on iron chairs in the Park to see Mrs Langtry walk past; and wherever Georgiana Lady Dudley drove there were crowds round her carriage when it pulled up, to see this vision of beauty, holding a large holland umbrella over the head of her lifeless husband.

Groups of beauties like the Moncrieffes, Grahams, Conynghams, de Moleynses, Lady Mary Mills, Lady Randolph Churchill, Mrs Arthur Sassoon, Lady Dalhousie, Lady March, Lady Londonderry and Lady de Grey were to be seen in the salons of the 'eighties. There is nothing at all like this in London today and I doubt if there is anyone now with enough beauty or temperament to provoke a fight in Rotten Row between gentlemen in high society (an incident of my youth which I was privileged to witness and which caused a profound sensation).

Queen Alexandra had a more perfect face than any of those I have mentioned; it is visible now, because the oval is still there, the frownless brows, the carriage and, above all, the grace both of movement and of gesture which made her the idol of her people.

London society is neither better nor worse than it was in the 'eighties; there is less talent and less intellectual ambition and much less religion; but where all the beauty has gone to I cannot think!

When the Princess of Wales walked into the Duchess of Manchester's boudoir that afternoon, I got up to go away, but the Duchess presented me to her and they invited me to stay and have tea, which I was delighted to do. I sat watching her, teacup in hand, and was thrilled with admiration.

Queen Alexandra's total absence of egotism and the warmth of her manner, prompted not by consideration, but by sincerity; her gaiety of heart and refinement – rarely to be seen in royal people – inspired me that day with a love for her from which I have never departed.

I had been presented to the Prince of Wales – before I met the

[1] Georgiana Countess of Dudley.

Princess – by Lady Dalhousie, in the Paddock at Ascot. He asked me if I would back my fancy for the Wokingham Stakes and have a bet with him on the race. We walked down to the rails and watched horses gallop past. One of them went down in great form; I verified him by his colours and found he was called Wokingham. I told the Prince that he was a sure winner; but out of so many entries no one was more surprised than I was when my horse came romping in. I was given a gold cigarette-case and went home much pleased.

King Edward had great charm and personality and enormous prestige; he was more touchy than King George and fonder of pleasure. He and Queen Alexandra, before they succeeded, were the leaders of London society; they practically dictated what people could and could not do; every woman wore a new dress when she dined at Marlborough House and we vied with each other in trying to please him.

Opinions differ as to the precise function of royalty, but no one doubts that it is a valuable and necessary part of our Constitution. Just as the Lord Mayor represents commerce, the Prime Minister the Government, and the Commons the people, the King represents society. Voltaire said we British had shown true genius in preventing our kings by law from doing anything but good. This sounds well, but we all know that laws do not prevent men from doing harm.

The two kings that I have known have had a high degree of both physical and moral courage and have shown a sense of duty unparallelled in the Courts of Europe. It is this that has given them their stability; and we must add that their truthfulness and simplicity of nature have won for them a lasting love.

They have been exceptionally fortunate in their private secretaries: Lord Knollys and Lord Stamfordham are liberal-minded men of the highest honour and discretion and I am proud to call them my friends.

Before I knew the Prince and Princess of Wales, I did not go to fashionable balls, but after that Ascot I was asked everywhere. I was quite unconscious of it at the time, but was told afterwards that people were beginning to criticise me; one or two incidents might have enlightened me had I been more aware of myself.

One night, when I was dining *tête-à-tête* with my old friend,

Godfrey Webb, in his flat in Victoria Street, my father sent the brougham for me with a message to ask if I would accompany him to supper at Lord and Lady Randolph Churchill's, where we had been invited to meet the Prince of Wales. I said I should be delighted if I could keep on the dress that I was wearing, but as it was late and I had to get up early next day I did not want to change my clothes; he said he supposed my dress would be quite smart enough, so we drove to the Randolph Churchills' house together.

I had often wanted to know Lord Randolph, but it was only a few days before the supper that I had had the good fortune to sit next to him at dinner. When he observed that he had been put next to a Miss, he placed his left elbow firmly on the table and turned his back upon me through several courses. I could not but admire the way he appeared to eat everything with one hand. I do not know whether it was the lady on his right or what it was that prompted him, but he ultimately turned round and asked me if I knew any politicians. I told him that, with the exception of himself, I knew them all intimately. This surprised him and after discussing Lord Rosebery – to whom he was devoted – he said:

'Do you know Lord Salisbury?'

I told him that I had forgotten his name in my list, but that I would like above everything to meet him; at which he remarked that I was welcome to all his share of him, adding:

'What do you want to know him for?'

MARGOT: 'Because I think he is amazingly amusing and a very fine writer.'

LORD RANDOLPH (*muttering something I could not catch about Salisbury lying dead at his feet*): 'I wish to God that I had *never* known him!'

MARGOT: 'I am afraid you resigned more out of temper than conviction, Lord Randolph.'

At this he turned completely round and, gazing at me, said:

'Confound your cheek! What do you know about me and my convictions? I hate Salisbury! He jumped at my resignation like a dog at a bone. The Tories are ungrateful, short-sighted beasts. I hope you are a Liberal?'

I informed him that I was and exactly what I thought of the

Tory party; and we talked through the rest of dinner. Towards the end of our conversation he asked me my name. I told him that, and after his manners to me in the earlier part of the evening, it was perhaps better that we should remain strangers. However, after a little chaff, we made friends and he said that he would come and see me in Grosvenor Square.

On the night of the supper-party, I was wearing a white muslin dress with transparent chemise sleeves, a fichu and a long skirt with a Nattier blue taffeta sash. I had taken a bunch of rose carnations out of a glass and pinned them into my fichu with three diamond ducks given me by Lord Carmichael (our Peeblesshire friend and neighbour).

On my arrival at the Churchills', I observed all the fine ladies wearing ball-dresses off the shoulder and their tiaras. This made me very conspicuous, and I wished profoundly that I had changed into something smarter before going out.

The Prince of Wales had not arrived and, as our hostess was giving orders to the White Hungarian Band, my father and I had to walk into the room alone.

I saw several of the ladies eyeing my toilette and, having painfully sharp ears, I heard some of their remarks:

'Do look at Miss Tennant! She is in her night-gown!'

'I suppose it is meant to be "ye olde Englishe pictury"! I wonder she has not let her hair down like the Juliets at the Oakham balls!'

Another, more charitable, said:

'I daresay no one told her that the Prince of Wales was coming. . . . Poor child! What a shame!'

And finally a man said:

'There is nothing so odd as the passion some people have for self-advertisement; it only shows what it is to be intellectual!'

At that moment our hostess came up to us with a charming *accueil*.

The first time I saw Lady Randolph was at Punchestown races, in 1887, where I went with my new friends, Mrs Bunbury, Hatfield Harter and Peter Flower. I was standing at the big double when I observed a woman next to me in a Black Watch tartan skirt, braided coat and astrackan hussar's cap. She had a forehead like a panther's and great wild eyes that looked through you; she was so arresting that I followed her about till I found someone who could tell me who she was.

Had Lady Randolph Churchill been like her face, she could have governed the world.

My father and I were much relieved at her greeting; and while we were talking the Prince of Wales arrived. The ladies fell into position, ceased chattering and made subterranean curtsies. He came straight up to me and told me I was to sit on the other side of him at supper. I said, hanging my head with becoming modesty and in a loud voice:

'Oh no, Sir, I am not dressed at all for the part! I had better slip away, I had no notion this was going to be such a smart party. . . . I expect some of the ladies here think I have insulted them by coming in my night-gown!'

I saw everyone straining to hear what the Prince's answer would be, but I took good care that we should move out of earshot. At that moment Lord Hartington[1] came up and told me I was to go in to supper with him. More than ever I wished I had changed my dress, for now everyone was looking at me with even greater curiosity than hostility.

The supper was gay and I had remarkable talks which laid the foundation of my friendship both with King Edward and the Duke of Devonshire. The Prince told me he had had a dull youth, as Queen Victoria could not get over the Prince Consort's death and kept up an exaggerated mourning. He said he hoped that when I met his mother I should not be afraid of her, adding, with a charming smile, that with the exception of John Brown everybody was. I assured him with perfect candour that I was afraid of no one. He was much amused when I told him that before he had arrived that evening some of the ladies had whispered that I was in my night-gown and I hoped he did not think me lacking in courtesy because I had not put on a ball-dress. He assured me that on the contrary he admired my frock very much and thought I looked like an old picture. This remark made me see uncomfortable visions of the Oakham ball and he did not dispel them by adding:

[1] The late Duke of Devonshire.

'You are so original! You must dance the cotillion with me.'

I told him that I could not possibly stay, it would bore my father stiff, as he hated sitting up late; also I was not dressed for dancing and had no idea there was going to be a ball. When supper was over, I made my best curtsy and, after presenting my father to the Prince, went home to bed.

Lord Hartington told me in the course of our conversation at supper that Lady Grosvenor[1] was by far the most dangerous syren in London and that he would not answer for any man keeping his head or his heart when with her, to which I entirely agreed.

When the London season came to an end we all went up to Glen.

[1] The Countess of Grosvenor.

IV · *Hunting*

In the winter of 1880 I went to stay with my sister, Lucy Graham Smith, in Wiltshire.

I was going out hunting for the first time, never having seen a fox, a hound or a fence in my life; my heart beat as my sisters superintending my toilette put the last hair-pin into a crinkly knot of hair; I pulled on my top-boots and, running down to the front door, found Ribblesdale, who was mounting me, waiting to drive me to the meet. Hounds met at Christian Malford station.

Not knowing that with the Duke of Beaufort's hounds everyone wore blue and buff, I was disappointed at the appearance of the field. No one has ever suggested that a touch of navy blue improves a landscape, and, although I had never been out hunting before, I had looked forward to seeing scarlet coats.

We moved off, jostling each other as thick as sardines, to draw the nearest cover. My mount was peacocking on the grass when suddenly we heard a 'Halloa!' and the whole field went hammering like John Gilpin down the hard high road.

Plunging through a gap, I dashed into the open country. Storm flung herself up to the stars over the first fence and I found myself seated on the wettest of wet ground, angry but unhurt; all the stragglers – more especially the funkers – agreeably diverted from pursuing the hunt, galloped off to catch my horse. I walked to a cottage; and nearly an hour afterwards Storm was returned to me.

After this contretemps my mount was more amenable and I determined that nothing should unseat me again. Not being hurt by a fall gives one a sense of exhilaration and I felt ready to face an arm of the sea.

The scattered field were moving aimlessly about, some looking for their second horses, some eating an early sandwich, some in groups, laughing and smoking and no one knowing anything about the hounds; I was a little away from the others and wondering – like all amateurs – why we were wasting so much time, when a fine old gentleman on a huge horse came up to me and said, with a sweet smile:

'Do you always whistle out hunting?'

MARGOT: 'I didn't know I was whistling. . . . I've never hunted before.'

STRANGER: 'Is this really the first time you've ever been out with hounds?'

MARGOT: 'Yes, it is.'

STRANGER: 'How wonderfully you ride! But I am sorry to see you have taken a toss.'

MARGOT: 'I fell off at the first fence, for though I've ridden all my life I've never jumped before.'

STRANGER: 'Were you frightened when you fell?'

MARGOT: 'No, my horse was. . . .'

STRANGER: 'Would you like to wear the blue and buff?'

MARGOT: 'It's pretty for women, but I don't think it looks sporting for men, though I see you wear it; but in any case I could not get the blue habit.'

STRANGER: 'Why not?'

MARGOT: 'Because the old Duke of Beaufort only gives it to women who own coverts; I am told he hates people who go hard and after today I mean to ride like the devil!'

STRANGER: 'Oh, do you? But is "the old Duke", as you call him, so severe?'

MARGOT: 'I've no idea; I've never seen him or any other duke!'

STRANGER: 'If I told you I could get you the blue habit, what would you say?'

MARGOT (*with a patronising smile*): 'I'm afraid I should say you were running hares!'

STRANGER: 'You would have to wear a top-hat, you know, and you would not like that! But, if you are going to ride like the devil, it might save your neck; and in any case it would keep your hair tidy.'

MARGOT (*anxiously pushing back stray curls*): 'Why, is my hair very untidy? It is the first time it has ever been up; and, when I was "thrown from my horse", as the papers call it, all the hair-pins got loose.'

STRANGER: 'It doesn't matter with your hair, it is so pretty; I think I shall call you Miss Fluffy! By the bye, what is your name?'

When I told him he was much surprised:

'Oh, then you are a sister-in-law of the Ancestor's, are you?'

This was the first time I even heard Ribblesdale called 'the Ancestor'; and, as I did not know what he meant, I asked:

'And who are you?'

To which he replied:

'I am the Duke of Beaufort and I am not running hares this time. I will give you the blue habit, but you know you will have to wear a top-hat.'

MARGOT: 'Good gracious! I hope I've said nothing to offend you? Do you always do this sort of thing when you meet anyone like me for the first time?'

DUKE OF BEAUFORT (*with a smile, lifting his hat*): 'Just as it is the first time you have ever hunted, so it is the first time I have ever met anyone like you.'

On the third day with the Beaufort hounds, my horse fell heavily in a ditch with me and, getting up, galloped away. I was picked up by a good-looking man, who took me into his house, gave me tea and drove me back in his brougham to Easton Grey; I fell passionately in love with him. He owned a horse called Lardy Dardy, on which he mounted me.

Charty and the others chaffed me much about my new friend, saying that my father would never approve of a Tory and that it was lucky he was married.

I replied, much nettled, that I did not want to marry anyone and that, though he was a Tory, he was not at all stupid and would get into the Cabinet.

This was my first shrewd political prophecy, for he is in the Cabinet now.

I cannot look at him without remembering that he was the first man I ever was in love with and that, at the age of seventeen, I said he would be in the Cabinet in spite of his being a Tory.

For pure unalloyed happiness those days at Easton Grey were undoubtedly the most perfect of my life. Lucy's sweetness to me, the beauty of the place, the wild excitement of riding over fences and the perfect certainty I had that I would ride better than anyone in the whole world gave me an insolent confidence which no earthquake could have shaken.

Off and on, I felt qualms over my lack of education; and, when I was falling into a happy sleep, dreaming I was overriding hounds, echoes of 'Pray, Mama', out of Mrs Markham, or early punishments of unfinished poems would play about my bed.

On one occasion at Easton Grey, unable to sleep for love of life, I leant out of the window into the dark to see if it was thawing. It was a beautiful night, warm and wet, and I forgot all about my education.

The next day, having no mount, I had procured a hireling from a neighbouring farmer, but to my misery the horse did not turn up at the meet; Mr Golightly, the parish priest, said I might drive about in his low black pony-carriage, called in those days a Colorado beetle, but hunting on wheels was no rôle for me and I did not feel like pursuing the field.

My heart sank as I saw the company pass me gaily down the road, preceded by the hounds, trotting with a staccato step and their noses in the air.

Just as I was turning to go home, a groom rode past in mufti, leading a loose horse with a lady's saddle on it. The animal gave a clumsy lurch; and the man, jerking it violently by the head, bumped it into my phaeton. I saw my chance.

MARGOT: 'Hullo, man! ... That's my horse! Whose groom are you?'

MAN (*rather frightened at being caught jobbing his lady's horse in the mouth*): 'I am Mrs Chaplin's groom, miss.'

MARGOT: 'Jump off; you are the very man I was looking for; tell me, does Mrs Chaplin ride this horse over everything?'

MAN (*quite unsuspicious and thawing at my sweetness and authority*): 'Bless your soul! Mrs Chaplin doesn't 'unt this 'orse! It's the Major's! She only 'acked it to the meet.'

MARGOT (*apprehensively and her heart sinking*): 'But can it jump? ... Don't they hunt it? ...'

MAN (*pulling down my habit skirt*): 'It's a 'orse that can very near jump anythink, I should say, but the Major says it shakes every tooth in 'is gums and she says it's pig-'eaded.'

It did not take me long to mount and in a moment I had left the man miles behind me. Prepared for the worst, but in high glee, I began to look about me: not a sign of the hunt! Only odd remnants of the meet, straggling foot-passengers, terriers straining at a strap held by drunken runners – some in old Beaufort coats, others in corduroy – one-horse shays of every description by the sides of the road and sloppy girls with sticks and Tammies standing in gaps of the fences straining their eyes across the fields to see the hounds.

My horse with a loose rein was trotting aimlessly down the road when, hearing a 'Halloa!' I pulled up and saw the hounds streaming towards me all together, so close that you could have covered them with a handkerchief.

What a scent! What a pack! Have I headed the fox? Will they cross the road? No! They are turning away from me! Now's the moment!!

I circled the Chaplin horse round with great resolution and trotted up to a wall at the side of the road; he leapt it like a stag; we flew over the grass, and the next fence, and after a little scrambling, I found myself in the same field with hounds. The horse was as rough as the boy said, but a wonderful hunter; it could not put a foot wrong and we had a great gallop over the walls, which only a few of the field saw.

When hounds checked, I was in despair; all sorts of ladies and gentlemen came riding towards me and I wondered painfully which of them would be Mr and which Mrs Chaplin. What was I to do? Suddenly remembering my new friend and patron, I peered about for the Duke; when I found him and told him of the awkward circumstances in which I had placed myself, he was so much amused that he made my peace with the Chaplins, who begged me to go on riding their horse. At the end of the day I was given the brush – a fashion completely abandoned in the hunting-field now – and I went home happy and tired.

V · Dresden

I wanted to be alone and I wanted to learn. After endless talks it was decided that I should go to Germany for four or five months and thus settle the problem of an unbegun but finishing education.

Looking back on this decision, I think it was a remarkable one. I had a passion for dancing and my father wanted me to go to balls; I had a genius for horses and adored hunting; I had such a wonderful hack that everyone collected at the Park rails when they saw me coming into the Row; but all this did not deflect me from my purpose and I went to Dresden alone with a stupid maid at a time when – if not in England, certainly in Germany – I might have passed as a moderate beauty.

Frau von Mach kept a ginger-coloured lodging-house high up in the Lüttichaustrasse. She was a woman of culture and refinement; her mother had been English and her husband, having gone mad in the Franco-Prussian war, had left her with three children. She had to work for her living and she cooked and scrubbed without a thought for herself from dawn till dark.

There were thirteen pianos on our floor and two or three permanent lodgers. The rest of the people came and went – men, women and boys of every nationality, professionals and amateurs – but I was too busy to care or notice who went or who came.

Although my mother was bold and right to let me go as a bachelor to Dresden, I could not have done it myself. Later on, like everyone else, I sent my stepdaughter and daughter to be educated in Germany for a short time, but they were chaperoned by a woman of worth and character: my German nursery-governess, who came to me when Elizabeth was four.

In parenthesis, I may mention that, in the early terrible days of the war, our thoughtful newspapers, wishing to make money out of public hysteria, had the bright idea of turning this simple, devoted woman into a spy. There was not a creature who did not laugh in his sleeve at this and openly make a stunt of it, but it had its political uses; and, after the Russians had been seen with snow on their boots by everyone in England, the gentlemen of the Press calculated that almost anything would be believed if it could be repeated often enough. And they were right; the spiteful and the silly disseminated lies about our governess from door to door with the kind of venom that belongs in equal proportions to the credulous, the cowards and the cranks. The greenhorns believed it and the funkers who saw a plentiful crop of spies in every bush found no difficulty in mobilising their terrors from my governess – already languishing in the Tower of London – to myself, who suddenly became a tennis-champion and an *habituée* of the German officers' camps!

The Dresden of my day was different from the Dresden of twenty years later. I never saw an English person the whole time I was there.

After settling into my new rooms, I wrote out for myself a severe *Stundenplan*, which I pinned over my head next to my alarum-clock, and at 6 every morning I woke up and dashed into the kitchen to have coffee with the solitary slavey; after that I practised the fiddle or piano till 8.30, when we had the pension breakfast; and the rest of the day was taken up by literature and drawing. I went to concerts or the opera by myself every night.

One day Frau von Mach came to me greatly distressed by a letter she had received from my mother begging her to take in no men lodgers while I was in the pension, as some of her friends in England had told her that I might elope with a foreigner. To this hour I do not know whether my mother was serious; but I wrote and told her that Frau von Mach's life depended on her lodgers, that there was only one permanent lodger – an old American called Loring, who never spoke to me – and that I had no time to elope. Many and futile were the efforts to make me return home; but, though I wrote to England regularly, I never alluded to any of them, as they appeared childish to me.

I made great friends with Frau von Mach and in loose moments

sat on her kitchen-table smoking cigarettes and eating black cherries;
we discussed Shakespeare, Wagner, Brahms, George Eliot, Bach,
Hegel; and the time flew.

One night I arrived early at the Opera House and was looking
about while the fiddles were tuning up. I wore my pearls and a
scarlet *crêpe-de-chine* dress and a black cloth cape with a hood on it,
which I put on over my head when I walked home in the rain. I was
having a frank stare at the audience, when I observed just opposite
me an officer in a white uniform. As the Saxon soldiers wore pale
blue, I wondered what army he could belong to.

He was a fine-looking man, with tailor-made shoulders, a small
waist and silver and black on his sword-belt. When he turned to the
stage, I looked at him through my opera-glasses. On closer inspec-
tion, he was even handsomer than I had thought. A lady joined
him in the box and he took off her cloak, while she stood up gazing
down at the stalls, pulling up her long black gloves. She wore a
row of huge pearls, which fell below her waist, and a black jet
décolleté dress. Few people wore low dresses at the opera and I
saw half the audience fixing her with their glasses. She was evidently
famous. Her hair was fox-red and pinned back on each side of her
temples with Spanish combs of gold and pearls; she surveyed the
stalls with cavernous eyes set in a snow-white face, and in her hand
she held a bouquet of lilac orchids. She was the best-looking woman
I saw all the time I was in Germany and I could not take my eyes off
her. The white officer began to look about the opera-house when
my red dress caught his eye. He put up his glasses and I instantly
put mine down. Although the lights were lowered for the overture,
I saw him looking at me for some time.

I had been in the habit of walking about in the *entr'actes* and,
when the curtain dropped at the end of the first act, I left the box.
It did not take me long to identify the white officer. He was not
accompanied by his lady, but stood leaning against the wall smoking
a cigar and talking to a man; as I passed him I had to stop for a
moment for fear of treading on his outstretched toes. He pulled
himself erect to get out of my way; I looked up and our eyes met;
I don't think I blush easily, but something in his gaze may have
made me blush. I lowered my eyelids and walked on.

The *Meistersinger* was my favourite opera and so it appeared to be of the Dresdeners; Wagner, having quarrelled with the authorities, refused to allow the *Ring* to be played in the Dresden Opera House, and everyone was tired of the swans and doves of *Lohengrin* and *Tannhauser*.

There was a great crowd that night and, as it was raining when we came out, I hung about, hoping to get a cab; I saw my white officer with his lady, but he did not see me; I heard him before he got into the brougham give elaborate orders to the coachman to put him down at some club.

After waiting for a little time, as no cab turned up, I pulled the hood of my cloak over my head and started to walk home; when the crowd scattered I found myself alone and turned up a street which led into the Lüttichaustrasse. Suddenly I became aware that I was being followed; I heard the even steps and the click of spurs of someone walking behind me; I should not have noticed this had I not halted under a lamp to pull on my hood, which the wind had blown off. When I stopped, the steps also stopped. I walked on, wondering if it had been my imagination, and again I heard the click of spurs coming nearer. The street being deserted, I was unable to endure it any longer; I turned round and there was the officer. His black cloak hanging loosely over his shoulders showed me the white uniform and silver belt. He saluted me and asked me in a curious Belgian French if he might accompany me home. I said;

'Oh, certainly! But I am not at all nervous in the dark.'

OFFICER (*stopping under the lamp to light a cigarette*): 'You like Wagner? Do you know him well? I find him long and loud.'

MARGOT: 'He is a little long, but so wonderful!'

OFFICER: 'Do you not feel tired, no? (*With emphasis*) I DO!'

MARGOT: 'No, I'm not at all tired.'

OFFICER: 'You would not like to go and have supper with me in a private room of the hotel, no?'

MARGOT: 'You are very kind, but I don't like supper; besides, it is late. (*Leaving his side to look at the number on the door*) I am afraid we must part here.'

OFFICER (*drawing a long breath*): 'But you said I might accompany you to your home!'

MARGOT (*with a slow smile*): 'I know I did, but this is my home.'

He looked disappointed and surprised, but taking my hand he kissed it, then stepping back saluted and said:

'*Pardonnez-moi! mademoiselle.*'

VI · *A Broken Engagement*

The first year I came out in London I did not receive many invitations to balls and knew but few people; what I really enjoyed was riding in the Row. I bought a beautiful hack for myself at Tattersalls, 15.1, bright bay with black points and so well-balanced that if I had ridden it with my face to its tail I should hardly have known the difference. I called it Tatts; it was bold as a lion, vain as a peacock and extremely moody. One day, when I was mounted to ride in the Row, my papa kept me waiting so long at the door of 40 Grosvenor Square that I thought I would ride Tatts into the front hall and give him a call; it only meant going up one step from the pavement to the porch and another through the double doors held open by the footmen. Unluckily, after a somewhat cautious approach by Tatts up the last step into the marble hall, he caught his reflection in a mirror. At this he instantly stood erect upon his hind legs, crashing my tall hat into the crystal chandelier. His four legs all gave way on the polished floor and down we went with a noise like thunder, the pony on the top of me, the chandelier on the top of him and my father and the footmen helpless spectators. I was up and on Tatt's head in a moment, but not before he had kicked a fine old English chest into a jelly. This misadventure upset my father's temper and my pony's nerve, as well as preventing me from dancing for several days.

* * *

My second scrape was more serious. I engaged myself to be married.

If any young Miss reads this autobiography and wants a little advice from a very old hand, I will say to her, when a man threatens to commit suicide after you have refused him, you may be quite

62

sure that he is a vain, petty fellow, or a great goose; if you felt any doubts about your decision before, you need have none after this and under no circumstances must you give way. To marry a man out of pity is folly; and, if you think you are going to influence the kind of fellow who had 'never had a chance, poor devil', you are profoundly mistaken. One can only influence the strong characters in life, not the weak; and it is the height of vanity to suppose that you can make an honest man of anyone. My fiancé was neither petty nor a goose, but a humorist; I do not think he meant me to take him seriously, but in spite of my high spirits I was very serious and he was certainly more in love with me than anyone had ever been before. He was a fine rider and mounted me with the Beaufort hounds.

When I told my mother of my engagement, she sank upon a settee, put a handkerchief to her eyes, and said:

'You might as well marry your groom!'

I struggled very hard to show her how worldly she was. Who wanted money? Who wanted position? Who wanted brains? Nothing in fact was wanted, except my will!

I was much surprised, a few days later, to hear from G., whom I met riding in the Row, that he had called every day of the week but been told by the footman that I was out. The under-butler, who was devoted to me, said sadly, when I complained:

'I am afraid, miss, your young gentleman has been forbidden the house.'

Forbidden the house! I rushed to my sister Charty and found her even more upset than my mother. She pointed out with some truth that Lucy's marriage and the obstinacy with which she had pursued it had gone far towards spoiling her early life; but 'the squire', as Graham Smith was called, although a character apart, was a man of perfect education and charming manners. He had beaten all the boys at Harrow, won a hundred steeplechases and loved books; whereas my young man knew little about anything but horses and, she added, would be no companion to me when I was ill or old.

I flounced about the room and said that forbidding him the house was grotesque and made me ridiculous in the eyes of the servants. I ended a passionate protest by telling her gravely that if

I changed my mind he would undoubtedly commit suicide. This awful news was received with an hilarity which nettled me.

CHARTY: 'I should have thought you had too much sense of humour and Mr G. too much common sense for either of you to believe this. He must think you very vain. . . .'

I did not know at all what she meant and said with the utmost gravity:

'The terrible thing is that I believe I have given him a false impression of my feelings for him; for, though I love him very much, I would never have promised to marry him if he had not said he was going to kill himself.' Clasping my two hands together and greatly moved, I concluded, 'If I break it off now and *anything* *should* happen, my life is over and I shall feel as if I had murdered him.'

CHARTY (*looking at me with a tender smile*): 'I should risk it, darling.'

*   *   *

I knew things could not go on as they were; scenes bored me and I was quite incapable of sustaining a campaign of white lies; so I reassured my friends and relieved my relations by telling the young man that I could not marry him. He gave me his beautiful mare, Molly Bawn, sold all his hunters and went to Australia. His hair when he returned to England two years later was grey. I have heard of this happening, but have only known of it twice in my life, once on this occasion and the other time when the boiler of the *Thunderer* burst in her trial trip; the engine was the first Government order ever given to my father's firm of Humphreys & Tennant and the accident made a great sensation. My father told me that several men had been killed and that young Humphreys' hair had turned white. I remember this incident very well, as when I gave papa the telegram in the billiard-room at Glen he covered his face with his hands and sank on the sofa in tears.

64

VII · *Dr Jowett*

————◦◦◦————

I shall open this chapter of my autobiography with a character-sketch of myself, written at Glen in one of our pencil-games in January 1888. Nearly everyone in the room guessed that I was the subject, but opinions differed as to the authorship. Some thought that our dear and clever friend, Godfrey Webb, had written it as a sort of joke.

'In appearance she was small, with rapid, nervous movements; energetic, never wholly ungraceful, but inclined to be restless. Her face did not betray the intelligence she possessed, as her eyes, though clear and well-shaped, were too close together. Her hawky nose was bent over a short upper lip and meaningless. The chin showed more definite character than her other features, being large, bony and prominent, and she had curly, pretty hair, growing well on a finely-cut forehead; the *ensemble* healthy and mobile; in manner easy, unselfconscious, emphatic, inclined to be noisy from over-keenness and perfectly self-possessed. Conversation graphic and exaggerated, eager and concentrated, with a natural gift of expression. Her honesty more a peculiarity than a virtue. Decision more of instinct than of reason; a disengaged mind wholly unfettered by prejudice. Very observant and a fine judge of her fellow-creatures, finding all interesting and worthy of her speculation. She was not easily depressed by antagonistic circumstances or social situations hostile to herself – on the contrary – her spirit rose in all losing games. She was assisted in this by having no personal vanity, the highest vitality and great self-confidence. She was self-indulgent, though not selfish, and had not enough self-control for her passion and impetuosity; it was owing more to dash and grit than to any fore-sight that she kept out of difficulties. She distrusted the dried-up advice of many people, who prefer coining evil to publishing good. She was lacking in awe, and no respecter of persons; loving old people because she never felt they were old. Warm-hearted, and with much power of devotion, thinking no trouble too great to take for those you love, and agreeing with Dr Johnson that friendships should be kept in constant repair. Too many interests and too many-sided. Fond of people, animals, books, sport, music, art and exercise. More Bohemian than exclusive and with a certain power of investing acquaintances and even bores with interest. Passionate love of Nature. Lacking in devotional, practising religion; otherwise sensitively religious. Sensible; not easily influenced for good or evil. Jealous, keen and faithful in affection. Great want of plodding perseverance, doing many things with promise and nothing well. A fine ear for music: no execution; a good eye for drawing: no knowledge or practice in perspective: more critical than constructive. Very cool and decided with horses. Good nerve, good whip and a fine rider. Intellectually self-made, ambitious, independent and self-willed. Fond of admiration and love from both men and women, and able to give it.'

I sent this to Dr Jowett with another character-sketch of Gladstone. After reading them, he wrote me this letter:

'BALL. COLL.,
'OCT. 23RD, 1890

'My Dear Margot,

'I return the book[1] which you entrusted to me: I was very much interested by it. The sketch of Gladstone is excellent. Pray write some more of it some time: I understand him better after reading it.

'The young lady's portrait of herself is quite truthful and not at all flattered: shall I add a trait or two? "She is very sincere and extremely clever; indeed, her cleverness almost amounts to genius. She might be a distinguished authoress if she would – but she wastes her time and her gifts scampering about the world and going from one country house to another in a manner not pleasant to look back upon and still less pleasant to think of twenty years hence, when youth will have made itself wings and fled away."

'If you know her, will you tell her with my love, that I do not

[1] A commonplace-book with a few written sketches of people in it.

like to offer her any more advice, but I wish that she would take counsel with herself. She has made a great position, though slippery and dangerous: will she not add to this a noble and simple life which can alone give a true value to it? The higher we rise, the more self-discipline, self-control and economy is required of us. It is a hard thing to be in the world but not of it; to be outwardly much like other people and yet to be cherishing an ideal which extends over the whole of life and beyond; to have a natural love for everyone, especially for the poor; to get rid of, not of wit or good humour, but of frivolity and excitement; to live "selfless" according to the Will of God and not after the fashions and opinions of men and women.'

Stimulated by this and the encouragement of Lionel Tennyson – a new friend – I was anxious to start a newspaper. When I was a little girl at Glen, there had been a schoolroom paper, called *The Glen Gossip: The Tennant Tatler, or The Peeblesshire Prattler*. I believe my brother Eddy wrote the wittiest verses in it; but I was too young to remember much about it or to contribute anything. I had many distinguished friends by that time, all of whom had promised to write for me. The idea was four or five numbers, to be illustrated by my sister Lucy Graham Smith, and a brilliant letter-press. The title of the paper gave us infinite trouble. We ended by adopting a suggestion of my own; and our new venture was to have been called *To-morrow*. This is the list of people who promised to write for me, and the names they suggested for the paper:

Lord and Lady Pembroke .	*Sympathetic Ink.*
	The Idle Pen.
	The Mail.
	The Kite.
	Blue Ink.
Mr A. Lyttelton .	. *The Hen.*
	The Cluck.
Mr Knowles . .	. *The Butterfly.*
Mr A. J. Balfour .	. *The New Eve.*
	Anonymous.
	Mrs Grundy.

Mr Oscar Wilde	. .	*The Life Improver.*
		Mrs Grundy's Daughter.
Lady Ribblesdale	. .	*Jane.*
		Psyche.
		The Mask.
Margot Tennant	. .	*The Mangle.*
		Eve.
		Dolly Varden.
		To-morrow.
Mr Webb	. . .	*The Petticoat.*
Mrs Horner	. . .	*She.*
Miss Mary Leslie	. .	*The Sphinx.*
		Eglantine.
		Blue Veil.
		Pinafore.
Sir A. West	. . .	*The Spinet.*
		The Spinning-Wheel.
Mr J. A. Symonds	. .	*Muses and Graces.*
		Causeries en peignoir.
		Woman's Wit and Humour.

The contributors on our staff were to have been Laurence Oliphant, J. K. Stephen, Mr Wilfrid Blunt, the Hon. George Curzon, George Wyndham, Godfrey Webb, Doll Liddell, Harry Cust, Mr Knowles (Editor of the *Nineteenth Century*), the Hon. A. Lyttelton, Mr A. J. Balfour, Oscar Wilde, Lord and Lady Ribblesdale, Mrs (now Lady) Horner, Sir Algernon West, Lady Frances Balfour, Lord and Lady Pembroke, Miss Betty Ponsonby (the present Mrs Montgomery), John Addington Symonds, Dr Jowett (the Master of Balliol), M. Coquelin, Sir Henry Irving, Miss Ellen Terry, Sir Edward Burne-Jones, Mr George Russell, Mrs Singleton (alias Violet Fane, afterwards Lady Currie), Lady de Grey, Lady Constance Leslie and the Hon. Lionel Tennyson.

Our programme for the first number was to have been the following:

TO-MORROW

Leader	. . .	Persons and Politics	. Margot Tennant.

The Social Zodiac .	Rise and Fall of Professional Beauties .	Lady de Grey.
Occasional Articles .	The Green-eyed Monster . .	Violet Fane (*nom de plume* of Mrs Singleton).
Occasional Notes .	Foreign and Colonial Gossip . . .	Harry Cust.
Men and Women .	Character Sketch .	Margot Tennant.
Story		Oscar Wilde.
Poem		Godfrey Webb.
Letters to Men		George Wyndham.
Books Reviewed		John Addington Symonds.
Conversations		Miss Ponsonby.

In spite of much discussion, our scheme came to nothing. I am sure Jowett was right, I wasted my time 'scampering about the world', but I made many friends in this way that I could not have made otherwise.

No one has had such wonderful friends as I have, but no one has suffered more at discovering the instability of human beings and how little power to love they possess.

The two friends I made at that time who had the most influence over me were Jowett (the Master of Balliol in 1888-89) and Lady Wemyss (the mother of the present Earl).

When I first met Lady Wemyss I saw that it was possible to have a great character without being a character-part. She told me that she frightened people, which distressed her. As I am not easily frightened, I was puzzled by this. After thinking it over, I was convinced that it was because she had a hard nut to crack within herself: she possessed a jealous, passionate, youthful temperament, a formidable standard of right and wrong, a distinguished and rather stern *accueil*, a low, slow utterance and terrifying sincerity. She was the kind of person I had dreamt of meeting and never knew that God had made. She once told me that I was the best friend man, woman or child could ever have. After this wonderful compliment, we formed a deep attachment, which lasted until her death. She had a unique power of devotion and fundamental humbleness. I kept every letter she ever wrote to me and try to hope that she loves me still.

It was through my beloved Lady Wemyss that I first met the Master of Balliol. One evening in 1888, after the men had come in from shooting, we were having tea in the large marble hall at Gosford.[1] I generally wore an accordion skirt at tea, as Lord Wemyss liked me to dance to him.

Someone was playing the piano and I was improvising in and out of the chairs, when, in the act of making a final curtsy, I caught my foot in my skirt and fell at the feet of an old clergyman seated in the window. As I got up, a loud 'Damn!' resounded through the room. Recovering my presence of mind, I said, looking up:

'You are a clergyman and I am afraid I have shocked you!'

'Not at all,' he replied. 'I hope you will go on; I like your dancing extremely.'

I provoked much amusement by asking the family afterwards if the parson whose presence I had failed to notice was their minister at Aberlady. I then learnt that he was the famous Rev. Benjamin Jowett, Master of Balliol.

When I met the Master in 1887, I was young and he was old; but, whether from insolence or insight, I never felt this difference. I do not think I was a good judge of age, as I have always liked older people than myself; and I imagine it was because of this un-consciousness that we became such wonderful friends. Jowett was younger than half the young people I know now and we understood each other perfectly. If I am hasty in making friends and skip the preface, I always read it afterwards.

A good deal of controversy has arisen over the Master's claim to greatness by some of the younger generation. It is not denied that Jowett was a man of influence. Men as different as Huxley, Symonds, Lord Lansdowne, Lord Bowen, Lord Milner, Sir Robert Morier and others have told me in reverent and affectionate terms how much they owed to him and to his influence. It is not denied that he was a kind man; infinitely generous, considerate and good about

[1] Gosford – the Earl of Wemyss' country place – is situated between Edinburgh and North Berwick.

money. It may be denied that he was a fine scholar of the first rank, such as Munro or Jebb, although no one denies his contribution to scholarship; but the real question remains: was he a great man? There are big men, men of intellect, men of talent and men of action; but the great man is difficult to find, and it needs – apart from discernment – a certain greatness to find him. The Almighty is a wonderful handicapper: He will not give us everything. I have never met a woman of supreme beauty with more than a mediocre intellect, by which I do not mean intelligence. There may be some, but I am only writing my own experiences and I have not met them. A person of magnetism, temperament and quick intelligence may have neither intellect nor character. I have known one man whose genius lay in his rapid and sensitive understanding, real wit, amazing charm and apparent candour, but whose meanness, ingratitude and instability injured everything he touched. You can only discover ingratitude or instability after years of experience, and few of us, I am glad to think, ever suspect meanness in our fellow-creatures; the discovery is as painful as finding a worm in the heart of a rose. A man may have a fine character and be taciturn, stubborn and stupid. Another may be brilliant, sunny and generous, but self-indulgent, heartless and a liar. There is no contradiction I have not met within men and women: the rarest combination is to find fundamental humbleness, freedom from self, intrepid courage, and the power to love; when you come upon these, you may be quite sure that you are in the presence of greatness.

Human beings are made up of a good many pieces. Nature, character, intellect and temperament: roughly speaking, these headings cover everyone. The men and women whom I have loved best have been those whose natures were rich and sweet; but, also, with a few exceptions, all of them have had gimcrack characters; and the qualities which I have loved in them have been ultimately submerged by self-indulgence.

The present Archbishop of Canterbury is one of these exceptions: he has a sweet and rich nature, a fine temper and is quite unspoilable. I have only one criticism to make of Randall Davidson: he has too much moderation for his intellect; but I daresay he would not have steered the Church through so many shallows if he had not had this attribute. I have known him since I was ten (he christened, confirmed, married and buried us all); and his faith in such qualities of head and heart as I possess has never wavered. He reminds me of Jowett in the soundness of his nature and his complete absence of vanity, although no two men were ever less alike. The first element of greatness is fundamental humbleness (this should not be confused with servility); the second is freedom from self; the third is intrepid courage, which, taken in its widest interpretation, generally goes with truth; and the fourth – the power to love – although I have put it last, is the rarest. If these go to the makings of a great man, Jowett possessed them all. He might have mocked at the confined comprehension of Oxford and exposed the arrogance, vanity and conventionality of the Church; intellectual scorn and even bitterness might have come to him; but, with infinite patience and imperturbable serenity, he preserved his faith in his fellow-creatures.

'There was in him a simple trust in the word of other men that won for him a devotion and service which discipline could never have evoked.'[1]

Whether his criticisms of the Bible fluttered the faith of the flappers in Oxford, or whether his long silences made the undergraduates more stupid than they would otherwise have been, I care little: I only know that he was what I call great and that he had an ennobling influence over my life.

He was apprehensive of my social reputation; and in our correspondence, which started directly we parted at Gosford, he constantly gave me wise advice. He was extremely simple-minded and had a pathetic belief in the fine manners, high tone, wide opportunities, and lofty example of the British aristocracy. It shocked him that I did not share it; I felt his warnings much as a duck swimming might feel the cluckings of a hen on a bank; nevertheless, I loved his exhortations. In one of his letters he begs me to give up the idea of shooting bears with the Prince of Wales in Russia. It was the first I had heard of it! In another of his letters to me he ended thus:

'But I must not bore you with good advice. Child, why don't

[1] I read these words the other day in the *Nation* and thought how much I should like to have had them written of me.

you make a better use of your noble gifts? And yet you do not do anything wrong – only what other people do, but with more success. And you are very faithful to your friends. And so, God bless you.'

He was much shocked by hearing that I smoked. This is what he says:

'What are you doing – breaking a young man's heart; not the first time nor the second, nor the third – I believe? Poor fellows! they have paid you the highest compliment that a gentleman can pay a lady, and are deserving of all love. Shall I give you a small piece of counsel? It is better for you and a duty to them that their disappointed passions should never be known to a single person, for as you are well aware, one confidante means everybody, and the good-natured world, who are of course very jealous of you, will call you cruel and a breaker of hearts, etc. I do not consider this advice, but merely a desire to make you see things as others see them or nearly. The Symonds girls at Davos told me that you smoked[!] at which I am shocked, because it is not the manner of ladies in England. I always imagine you with a long hookah puffing, puffing, since I heard this; give it up, my dear Margaret – it will get you a bad name.

'Please do observe that I am always serious when I try to make fun. I hope you are enjoying life and friends and the weather: and believe me

'Ever yours truly,

'B. JOWETT.'

He asked me once if I ever told anyone that he wrote to me, to which I answered:

'I should rather think so! I tell every railway-porter!'

This distressed him. I told him that he was evidently ashamed of my love for him, but that I was proud of it.

JOWETT (*after a long slience*): 'Would you like to have your life written, Margaret?'

MARGOT: 'Not much, unless it told the whole truth about me, and everyone, and was indiscreet. If I could have a biographer like Froude or Lord Hervey, it would be divine, as no one would be bored by reading it. Who will you choose to write your life, Master?'

73

JOWETT: 'No one will be in a position to write my life, Margaret.' (For some time he called me Margaret; he thought it sounded less familiar than Margot.)

MARGOT: 'What nonsense! How can you possibly prevent it? If you are not very good to me, I may even write it myself!'

JOWETT (*smiling*): 'If I could have been sure of that, I need not have burnt all my correspondence! But you are an idle young lady and would certainly never have concentrated on so dull a subject.'

MARGOT (*indignantly*): 'Do you mean to say you have burnt all George Eliot's letters, Matthew Arnold's, Swinburne's, Temple's and Tennyson's?'

JOWETT: 'I have kept one or two of George Eliot's and Florence Nightingale's; but great men do not write good letters.'

MARGOT: 'Do you know Florence Nightingale? I wish I did.'

JOWETT (*evidently surprised that I had never heard the gossip connecting his name with Florence Nightingale*): 'Why do you want to know her?'

MARGOT: 'Because she was in love with my friend George Pembroke's[1] father.'

JOWETT: 'I do not think she will care for you, but would you mind that?'

MARGOT: 'Oh, not at all! I am quite unfeminine in those ways. When people leave the room, I don't say to myself, "I wonder if they like me", but, "I wonder if I like them."'

This made an impression on the Master, or I should not have remembered it. Some weeks after this he took me to see Florence Nightingale in her house in South Street. Groups of hospital-nurses were waiting outside in the hall to see her. When we went in I noted her fine, handsome, well-bred face. She was lying on a sofa, with a white shawl round her shoulders and, after shaking hands with her, the Master and I sat down. She pointed to the beautiful Richmond print of Sidney Herbert, hanging above her mantle-piece, and said to me:

'I am interested to meet you, as I hear George Pembroke, the son of my old and dear friend, is devoted to you. Will you tell me what he is like?'

[1] George Earl of Pembroke, uncle of the present Earl.

I described Lord Pembroke, while Jowett sat in stony silence till we left the house.

One day, a few months after this visit, I was driving in the vicinity of Oxford with the Master and I said to him:

'You never speak of your relations to me and you never tell me whether you were in love when you were young; I have told you so much about myself!'

JOWETT: 'Have you ever heard that I was in love with anyone?'

I did not like to tell him that, since our visit to Florence Nightingale, I had heard that he had wanted to marry her, so I said:

'Yes, I have been told you were in love once.'

JOWETT: 'Only once?'

MARGOT: 'Yes.'

Complete silence fell upon us after this. I broke it at last by saying:

'What was your lady-love like, dear Master?'

JOWETT: 'Violent . . . very violent.'

After this disconcerting description, we drove back to Balliol.

Mrs Humphry Ward's novel, *Robert Elsmere*, had just been published and was dedicated to my sister Laura and Thomas Hill Green, Jowett's rival in Oxford. This is what the Master wrote to me about it:

'NOV. 28, 1888

'Dear Miss Tennant,

'I have just finished examining for the Balliol Scholarships: a great institution of which you may possibly have heard. To what shall I liken it? It is not unlike a man casting into the sea a great drag-net, and when it is full of fish, pulling it up again and taking out fishes, good, bad and indifferent, and throwing the bad and indifferent back again into the sea. Among the good fish there have been Archbishop Tait, Dean Stanley, A. H. Clough, Mr Arnold, Lord Coleridge, Lord Justice Bowen, Mr Ilbert, etc., etc., etc. The institution was founded about sixty years ago.

'I have been dining alone rather dismally, and now I shall imagine that I receive a visit from a young lady about twenty-three years of age, who enlivens me by her prattle. Is it her or her angel? But I believe that she is an angel, pale, volatile and like Laodamia in Wordsworth, ready to disappear at a moment's notice. I could write a description of her, but am not sure that I could do her justice.

'I wish that I could say anything to comfort you, my dear Margot, or even to make you laugh. But no one can comfort another. The memory of a beautiful character is "a joy for ever", especially of one who was bound to you in ties of perfect amity. I saw what your sister[1] was from two short conversations which I had with her, and from the manner in which she was spoken of at Davos.

'I send you the book[2] which I spoke of, though I hardly know whether it is an appropriate present; at any rate I do not expect you to read it. It has taken me the last year to revise and, in parts, re-write it. The great interest of it is that it belongs to a different age of the human mind, in which there is so much like and also unlike ourselves. Many of our commonplaces and common words are being thought out for the first time by Plato. Add to this that in the original this book is the most perfect work of art in the world. I wonder whether it will have any meaning or interest for you.

'You asked me once whether I desired to make a Sister of Charity of you. Certainly not (although there are worse occupations); nor do I desire to make anything. But your talking about plans of life does lead me to think of what would be best and happiest for you. I do not object to the hunting and going to Florence and Rome, but should there not be some higher end to which these are the steps? I think that you might happily fill up a great portion of your life with literature (I am convinced that you have considerable talent and might become eminent) and a small portion with works of benevolence, just to keep us in love and charity with our poor neighbours; and the rest I do not grudge to society and hunting. Do you think that I am a hard task-master? Not very, I think. More especially as you will not be led away by my good advice. You see that I cannot bear to think of you hunting and ballet-dancing when you are "fair, fat and forty-five". Do prepare yourself for that awful age.

'I went to see Mrs H. Ward the other day: she insists on doing battle with the Reviewer of *Robert Elsmere*. Rose is intended for you, Catherine for your sister Laura, the Squire for Mark Pattison,

---

[1] Mrs Gordon Duff.   [2] Plato's *Republic*.

the Provost for me, etc., and Mr Grey for Professor Green. All the portraits are about equally unlike the originals.

'Good-bye, you have been sitting with me for nearly an hour, and now, like Laodamia or Protesilaus, you disappear. I have been the better for your company. One serious word: May God bless you and help you in this and every other great hurt of life.

'Ever yours,

'B. JOWETT.'

I will publish all his letters to me together, as, however delightful letters may be, I find they bore me when they are scattered all through an autobiography.

'MARCH 11TH, 1889

'My Dear Margaret,

'As you say, friendships grow dull if two persons do not care to write to one another. I was beginning to think that you resented my censorious criticisms on your youthful life and happiness.

'Can youth be serious without ceasing to be youth? I think it may. The desire to promote the happiness of others rather than your own may be always "breaking in". As my poor sister (of whom I will talk to you some day) would say: "When others are happy, then I am happy." She used to commend the religion of Sydney Smith – "Never to let a day pass without doing a kindness to somebody" – and I think that you understand something about this; or you would not be so popular and beloved.

'You ask me what persons I have seen lately: I doubt whether they would interest you. Mr Welldon, the Headmaster of Harrow, a very honest and able man with a long life before him, and if he is not too honest and open, not unlikely to be an Archbishop of Canterbury. Mr J. M. Wilson, Headmaster of Clifton College – a very kind, genial and able man – there is a great deal of him and in him – not a man of good judgment, but very devoted – a first-rate man in his way. Then I have seen a good deal of Lord Rosebery – very able, shy, sensitive, ambitious, the last two qualities rather at war with each other – very likely a future Prime Minister. I like Lady Rosebery too – very sensible and high-principled, not at all inclined to give up her Judaism to please the rest of the world.

They are rather overloaded with wealth and fine houses: they are both very kind. I also like Lady Leconfield,[1] whom I saw at Mentone. Then I paid a visit to Tennyson, who has had a lingering illness of six months, perhaps fatal, as he is eighty years of age. It was pleasing to see how he takes it, very patient and without fear of death, unlike his former state of mind. Though he is so sensitive, he seemed to me to bear his illness like a great man. He has a volume of poems waiting to come out – some of them as good as he ever wrote. Was there ever an octogenarian poet before?

'Doctor Johnson used to say that he never in his life had eaten as much fruit as he desired. I think I never talked to you as much as I desired. You once told me that you would show me your novel.[2] Is it a reality or a myth? I should be interested to see it if you like to send me that or any other writings of yours.

'*Robert Elsmere*, as the authoress tells me, has sold 60,000 in England and 400,000 in America! It has considerable merit, but its success is really due to its saying what everybody is thinking. I am astonished at her knowing so much about German theology – she is a real scholar and takes up things of the right sort. I do not believe that Mrs Ward ever said "She had pulverised Christianity". These things are invented about people by the orthodox, i.e., the infidel world, in the hope that they will do them harm. What do you think of being "laughed to death"? It would be like being tickled to death.

'Good-bye,

'Ever yours truly,

'B. JOWETT.'

'BALLIOL COLLEGE,
'MAY 22ND, 1891

'My Dear Margaret,

'It was very good of you to write me such a nice note. I hope you are better. I rather believe in people being able to cure themselves of many illnesses if they are tolerably prudent and have a great spirit.

---

[1] Lady Leconfield is a sister of Lord Rosebery's and one of my dearest friends.
[2] I began two, but they were not at all interesting and have long since disappeared.

'I liked your two friends who visited me last Sunday, and shall hope to make them friends of mine. Asquith is a capital fellow, and has abilities which may rise to the highest things in the law and politics. He is also very pleasant socially. I like your lady friend. She has both "Sense and Sensibility", and is free from "Pride and Prejudice". She told me that she had been brought up by an Evangelical grandmother, and is none the worse for it.

'I begin to think bed a very nice place, and I see a great deal of it, not altogether from laziness, but because it is the only way in which I am able to work.

'I have just read the life of Newman, who was a strange character. To me he seems to have been the most artificial man of our generation, full of ecclesiastical loves and hatred. Considering what he really was, it is wonderful what a space he has filled in the eyes of mankind. In speculation he was habitually untruthful and not much better in practice. His conscience had been taken out, and the Church put in its place. Yet he was a man of genius, and a good man in the sense of being disinterested. Truth is very often troublesome, but neither the world nor the individual can get on without it.

'Here is the postman appearing at 12 o'clock, as disagreeable a figure as the tax-gatherer.

'May you have good sleep and pleasant dreams. I shall still look forward to seeing you with Lady Wemyss.

'Believe me always,
'Yours affectionately,
'B. Jowett.'

'BALLIOL COLLEGE,
'SEP. 8, 1892

'My Dear Margaret,

'Your kind letter was a very sweet consolation to me. It was like you to think of a friend in trouble.

'Poor Nettleship, whom we have lost, was a man who cannot be replaced – certainly not in Oxford. He was a very good man, and had a considerable touch of genius in him. He seems to have died bravely, telling the guides not to be cowards, but to save their lives. He also sang to them to keep them awake, saying (this was so like him) that he had no voice, but that he would do his best. He probably sang that song of Salvator Rosa's which we have so often heard from him. He was wonderfully beloved by the undergraduates, because they knew that he cared for them more than for anything else in the world.

'Of his writings there is not much, except what you have read, and a long essay on Plato in a book called *Hellenica* – very good. He was beginning to write, and I think would have written well. He was also an excellent speaker and lecturer – Mr Asquith would tell you about him.

'I have received many letters about him – but none of them has touched me as much as yours. Thank you, dear.

'I see that you are in earnest about writing – no slipshod or want of connection. Writing requires boundless leisure, and is an infinite labour, yet there is also a very great pleasure in it. I shall be delighted to read your sketches.'

'BALLIOL COLLEGE,
'DEC. 27TH, 1892

'My Dear Margaret,

'I have been reading Lady Jeune's two articles. I am glad that you did not write them and have never written anything of that sort. These criticisms on Society in which some of us "live and move and have our being" are mistaken. In the first place, the whole fabric of society is a great mystery, with which we ought not to take liberties, and which should be spoken of only in a whisper when we compare our experiences, whether in a walk or *tête-à-tête*, or "over the back hair" with a faithful, reserved confidante. And there is also a great deal that is painful in the absence of freedom in the division of ranks, and the rising or falling from one place in it to another. I am convinced that it is a thing not to be spoken of; what we can do to improve it or do it good – whether I, the head of a college at Oxford, or a young lady of fashion (I know that you don't like to be called *that*) – must be done quite silently.

'Lady Jeune believes that all the world would go right, or at least be a great deal better, if it were not for the Nouveaux Riches.

Some of the Eton masters talk to me in the same way. I agree with our dear friend, Lady Wemyss, that the truth is "the old poor are so jealous of them". We must study the arts of uniting Society as a whole, not clinging to any one class of it – what is possible and desirable to what is impossible and undesirable.

'I hope you are none the worse for your great effort. You know it interests me to hear what you are about if you have time and inclination to write. I saw your friend, Mr Asquith, last night: very nice and not at all puffed up with his great office.[1] The fortunes of the Ministry seem very doubtful. There is a tendency to follow Lord Rosebery in the Cabinet. Some think that the Home Rule Bill will be pushed to the second reading, then dropped, and a new shuffle of the cards will take place under Lord Rosebery: this seems to me very likely. The Ministry has very little to spare and they are not gaining ground, and the English are beginning to hate the Irish and the Priests.

'I hope that all things go happily with you. Tell me some of your thoughts. I have been reading Mr Milner's book with great satisfaction – most interesting and very important. I fear that I have written you a dull and meandering epistle.

'Ever yours,

'B. JOWETT.'

'BALLIOL COLLEGE,

'FEB. 13, 1893

'My Dear Margaret,

'I began at ten minutes to twelve last night to write to you, but as the postman appeared at five minutes to twelve, it was naturally cut short. May I begin where I left off? I should like to talk to you about many things. I hope you will not say, as Johnson says to Boswell, "Sir, you have only two subjects, yourself and me, and I am heartily sick of both."

'I have been delighted with Mr Asquith's success. He has the certainty of a great man in him – such strength and simplicity and independence and superiority to the world and the clubs. You seem to me very fortunate in having three such friends as Mr Asquith,

[1] The Home Office.

Mr Milner and Mr Balfour. I believe that you may do a great deal for them, and they are probably the first men of their time, or not very far short of it.

'Mr Balfour is not so good a leader of the House of Commons in opposition as he was when he was in office. He is too aggressive and not dignified enough. I fear that he will lose weight. He had better not coquette with the foolish and unpractical thing "Bimetallism", or write books on "Philosophic Doubt"; for there are many things which we must certainly believe, are there not? Quite enough either for the highest idealism or for ordinary life. He will probably, like Sir R. Peel, have to change many of his opinions in the course of the next thirty years and he should be on his guard about this, or he will commit himself in such a manner that he may have to withdraw from politics (about the currency, about the Church, about Socialism).

'Is this to be the last day of Gladstone's life in the House of Commons? It is very pathetic to think of the aged man making his last great display almost in opposition to the convictions of his whole life. I hope that he will acquit himself well and nobly, and then it does not much matter whether or no he dies like Lord Chatham a few days afterwards. It seems to me that his Ministry have not done badly during the last fortnight. They have, to a great extent, removed the impression they had created in England that they were the friends of disorder. Do you know, I cannot help feeling I have more of the Liberal element in me than of the Conservative? This rivalry between the parties, each surprising the other by their liberality, has done a great deal of good to the people of England.'

'HEADINGTON HILL,
'NEAR OXFORD,
'JULY 30TH, 1893

'My Dear Margaret,
'Did you ever read these lines? –

> *"'Tis said that marriages are made above –*
> *It may be so, some few, perhaps, for love.*
> *But from the smell of sulphur I should say*
> *They must be making* matches *here all day."*

'(Orpheus returning from the lower world in a farce called *The Olympic Devils*, which used to be played when I was young.)

'Miss Nightingale talks to me of "the feelings usually called love", but then she is a heroine, perhaps a goddess.

'This love-making is a very serious business, though society makes fun of it, perhaps to test the truth and earnestness of the lovers.

'Dear, I am an old man, what the poet calls "on the threshold of old age" (Homer), and I am not very romantic or sentimental about such things, but I would do anything I could to save anyone who cares for me from making a mistake.

'I think that you are quite right in not running the risk without a modest abode in the country.

'The real doubt about the affair is the family; will you consider this and talk it over with your mother? The other day you were at a masqued ball, as you told me – a few months hence you will have, or rather may be having, the care of five children, with all the ailments and miseries and disagreeables of children (unlike the children of some of your friends) and not your own, although you will have to be a mother to them, and this state of things will last during the greatest part of your life. Is not the contrast more than human nature can endure? I know that it is, as you said, a nobler manner of living, but are you equal to such a struggle? If you are, I can only say, "God bless you, you are a brave girl." But I would not have you disguise from yourself the nature of the trial. It is not possible to be a leader of fashion and to do your duty to the five children.

'On the other hand, you have at your feet a man of outstanding ability and high character, and who has attained an extraordinary position – far better than any aristocratic lath or hop-pole; and you can render him the most material help by your abilities and knowledge of the world. Society will be gracious to you because you are a *grata persona*, and everybody will wish you well because you have made the sacrifice. You may lead a much higher life if you are yourself equal to it.

'Today I read Hume's life – by himself – very striking. You will find it generally at the beginning of his History of England. There have been saints among infidels too, e.g., Hume and Spinoza, on behalf of whom I think it a duty to say something, as the Church has devoted them to eternal flames. To use a German phrase, "They were 'Christians in unconsciousness'. " That describes a good many people. I believe that as Christians we should get rid of a good many doubtful phrases and speak only through our lives.

'Believe me, my dear Margaret,

'Yours truly and affectionately,

'B. JOWETT.'

'BALLIOL,

'SUNDAY, 1893

'My Dear Margaret,

'I quite agree with you that what we want most in life is rest and peace. To act up to our best lights, that is quite enough; there need be no trouble about dogmas, which are hardly intelligible to us, nor ought there to be any trouble about historical facts, including miracles, of which the view of the world has naturally altered in the course of ages. I include in this such questions as whether Our Lord rose from the dead in any natural sense of the words. It is quite a different question, whether we shall imitate Him in His life.

'I am glad you think about these questions, and shall be pleased to talk to you about them. What I have to say about religion is contained in two words: Truth and Goodness, but I would not have one without the other, and if I had to choose between them, might be disposed to give Truth the first place. I think, also, that you might put religion in another way, as absolute resignation to the Will of God and the order of nature. There might be other definitions, equally true, but none suited better than another to the characters of men, such as the imitation of Christ, or the truth in all religions, which would be an adequate description of it. The Christian religion seems to me to extend to all the parts and modes of life, and then to come back to our hearts and conscience. I think that the best way of considering it, and the most interesting, is to view it as it may be seen in the lives of good men everywhere, whether Christians or so-called heathens – Socrates, Plato, Marcus Aurelius, St Augustine, as well as in the lives of Christ, or Bunyan, or Spinoza. The study of religious biography seems to me one of the best modes of keeping up Christian feeling.

'As to the question of Disestablishment, I am not like Mr Balfour, I wobble rather, yet, on the whole, I agree with Mr Gladstone, certainly about the Welsh Church. Churches are so worldly and so much allied to the interests of the higher classes. I think that a person who belongs to a Church should always endeavour to live above his Church, above the sermon and a good part of the prayer, above the Athanasian Creed, and the form of Ordination, above the passions of party feelings and public meetings. The best individuals have always been better than Churches, though I do not go so far as a German professor, who thinks that people will never be religious until they leave off going to church, yet I am of opinion that in every congregation the hearers should attempt to raise themselves above the tone of the preacher and of the service.

'I am sorry to hear that Mr Balfour, who has so much that is liberal in him, is of an extreme opposite opinion. But I feel that I have talked long enough on a subject which may not interest you, but of which I should like to talk to you again when we meet. It seems to me probable that the Church *will* be disestablished, because it has been so already in most countries of Europe, and because the school is everywhere taking its place.

'I shall look forward to your coming to see me, if I am seriously ill – "Be with me when my light is low' . But I don't think that this illness which I at present have is serious enough to make any of my friends anxious, and it would be rather awkward for my friends to come and take leave of me if I recovered, which I mean to do, for what I think a good reason – because I *still* have a good deal to do.

'B. JOWETT.'

My beloved friend died in 1893. I have mourned him ever since.

The year before his death he had the dangerous illness to which he alludes in the above letter. Everyone thought he would die. He dictated farewell letters to all his friends by his secretary and housekeeper, Miss Knight. On receiving mine from him at Glen, I was so much annoyed at its tone that I wired:

'JOWETT, BALLIOL COLLEGE, OXFORD.

'I refuse to accept this as your farewell letter to me you have been listening to some silly woman and believing what she says. Love.

'MARGOT.'

This telegram had a magical effect: he got steadily better and wrote me a wonderful letter. I remember the reason that I was vexed was because he believed a report that I had knocked up against a foreign potentate in Rotten Row for a bet, which was not only untrue but ridiculous; and I was getting a little impatient of the cattishness and credulity of the West End of London.

*   *   *

My week-ends at Balliol were different to my other visits. The Master took infinite trouble over them. Once on my arrival he asked me which of one or two men I would like to sit next to at dinner. I said I should prefer Mr Huxley or Lord Bowen; to which he replied:

'I would like you to have on your other side, either tonight or tomorrow, my friend Lord Selborne.

MARGOT (*with surprise*): 'Since when is he your friend? I was under the impression you disliked him.'

JOWETT: 'Your impression was right, but even the youngest of us are sometimes wrong, as Dr Thompson said, and I look upon Lord Selborne now as a friend. I hope I said nothing against him.'

MARGOT: 'Oh dear no! You only said he was fond of hymns, and had no sense of humour.'

JOWETT (*snappishly*): 'If that is so, Margaret, I made an extremely foolish remark. I will put you between Lord Bowen and Sir Alfred Lyall. Was it not strange that you should have said of Lyall to Huxley that he reminded you of a faded Crusader and that you suspected him of wearing a coat of mail under his broad-cloth, to which you will remember Huxley remarked, "You mean a coating of female, without which no man is saved!" Your sister, Lady Ribblesdale, said the very same thing to me about him.'

This interested me, as Charty and I had not spoken to each other of Sir Alfred Lyall, who was a new acquaintance of ours.

MARGOT: 'I am sure, Master, you did not give her the same answer as Mr Huxley gave me; you don't think well of my sex, do you?'

JOWETT: 'You are not the person to reproach me, Margaret; only the other week I reproved you for saying women were often dull, sometimes dangerous and always dishonourable. I might have added they were rarely reasonable and always courageous. Would you agree to this?'

MARGOT: 'Yes.'

I sat between Sir Alfred Lyall and Lord Bowen that night at dinner. There was more bouquet than body about Sir Alfred and, to parody Gibbon, Lord Bowen's mind was not clouded by enthusiasm; but two more agreeable companions could not have been met.

After dinner, Mr Huxley came across the room to me and said that the Master had confessed he had done him out of sitting next to me, so would I talk to him? We sat down together, and our conversation opened upon religion.

There was not much *juste milieu* about Mr Huxley. He began by saying God was only there because people believed in Him, and that the fastidious incognito, 'I am that I am,' was His idea of humour, etc., etc.; and ended by saying he did not believe any man of action had ever been inspired by religion. I thought I would call in Lord Bowen to my assistance. He was standing aimlessly in the middle of the room, and instantly responded to my invitation. Pushing a chair towards him, I said:

'Mr Huxley challenges me to produce any man of action who has been directly inspired by religion.'

BOWEN (*with a sleek smile*): 'Between us we should be able to answer him, Miss Tennant, I think. Who is your man?'

Every idea seemed to scatter out of my brain and I suggested at random:

'Gordon.'

I might have been reading his thoughts, for it so happened that Mr Huxley adored General Gordon.

HUXLEY: 'Ah! There you rather have me!' he said, and changing the position of his chair, as if to engage Bowen in a *tête-à-tête*, he continued:

'My dear Bowen, Gordon was the most remarkable man I ever

met. I knew him well; he was sincere and disinterested, quite incapable of saying anything he did not think. You will hardly believe me, but one day he said in tones of passionate conviction, that if he were to walk round the corner of the street and have his brains shot out, he would only be transferred to a wider sphere of government.'

BOWEN: 'Would the absence of brains have been of any help to him?'

After this, our mutual good humour was restored and I only had time for a word with Mrs Green before the evening was ruined by Jowett taking us across the quad to hear moderate music in the hideous new Balliol hall.

*   *   *

Of all the Master's women friends, I preferred Mrs T. H. Green (John Addington Symonds' sister). She is among the rare women who have all the qualities which in moments of exasperation I deny to them.

I spent my last weekend at Balliol when Jowett's health appeared to have completely recovered. On the Monday, after his guests had gone, I went as usual into his study, to talk to him. My wire on receiving his death-bed letter had amused but distressed him; and on my arrival he pressed me to tell him what it was he had written that had offended me. I told him I was not offended, only hurt. He asked me what the difference was. I wish I could have given him the answer that my daughter Elizabeth gave Lord Grey[1] when he asked her the same question, walking in the garden at Fallodon on the occasion of her first country-house visit:

'The one touches your vanity and the other your heart.'

I do not know what I replied, but I told him I was quite unoffendable and without touchiness, but that his letter appeared to me to have all the faults of a school-master and a cleric in it and not the love of a friend. He listened with his usual patience and expressed his regret.

On the Monday morning of which I am writing, I had made up my mind that, as I had spoilt many good conversations by talking too much myself, I would hold my tongue and let the Master for

[1] Viscount Grey of Fallodon.

once make the first move. I had not had much experience of his classical silences and had often defended him from the charge; but it was time to see what would happen if I talked less.

When we got into the room and he had shut the door, I absently selected the only comfortable chair and we sat down next to each other. A long and quelling silence followed the lighting of my cigarette. Feeling rather at a loose end, I thought out a few stage-directions – 'here business with handkerchief, etc.,' – and adjusted the buckles on my shoes. I looked at some photographs and fingered paper-knife and odds and ends on the table near me. The oppressive silence continued. I strolled to the book-shelves and, under cover of a copy of *Country Conversations*, peeped at the Master. He appeared to be transfixed and quite unaware of my existence.

'Nothing doing,' said I to myself, putting back the book.

Something had switched him off as if he had been the electric light.

With considerable impatience, I said at last:

'Really, Master, there is very little excuse for your silence! Surely you have something to say to me, something to tell me; you have had an experience since we talked to each other that I have never had: you have been near Death.'

JOWETT (*not in any way put out and with great deliberation*): 'I felt no rapture . . . no bliss. . . . My dear child, you must believe in God in spite of what the clergy tell you.'

VIII · *Gladstone and Salisbury*

The political event that caused the greatest sensation when I was a girl was the murder of Mr Burke and Lord Frederick Cavendish on 6th May 1882. We were in London at the time; and the news came through on a Sunday. Alfred Lyttelton told me that Lady Frederick Cavendish's butler had broken it to him by rushing into his room and saying:

'They have knifed his lordship!'

The news spread from West to East and North to South; groups of people stood talking in the middle of the streets without their hats, and everyone felt that this terrible outrage was bound to have consequences far beyond the punishment of the criminals.

Just as I ask myself what would have been the outcome of the Paris Conference if the British had made the League of Nations a genuine first plank in their programme instead of a last postscript, so I wonder what would have happened if Chamberlain had stuck to Gladstone in 1885-86. Gladstone had all the playing–cards – as President Wilson had – and was not likely to under-declare his hand, but he was a much older man and I cannot but think that if they had remained together Chamberlain would not have been thrown into the arms of the Tories and the reversion of the Premiership must have gone to him. It seems strange to me that the leaders of the great Conservative party have so often been hired bravos or wandering minstrels with whom it can share no common conviction. I never cease wondering why it cannot produce a man of its own, and there must be something inherent in its creed that produces such sterility.

When Mr Gladstone went in for Home Rule, society was rent from top to bottom, and even the most devoted friends quarrelled over it. Our family was as much divided as any other.

One day, when Lord Spencer was staying at Glen, I was sent out of the room at dinner for saying that Gladstone had made a Balaclava blunder with his stupid Home Rule; we had all got so heated over the discussion that I was glad enough to obey my papa. A few minutes later he came out full of penitence to see if he had hurt my feelings and found me sitting on the billiard-table smoking one of his best cigars. I gave him a good hug and told him I would join him later on. He said he was only too glad that his cigars were appreciated and returned to the dining-room in high spirits to talk to Lord Spencer.

Events have proved that I was entirely wrong about Home Rule. Now that we have discovered what the consequences are of withholding from Ireland the self-government which for generations she has asked for, can we doubt that Gladstone should have been vigorously backed in his attempt to still the controversy? As it is, our follies in Ireland have cursed the political life of this country for years. Someone has said, '*L'Irlande est une maladie incurable mais jamais mortelle*': and, if she can survive the present régime, no one will doubt the truth of the saying.

In May, June and July, 1914, within three months of the war, every donkey in London was cutting or trying to cut us, for wishing to settle this very same Irish question. My presence at a ball with Elizabeth – who was seventeen – was considered not only provocative to others but a danger to myself. All the brains of all the landlords in Ireland, backed by half the brains of half the landlords in England, had ranged themselves behind Sir Edward Carson, his army and his Covenant. Earnest Irish patriots had turned their fields into camps and their houses into hospitals; aristocratic females had been making bandages for months, when von Kühlmann, Secretary of the German Embassy in London, went over to pay his first visit to Ireland. On his return he told me with conviction that, from all he had heard and seen out there during a long tour, nothing but a miracle could avert civil war, to which I replied:

'Shocking as that would be, it would not break England.'

Our follies in Ireland have cursed not only the political but the social life of this country.

It was not until the political ostracisms over Home Rule began all over again in 1914 that I realised how powerful socially my friends and I were in the 'eighties.

Mr Balfour once told me that, before our particular group of friends – generally known as the Souls – appeared in London, prominent politicians of opposite parties seldom if ever met one another; and he added:

'No history of our time will be complete unless the influence of the Souls upon society is dispassionately and accurately recorded.'

The same question of Home Rule that threw London back to the old parochialisms in 1914 was at its height in 1886 and 1887; but at our house in Grosvenor Square and later in those of the Souls, everyone met – Randolph Churchill, Gladstone, Asquith, Morley, Chamberlain, Balfour, Rosebery, Salisbury, Hartington, Harcourt and, I might add, jockeys, actors, the Prince of Wales and every ambassador in London. We never cut anybody – not even our friends – or thought it amusing or distinguished to make people feel uncomfortable; and our decision not to sacrifice private friendship to public politics was envied in every capital in Europe. It made London the centre of the most interesting society in the world and gave men of different tempers and opposite beliefs an opportunity of discussing them without heat and without reporters. There is no individual or group among us powerful enough to succeed in forming a salon of this kind today.

The daring of such a change in society cannot be over-estimated, but the unconscious and accidental grouping of brilliant, sincere and loyal friends like ourselves gave rise to so much jealousy and discussion that I shall devote a later chapter to the Souls.

It was at No. 40 Grosvenor Square that Gladstone met Lord Randolph Churchill, after he had made himself famous by attacking and abusing the 'Grand Old Man' with such virulence that everyone thought it impossible that they could ever meet in intimacy again. I was not awed by this, but invited them to a luncheon-party which they both accepted. I need hardly say that when they met they talked with fluency and interest, for it was as impossible for Mr Gladstone to be *gauche* or rude as it was for anyone to be ill at ease with Lord Randolph Churchill. The news of their lunching with us spread all over London; and the West End buzzed round me with questions: all the political ladies including the Duchess of Manchester, were torn with curiosity to know whether Randolph was going to join the Liberal Party. I refused to gratify their curiosity, but managed to convey a general impression that at any moment our ranks having lost Mr Chamberlain, were going to be reinforced by Lord Randolph Churchill, and our house became a centre of political interests.

*   *   *

The Duchess of Manchester (who became the Duchess of Devonshire) was the last great political lady in London society as I have known it. The secret of her power lay not only in her position – many people are rich and grand, gay and clever, and live in big houses – but in her elasticity, her careful criticisms, her sense of justice, and her discretion. She not only kept her own but other people's secrets; and she added to considerable effrontery intrepid courage and real kindness. She was powerful enough to entertain both the great political parties which few can do. You met everyone at her house, but she told me that before 1886-87 political opponents hardly ever saw one another and society was much duller. I have heard her reprove and mildly ridicule all her guests both at Compton Place and at Chatsworth, from the Prince of Wales to the Prime Minister. I asked her once what she thought of a certain famous political lady, whose arrogance and vulgarity had annoyed us all, to which she answered:

'I dislike her too much to be a good judge of her.'

One evening many years after the time of which I am writing, she was dining with us, and we were talking alone.

'Margot,' she said, 'you and I are very much alike.'

It was impossible to imagine two more different beings than myself and the Duchess of Devonshire – morally, physically or intellectually – so I asked her what reason she had for thinking so, to which she replied:

'We have both married angels; when Hartington dies he will go straight to Heaven' – pointing her first finger high above her head – 'and when Mr Asquith dies he will go straight there, too: not so

93

Lord Salisbury', pointing her finger with a diving movement to the floor.

One day in 1901 my husband and I were staying at Chatsworth. There was a huge house-party, including Arthur Balfour and Mr Chamberlain. Before going down to dinner, Henry came into my bedroom and told me he had had a telegram to say that Queen Victoria was very ill and he feared the worst; he added that it was a profound secret and that I was to tell no one. After dinner I was asked by the Duchess' granddaughters – Lady Aldra and Lady Mary Acheson – to join them at planchette, so, to please them, I put my hand upon the board. I was listening to what the Duchess was saying and my mind was a blank. After the girls and I had scratched about for a little time, one of them took the paper off the board and read out loud:

' "The Queen is dying": what Queen can that be?' she added.

We gathered round her and all looked at the writing; and there I read distinctly out of a lot of hieroglyphics:

'The Queen is dying.'

If the three of us had combined to try to write this and had poked about all night, we could not have done it.

I have had many interesting personal experiences of untraceable communication and telepathy and I think that people who set themselves against all this side of life are excessively stupid; but I do not connect them with religion any more than with Marconi and I shall always look upon it as strange that people can find consolation in the rubbish they listen to in the dark at séances.

To return to Chatsworth. Our host, the Duke of Devonshire, was a man whose like we shall never see again; he stood by himself and could have come from no country in the world but England. He had the figure and appearance of an artisan, with the brevity of a peasant, the courtesy of a king and the noisy sense of humour of a Falstaff. He gave a great, wheezy guffaw at all the right things and was possessed of endless wisdom. He was perfectly disengaged from himself, fearlessly truthful and without pettiness of any kind.

Bryan, the American politician, who came over here and heard all our big guns speak – Rosebery, Chamberlain, Asquith, etc. – when asked what he thought, said that a Chamberlain was not unknown to them in America, and that they could produce a Rosebery or an Asquith, but that a Hartington no man could find. His speaking was the finest example of pile-driving the world had ever seen.

*　　*　　*

As I have said before, we were not popular in Peeblesshire. My papa and his vital family disturbed the county conventions; and all Liberals were looked upon as aliens by the Scottish aristocracy of those days. At election times the mill-hands of both sexes were locked up for fear of rows, but in spite of this the locks were broken and the rows were perpetual. When my father turned out the sitting Tory, Sir Graham Montgomery, in 1880, there were high jinks in Peebles. I pinned the Liberal colours, with the deftness of a pickpocket, to the coat-tails of several of the unsuspecting Tory landlords, who had come from great distances to vote. This delighted the electors, most of whom were feather-stitching up and down the High Street, more familiar with drink than jokes.

The first politicians of note that came to stay with us at Glen were Mr Chamberlain and Sir Charles Dilke. Just as, later on, my friends (the Souls) discussed which would go farthest, George Curzon, George Wyndham or Harry Cust, so in those days people were asking the same question about Chamberlain and Dilke. To my mind it wanted no witch to predict that Chamberlain would beat not only Dilke but other men; and it appeared to me that Gladstone made a profound mistake in not making him a Secretary of State in his Government of 1886.

Mr Chamberlain never deceived himself, which is more than could be said of some of the famous politicians of that day. He also possessed a rare measure of intellectual control. Self-mastery was his idiosyncrasy and was particularly noticeable in his speaking; he encouraged in himself such scrupulous economy of gesture, movement and colour that, after hearing him many times, I came to the definite conclusion that Chamberlain's opponents were snowed under by his accumulated moderation. Whatever Dilke's native impulses were, no one could say that he controlled them. Besides a defective sense of humour, he was fundamentally commonplace and had no key to his mind, which makes everyone ultimately dull.

My father, being an ardent Radical, with a passion for anyone that Gladstone patronized, had made elaborate preparations for Dilke's reception; and when he arrived at Glen he was given a warm welcome while we all sat down to tea. After hearing him talk uninterruptedly for hours and watching his stuffy face and protruding eyes, I said to Laura:

'He may be a very clever man, but he has not a ray of humour and hardly any sensibility. If he were a horse, I would certainly not buy him!'

With which she entirely agreed.

On the second night of his visit, our distinguished guest met Laura in the passage on her way to bed; he said to her:

'If you will kiss me, I will give you a signed photograph of myself.'

To which she answered:

'It is awfully good of you, Sir Charles, but I would rather not, for what on earth should I do with the photograph?'

*   *   *

Mr Gladstone was the dominating politician of the day, and excited more adoration and hatred than anyone.

After my first visit to Hawarden, he sent me the following poem, which he had written the night before I left:

MARGOT

When Parliament ceases and comes the recess,
And we seek in the country rest after distress,
As a rule upon visitors place an embargo,
But make an exception in favour of Margot.

For she brings such a treasure of movement and life,
Fun, spirit and stir, to folk weary with strife.
Though young and though fair, who can hold such a cargo
Of all the good qualities going as Margot?

Up hill and down dale, 'tis a capital name
To blossom in friendship, to sparkle in fame;
There's but one objection can light upon Margot,
Its likeness in rhyming, not meaning, to argot.

Never mind, never mind, we will give it the slip,
'Tis not argot, the language, but Argo, the ship;
And by sea or by land, I will swear you may far go
Before you can hit on a double for Margot.

W. E. G.

December 17th, 1889.

I received this at Glen by the second post on the day of my arrival – too soon for me to imagine my host had written it, so I wrote to our dear old friend, Godfrey Webb – always under suspicion of playing jokes upon us – to say he had overdone it this time, as Gladstone had too good a handwriting for him to caricature convincingly. When I found that I was wrong, I wrote to my poet:

'DEC. 19TH, 1889

'Very Dear and Honoured Mr Gladstone,

'At first I thought your poem must have been a joke, written by someone who knew of my feelings for you and my visit to Hawarden; but, when I saw the signature and the post-mark, I was convinced it could be but from you. It has had the intoxicating effect of turning my head with pleasure; if I began I should never cease thanking you. Getting four rhymes to my name emphasizes your uncommon genius, I think! And Argo the ship is quite a new idea and a charming one. I love the third verse: that Margot is a capital name to blossom in friendship and sparkle in fame. You must allow me to say that you are ever such a dear. It is impossible to believe that you will be eighty tomorrow, but I like to think of it, for it gives most people an opportunity of seeing how life should be lived without being spent.

'There is no blessing, beauty or achievement that I do not wish you.

'In truth and sincerity,
'Yours,
'MARGOT TENNANT.'

A propos of this, twelve years later I received the following letter from Lord Morley:

'THE RED HOUSE, HAWARDEN, CHESTER,
'JULY 18TH, 1901

'I have just had such a cheerful quarter-of-an-hour – a packet of *your* letters to Mr G. Think ! – I've read them all! – and they bring the writer back to me with queer and tender vividness. Such a change from Bishops!!! Why do you never address *me* as "Very dear and honoured Sir"? I'm not quite eighty-five yet, but I soon shall be.

'Ever yours,
'JOHN MORLEY.'

I have heard people say that the Gladstone family never allowed him to read a newspaper with anything hostile to himself in it; all this is the greatest rubbish; no one interfered with his reading. The same silly things were said about the great men of that day as of this and will continue to be said; and the same silly geese will believe them. I never observed that Gladstone was more easily flattered than other men. He *was* more flattered and by more people, because he was a bigger man and lived a longer life; but he was remarkably free from vanity of any kind. He would always laugh at a good thing, if you chose the right moment in which to tell it to him; but there were times when he was out of temper with fun.

One day, when he and I were talking of Jane Welsh Carlyle, I told him that a friend of Carlyle's, an old man whom I met at Balliol, had told me that one of his favourite stories was of an Irishman who, when asked where he was driving his pig to, said:

'Cark. . . .' (Cork).

'But,' said his interlocutor, 'your head is turned to Mullingar! . . .'

To which the man replied:

'Whist! He'll hear ye!'

This delighted Mr Gladstone. I also told him one of Jowett's favourite stories, of how George IV went down to Portsmouth for some big function and met a famous admiral of the day. He clapped him on the back and said in a loud voice:

'Well, my dear Admiral, I hear you are the greatest blackguard in Portsmouth!'

At which the Admiral drew himself up, saluted the King and said:

'I hope, Sir, *you* have not come down here to take away my reputation.'

I find in an old diary an account of a drive I had with Mr Gladstone after my sister Laura died. This is what I wrote:

'On Saturday 20th May 1886, Mr and Mrs Gladstone came to pay us a visit at 40 Grosvenor Square. Papa had been arranging the drawing-room preparatory to their arrival and was in high spirits. I was afraid he might resent my wish to take Mr Gladstone up to my room after lunch and talk to him alone. However, Aunty Pussy – as we called Mrs Gladstone – with a great deal of winking, led papa away and said to mamma:

' "William and Margot are going to have a little talk!"

'I had not met or seen Mr Gladstone since Laura's death.

'When he had climbed up to my boudoir, he walked to the window and admired the trees in the square, deploring their use-lessness and asking whether the street lamp – which crossed the square path in the line of our eyes – was a child.

'I asked him if he would approve of the square railings being taken away and the grass and trees made into a *place* with seats, such as you see in foreign towns, not merely for the convenience of sitting down, but for the happiness of invalids and idlers who court the shade or the sun. This met with his approval, but he said with some truth that the only people who could do this – or prevent it – were "the resident aristocracy".

'He asked if Laura had often spoken of death. I said yes and that she had written about it in a way that was neither morbid nor terrible. I showed him some prayers she had scribbled in a book, against worldliness and high spirits. He listened with reverence and interest. I don't think I ever saw his face wear the expression that Millais painted in our picture as distinctly as when, closing the book, he said to me:

' "It requires very little faith to believe that so rare a creature as your sister Laura is blessed and with God."

'Aunty Pussy came into the room and the conversation turned to Laurence Oliphant's objection to visiting the graves of those we love. They disagreed with this and he said:

' "I think, on the contrary, one should encourage oneself to find

99

consolation in the few tangible memories that one can claim; it should not lessen faith in their spirits; and there is surely a silent lesson to be learnt from the tombstone."

'Papa and mamma came in and we all went down to tea. Mr G., feeling relieved by the change of scene and topic, began to talk and said he regretted all his life having missed the opportunity of knowing Sir Walter Scott, Dr Arnold and Lord Melbourne. He told us a favourite story of his. He said:

' "An association of ladies wrote and asked me to send them a few words on that unfortunate Mary Queen of Scots. In the penury of my knowledge and the confusion arising from the conflicting estimates of poor Mary, I though I would write to Bishop Stubbs. All he replied was, 'Mary is looking up.' " '

'After this I drove him back to Downing Street in my phaeton, round the Park and down Knightsbridge. I told him I found it difficult to judge of people's brains if they were very slow.

'MR GLADSTONE: "I wish, then, that you had had the privilege of knowing Mr Cobden; he was at once the slowest and quite one of the cleverest men I ever met. Personally I find it far easier to judge of brains than character; perhaps it is because in my line of life motives are very hard to fathom and constant association with intelligence and cultivation leads to a fair toleration and criticism of all sorts and conditions of men."

'He talked of Bright and Chamberlain and Lord Dalhousie, who, he said, was one of the best and most conscientious men he had ever known. He told me that, during the time he had been Prime Minister, he had been personally asked for every great office in the State, including the Archbishopric of Canterbury, and this not by maniacs but by highly respectable men, sometimes even his friends. He said that Goschen's critical power was sound and subtle, but that he spoilt his speeches by a touch of bitterness. Mr Parnell, he said, was a man of genius, born to great things. He had power, decision and reserve; he saw things as they were and had confidence in himself.

'I made him smile by telling him how Lord Kimberley told me that one day in Dublin, when he was Viceroy, he had received a letter which began:

' "My Lord, Tomorrow we intend to kill you at the corner of Kildare Street; but we would like you to know there is nothing personal in it!"

'He talked all the way down Piccadilly about the Irish character, its wit, charm, grace and intelligence. I nearly landed my phaeton into an omnibus in my anxiety to point out the ingratitude and want of purpose of the Irish; but he said that in the noblest of races the spirit of self-defence had bred mean vices and that generation after generation were born in Ireland with their blood discoloured by hatred of the English Government.

' "Tories have no hope and no faith," he continued; "the best of them have class-interest and the spirit of antiquity, but the last has been forgotten and only class-interest remains. Disraeli was a great Tory. It grieves me to see people believing in Randolph Churchill as his successor, for he has none of the genius, patience or insight which Dizzy had in no small degree."

'Mr Gladstone told me that he was giving a dinner to the Liberal party that night and added:

' "If Hartington is in a good humour, I intend to say to him, 'Don't move a vote of want of confidence in me after dinner, or you will very likely carry it.' "

'He laughed at this, and told me some days after that Lord Hartington had been delighted with the idea.

'He strongly advised me to read a little book by one Miss Tollet, called *Country Conversations*, which had been privately printed, and deplored the vast amount of poor literature that was circulated, "when an admirable little volume like this cannot be got by the most ardent admirers now the authoress is dead." ' (I often wish I had been able to tell Mr Gladstone that Jowett left me this little book and his Shakespeare in his will.)

'We drove through the Green Park and I pulled up on the Horse Guards Parade at the garden-gate of 10 Downing Street. He got out of the phaeton, unlocked the gate and, turning round, stood with his hat off and his grey hair blowing about his forehead, holding a dark, homespun cape close round his shoulders. He said with great grace that he had enjoyed his drive, that he hoped it would occur again and that I had a way of saying things and a tone of voice that would always remind him of my sister Laura. His dear old face looked furrowed with care and the outline of it was sharp as a profile. I said good-bye to him and drove away; perhaps it was the light of the setting sun, or the wind, or perhaps something else, but my eyes were full of tears.'

My husband, in discussing with me Gladstone's sense of humour told me the following story:

'During the Committee Stage of the Home Rule Bill in the session of 1893, I was one evening in a very thin House, seated by the side of Mr Gladstone on the Treasury Bench, of which we were the sole occupants. His eyes were half-closed and he seemed to be absorbed in following the course of a dreary discussion on the supremacy of Parliament. Suddenly he turned to me with an air of great animation and said, in his most solemn tones,"Have you ever considered who is the ugliest man in the party opposite?"

MR ASQUITH: 'Certainly; it is without doubt X.' (naming a famous Anglo-Indian statesman).

MR GLADSTONE: 'You are wrong. X. is no doubt an ugly fellow, but a much uglier is Y.' (naming a Queen's Counsel of those days).

MR ASQUITH: 'Why should you give him the preference?'

MR GLADSTONE: 'Apply a very simple test. Imagine them both magnified on a colossal scale. X.'s ugliness would then begin to look dignified and even impressive, while the more you enlarged Y. the meaner he would become.'

*   *   *

I have known seven Prime Ministers – Gladstone, Salisbury, Rosebery, Campbell-Bannerman, Arthur Balfour, Asquith and Lloyd George – every one of them as different from the others as possible. I asked Arthur Balfour once if there was much difference between him and his uncle. I said:

'Lord Salisbury does not care fanatically about culture or literature. He may like Jane Austen, Scott or Sainte-Beuve, for all I know, but he is not a scholar; he does not care for Plato, Homer, Virgil or any of the great classics. He has a wonderful sense of humour and is a beautiful writer of fine style; but I should say he is above everything a man of science and a Churchman. All this can be said equally well of you.'

To which he replied:

'There is a difference. My uncle is a Tory . . . and I am a Liberal.'

I delighted in the late Lord Salisbury, both in his speaking and in his conversation. I had a kind of feeling that he could always score off me with such grace, good humour and wit that I would never discover it. He asked me once what my husband thought of his son Hugh's speaking, to which I answered:

'I will not tell you, because you don't know anything about my husband and would not value his opinion. You know nothing about our House of Commons either, Lord Salisbury; only the other day you said in public that you had never seen even Parnell.'

LORD SALISBURY (*pointing to his waistcoat*): 'My figure is not adapted for the narrow seats in your peers' gallery, but I can assure you you are doing me an injustice. I was one of the first to predict that Mr Asquith would have a great future. I see no one of his generation, or even among the younger men, at all comparable to him. Will you not gratify my curiosity by telling me what he thinks of my son Hugh's speaking?'

I was luckily able to say that my husband considered Lord Hugh Cecil the best speaker in the House of Commons and indeed anywhere, at which Lord Salisbury remarked:

'Do you think he would say so if he heard him speak on subjects other than the Church?'

I assured him that he had heard him on many subjects and that his opinion remained unchanged. He thought that, if they could unknot themselves and cover more ground, both he and his brother, Bob Cecil, had great futures.

I asked Lord Salisbury if he had often heard Chamberlain speak (Chamberlain was Secretary of State for the Colonies at the time).

LORD SALISBURY: 'It is curious you should ask me this, as I heard him this afternoon.'

MARGOT: 'Where did you hear him? And what was he speaking about?'

LORD SALISBURY: 'I heard him at Grosvenor House. Let me

see . . . what was he speaking about? . . . (*reflectively*) Australian washerwomen, I think . . . or some such thing. . . .'

MARGOT: 'What did you think of it?'

LORD SALISBURY: 'He made a good, businesslike speech.'

MARGOT: 'I suppose at this moment Mr Chamberlain is as much hated as Gladstone ever was?'

LORD SALISBURY: 'There is a difference. Mr Gladstone was hated, but he was very much loved. Does anyone love Mr Chamberlain?'

One day after this conversation he came to see me, bringing with him a signed photograph of himself. We of the Liberal Party were much exercised over the shadow of Protection which had been presented to us by the then Chancellor of the Exchequer putting a tax on corn. The Conservative Party, with Mr Balfour as its Prime Minister, was not doing well. We opened the conversation upon his nephew and the fiscal question. I was shocked at his apparent detachment, and said:

'But do you mean to tell me you don't think there is any danger of England becoming Protectionist?'

LORD SALISBURY (*with a sweet smile*): 'Not the slightest! There will always be a certain number of foolish people who will be Protectionists, but they will easily be overpowered by the wise ones. Have you ever known a man of first-rate intellect in this country who was a Protectionist?'

MARGOT: 'I never thought of it, but Lord Milner is the only one I can think of for the moment.'

He entirely agreed with me and said:

'No, you need not be anxious. Free Trade will always win against Protection in this country. This will not be the trouble of the future.'

MARGOT: 'Then what will be?'

LORD SALISBURY: 'The House of Lords is the difficulty that I foresee.'

I was surprised and incredulous and said quietly:

'Dear Lord Salisbury, I have heard of the House of Lords all my life! But, stupid as it has been, no one will ever have the power to alter it. Why do you prophesy that it will cause trouble?'

LORD SALISBURY: 'You may think me vain, Mrs Asquith, but,

as long as I am there, nothing will happen. I understand my lords thoroughly; but, when I go, mistakes will be made: the House of Lords will come into conflict with the Commons.'

MARGOT: 'You should have taught it better ways! I am afraid it must be your fault!'

LORD SALISBURY (*smiling*): 'Perhaps; but what do *you* think will be the next subject of controversy?'

MARGOT: 'If what you say is true, and Protection *is* impossible in this country, I think the next row will be over the Church of England; it is in a bad way.'

I proceeded to denounce the constant building of churches while the parsons' pay was so cruelly small. I said that few good men could afford to go into the Church at all; and the assumed voices, both in the reading and in the preaching, got on the nerves of everyone who cared to listen to such a degree that the churches were becoming daily duller and emptier.

He listened with patience to all this and then got up and said:

'Now I must go; I shall not see you again.'

Something in his voice made me look at him.

'You aren't ill, are you?' I asked with apprehension.

To which he replied:

'I am going into the country.'

I never saw him again, and, when I heard of his death, I regretted I had not seen him oftener.

IX · *Rosebery, C. B., and Balfour*

———— ∘⊙∘ ————

The next Prime Minister, whom I knew better than either Mr Gladstone or Lord Salisbury, was Lord Rosebery.

I will here relate how I first met him.

When I was a little girl, my mother took us to stay at Thomas' Hotel, Berkeley Square, to have a course of dancing lessons from the fashionable and famous M. d'Egville. These lessons put me in high spirits, because my master told me I could always make a living on the stage. His remarks were justified by a higher authority ten years later: the beautiful Kate Vaughan of the Gaiety Theatre.

I made her acquaintance in this way: I was a good amateur actress and with the help of Miss Annie Schletter, a friend of mine who is on the English stage now, I thought we might act Molière's *Précieuses Ridicules* together for a charity matinée. Coquelin – the finest actor of Molière that ever lived – was performing in London at the time and promised he would not only coach me in my part but lend his whole company for our performance. He gave me twelve lessons and I worked hard for him. He was intensely particular; and I was more nervous over those lessons than I ever felt riding over high timber. My father was so delighted at what Coquelin said to him about me and my acting that he bought a fine early copy of Molière's plays which he made me give him. I enclose his letter of refusal:

'My dearest little Margot,

'Je suis très mécontent de vous. Je croyais que vous me traitiez tout à fait en ami, car c'était en ami que j'avais accepté de vous offrir quelques indications sur les Précieuses . . . et voilà que vous m'envoyez un énorme cadeau . . . imprudence d'abord, parce que j'ai tous les beaux Molières qui existent, et ensuite parce qu'il ne fallait pas envoyer ombre de quoi que ce soit à votre ami Coq.

'Je vais tout faire, malgré cela, pour aller vous voir un instant aujourd'hui, mais je ne suis pas certain d'y parvenir.

'Remerciez votre amie Madelon et dites-lui bien qu'elle non plus ne me doit absolument rien.

'J'aime mieux un tout petit peu de la plus légère gratitude que n'importe quoi. Conservez, ma chère Margot, un bon souvenir de ce petit travail qui a dû vous amuser beaucoup et qui nous a réunis dans les meilleurs sentiments du monde; continuons nous les meilleurs sentiments du monde; continuons nous cette sympathie que je trouve moi tout à fait exquise – et croyez qu'en la continuant de votre côté, vous serez mille fois plus que quitte envers votre très dévoué.'

'COQ.'

Coquelin the younger was our stage-manager and acted the principal part. When it was over and the curtain went down, 'Freddy Wellesley's[1] band' was playing Strauss valses in the *entr'acte*, while the audience was waiting for Kate Vaughan to appear in a short piece called *The Dancing Lesson*, the most beautiful solo dance ever seen. I was alone on the stage and, thinking that no one could see me, I slipped off my Molière hoop of flowered silk and let myself go, in lace petticoats, to the wonderful music. Suddenly I heard a rather Cockney voice say from the wings:

'My Lord! How you can dance! Who taught you, I'd like to know?'

I turned round and saw the lovely face of Kate Vaughan. She wore a long, black, clinging *crêpe-de-chine* dress and a little black bonnet with a velvet bow over one ear; her white throat and beautiful arms were bare.

'Why,' she said, 'you could understudy me, I believe! You come round and I'll show you my parts and *you* will never lack for goldie boys!'

I remember the expression, because I had no idea what she meant by it. She explained that, if I became her understudy at the Gaiety, I would make my fortune. I was surprised that she had taken me

[1] The Hon. F. Wellesley, a famous beau and the husband of Kate Vaughan.

for a professional, but not more so than she was when I told her that I had never had a lesson in ballet-dancing in my life.

My lovely coach, however, fell sick and had to give up the stage. She wrote me a charming letter, recommending me to her own dancing-master M. d'Auban, under whom I studied for several years.

One day, on returning from my early dancing-lessons to Thomas' Hotel, I found my father talking to Lord Rosebery. He said I had better run away; so, after kissing him and shaking hands with the stranger, I left the room. As I shut the door, I heard Lord Rosebery say:

'Your girl has beautiful eyes.'

I repeated this upstairs, with joy and excitement, to the family, who, being in a good humour, said they thought it was true enough if my eyes had not been so close together. I took up a glass, had a good look at myself and was reluctantly compelled to agree.

I asked my father about Lord Rosebery afterwards and he said:

'He is far the most brilliant young man living and will certainly be Prime Minister one day.'

Lord Rosebery was born with almost every advantage: he had a beautiful smile, an interesting face, a remarkable voice and natural authority. When at Oxford, he had been too much interested in racing to work and was consequently sent down – a punishment shared at a later date and on different grounds by another distinguished statesman, the present Viscount Grey – but no one could say he was not industrious at the time that I knew him and a man of education. He made his fame first by being Mr Gladstone's chairman at the political meetings in the great Midlothian campaign, where he became the idol of Scotland. Whenever there was a crowd in the streets or at the station, in either Glasgow or Edinburgh, and I enquired what it was all about, I always received the same reply:

'Rozbury!'

I think Lord Rosebery would have had a better nervous system and been a happier man if he had not been so rich. Riches are over-estimated in the Old Testament: the good and successful man receives too many animals, wives, apes, she-goats and peacocks. The values are changed in the New: Christ counsels a different perfection and promises another reward. He does not censure the man of great possessions, but He points out that his riches will hamper him in his progress to the Kingdom of Heaven and that he would do better to sell all; and concludes with the penetrating words:

'Of what profit is it to a man if he gain the whole world and lose his own soul?'

(The soul here is freedom from self.)

Lord Rosebery was too thin-skinned, too conscious, to be really happy. He was not self-swayed like Gladstone, but he was self-enfolded. He came into power at a time when the fortunes of the Liberal party were at their lowest; and this, coupled with his peculiar sensibility, put a strain upon him. Some people thought that he was a man of genius, morbidly sensitive, shrinking from public life and the Press, cursed with insufficient ambition, sudden, baffling, complex and charming. Others thought that he was a man irresistible to his friends and terrible to his enemies, dreaming of Empire, besought by kings and armies to put countries and continents straight, a man whose notice blasted or blessed young men of letters, poets, peers or politicians, who at once scared and compelled everyone he met by his freezing silence, his playful smile, or the weight of his moral indignation: the truth being that he was a mixture of both.

Lord Salisbury told me he was the best occasional speaker he had ever heard; and certainly he was an exceptionally gifted person. He came to Glen constantly in my youth and we all worshipped him. No one was more alarming to the average stranger or more playful and affectionate in intimacy than Lord Rosebery.

An announcement in some obscure paper that he was engaged to be married to me came between us in later years. He was seriously annoyed and thought I ought to have contradicted this. I had never even heard the report till I got a letter in Cairo from Paris, asking if I would not agree to the high consideration and respectful homages of the writer and allow her to make my chemises. After this, the matter went completely out of my head, till, meeting him one day in London, I was greeted with such frigid self-suppression that I felt quite exhausted. A few months later, our thoughtful Press said I was engaged to be married to Mr Arthur Balfour. As I had seen nothing of Lord Rosebery since he had gone into a period of mourning, I was acclimatized to doing without him, but to lose Arthur's friendship would have been an irreparable personal loss to me. I need not have been afraid, for this was just the kind of rumour that challenged his insolent indifference to the public and the Press. Seeing me come into Lady Rothschild's ball-room one night, he left the side of the man he was conversing with and in an elastic step stalked down the empty parquet floor to greet me. He asked me to sit down next to him in a conspicuous place; and we talked through two dances. I was told afterwards that someone who had been watching us said to him:

'I hear you are going to marry Margot Tennant.'

To which he replied:

'No, that is not so. I rather think of having a career of my own.'

*   *   *

Lord Rosebery's two antagonists, Sir William Harcourt and Sir Henry Campbell-Bannerman, were very different men.

Sir William ought to have lived in the eighteenth century. To illustrate his sense of humour: he told me that women should be played with like fish; only in the one case you angle to make them rise and in the other to make them fall. He had a great deal of wit and nature, impulsive generosity of heart and a temperament that clouded his judgment. He was a man to whom life had added nothing; he was perverse, unreasonable, brilliant, boisterous and kind when I knew him; but he must have been all these in the nursery.

At the time of the split in our party over the Boer War, when we were in opposition and the phrase 'methods of barbarism' became famous, my personal friends were in a state of the greatest agitation. Lord Spencer, who rode with me nearly every morning, deplored the attitude which my husband had taken up. He said it would be fatal to his future, dissociating himself from the Pacifists and the Pro-Boers, and that he feared the Harcourts would never speak to us again. As I was devoted to the latter, and to their son Lulu and his wife May – still my dear and faithful friends – I felt full of apprehension. We dined with Sir Henry and Lady Lucy one night and found Sir William and Lady Harcourt were of the company.

I had no opportunity of approaching either of them before dinner, but, when the men came out of the dining-room, Sir William made a bee-line for me. Sitting down, he took my hand in both of his and said:

'My dear little friend, you need not mind any of the quarrels! The Asquith evenings or the Rosebery afternoons, all these things will pass; but your man is the man of the future!'

These were generous words, for, if Lord Morley, my husband and others had backed Sir William Harcourt instead of Lord Rosebery when Gladstone resigned, he would certainly have become Prime Minister.

*   *   *

I never knew Sir Henry Campbell-Bannerman well, but whenever we did meet we had great laughs together. He was essentially a *bon vivant*, a *boulevardier* and a humorist. At an official luncheon given in honour of some foreign Minister, Campbell-Bannerman, in an admirable speech in French – a language with which he was familiar – described Arthur Balfour, who was on one side of him, as *l'enfant gâté* of English politics and Chamberlain, who was also at the lunch, as *l'enfant terrible*.

On the opening day of Parliament, 14th February 1905, he made an amusing and telling speech. It was *à propos* of the fiscal controversy which was raging all over England and which was destined to bring the Liberal party into power at the two succeeding general elections. He said that Arthur Balfour was 'like a general who, having given the command to his men to attack, found them attacking one another; when informed of this, he shrugs his shoulders and says that he can't help it if they will misunderstand his orders!'

In spite of the serious split in the Liberal Party over the Boer War, involving the disaffection of my husband, Grey and Haldane, Campbell-Bannerman became Prime Minister in 1905.

He did not have a coupon election by arrangement with the Conservative Party to smother his opponents, but asked Henry, before he consulted anyone, what office he would take for himself and what he thought suitable for other people in his new Cabinet. Only men of a certain grandeur of character can do these things, but everyone who watched the succeeding events would agree that Campbell-Bannerman's generosity was rewarded.

When C.B. – as he was called – went to Downing Street, he was a tired man; his wife was a complete invalid and his own health had been undermined by nursing her. As time went on, the late hours in the House of Commons began to tell upon him and he relegated more and more of his work to my husband.

One evening he sent for Henry to go and see him at 10 Downing Street and, telling him that he was dying, thanked him for all he had done, particularly for his great work on the South African constitution. He turned to him and said:

'Asquith, you are different from the others and I am glad to have known you . . . God bless you!'

C.B. died a few hours after this.

*   *   *

I now come to another Prime Minister, Arthur Balfour.

When Lord Morley was writing the life of Gladstone, Arthur Balfour said to me:

'If you see John Morley, give him my love and tell him to be bold and indiscreet.'

A biography must not be a brief either for or against its client and it should be the same with an autobiography. In writing about yourself and other living people you must take your courage in both hands. I had thought of putting as a motto on the title-page of this book, 'As well be hanged for a sheep as a lamb'; but I gave it up when my friends gave me away, and I saw it quoted as my chosen motto in the newspapers.

If I have written any words here that wound a friend or an enemy, I can only refer them to my general character and ask to be judged by it. I am not tempted to be spiteful, and have never consciously hurt anyone in my life; but in this book I must write what I think without fear or favour and with a strict regard to unmodelled truth.

Arthur Balfour was never a standard bearer. He was a self-indulgent man of simple tastes. For the average person he was as puzzling to understand and as difficult to know as he was easy for me and many others to love. You may say that no average man can know a Prime Minister intimately; but most of us have met strangers whose minds we understood and whose hearts we reached without knowledge and without effort; and some of us have had an equally surprising and more painful experience when, after years of love given and received, we find the friend upon whom we had counted has become a stranger.

Mr Balfour was difficult to understand, because I was never sure that he needed me, and difficult to know intimately, because of his formidable detachment. The most that many of us could hope for was that he had a taste in us as one might have in clocks or china.

He was blessed or cursed at his birth, according to individual opinion, by two assets: charm and wits. The first he possessed to a greater degree than any man, except John Morley, that I have ever met. His social distinction, exquisite attention, intellectual tact, cool grace and lovely bend of the head made him not only a flattering listener but an irresistible companion. The disadvantage of charm – which makes me say cursed or blessed – is that it inspires everyone to combine and smooth the way for you throughout life. As the earnest housemaid removes dust, so all his friends and relations kept disagreeable things from his path; and this gave him more leisure in his life than anyone ought to have.

His wits, with which I say that he was also cursed or blessed – quite apart from his brains – gave him confidence in his improvisings and the power to sustain any opinion on any subject – whether he held the opinion or not – with equal brilliance, plausibility and success, according to his desire to dispose of you or the subject. He either finessed with the ethical basis of his intellect, or had none. This made him unintelligible to the average man, unforgivable to the fanatic and a god to the blunderer.

On one occasion my husband and I went to a lunch given by old Mr McEwan, to meet Mr Frank Harris. I might have said what my sister Laura did, when asked if she had enjoyed herself at a similar meal, 'I would not have enjoyed it if I hadn't been there', as, with the exception of Arthur Balfour, I did not know a soul in the room. He sat like a prince – with his sphinx-like imperviousness to bores – courteous and concentrated on the languishing conversation. I made a few gallant efforts; and my husband, who is particularly good on these selfconscious occasions, did his best . . . but to no purpose.

Frank Harris, in a general disquisition to the table, at last turned to Arthur Balfour and said, with an air of finality:

'The fact is, Mr Balfour, all the faults of the age come from Christianity and journalism.'

To which Arthur replied with rapier quickness and a child-like air:

'Christianity, of course . . . but why journalism?'

When men said, which they have done now for over thirty years, that Arthur Balfour was too much of a philosopher to be really interested in politics, I always contradicted them. With his intellectual taste, perfect literary style and keen interest in philosophy and religion, nothing but a great love of politics could account for his not having given up more of his time to writing. People thought that he was not interested because he had nothing active in his political aspirations; he saw nothing that needed changing. Low wages, drink, disease, sweating and overcrowding did not concern him; they left him cold and he had not the power to express a moral indignation which he was too detached to feel.

He was a great Parliamentarian, a brilliant debater and a famous Irish Secretary in difficult times, but his political energies lay in tactics. He took a Puck-like pleasure in watching the game of party politics, not in the interests of any particular political party, nor from *esprit de corps*, but from taste. This was conspicuous during the fiscal controversy in the years of 1903 to 1906, but anyone with observation could watch this peculiarity carried to a fine art wherever and whenever the Government to which he might be attached was in a tight place.

Politically, what he cared most about were problems of national safety. He inaugurated the Committee of Defence and appointed as its permanent Chairman the Prime Minister of the day; everything connected with the size of the army and navy interested him. The size of your army, however, must depend on the aims and quality of your diplomacy; and, if you have Junkers in your Foreign Office and jesters on your War Staff, you must have permanent conscription. It is difficult to imagine anyone in this country advocating a large standing army plus a navy, which is vital to us; but such there were and such there will always be. With the minds of these militarists, protectionists and conscriptionists, Arthur Balfour had nothing in common at any time. He and the men of his opinions were called the Blue Water School; they deprecated fear of invasion and in consequence were violently attacked by the Tories. But, in spite of an army-corps of enthusiasts kept upon our coasts to watch the traitors with towels signalling to the sea, with full instructions where to drive the county cows to, no German army during the Great War attempted to land upon our shores; thus amply justifying Balfour's views.

The artists who have expressed with the greatest perfection human experience, from an external point of view, he delighted in. He preferred appeals to his intellect rather than claims upon his feelings. Handel in music, Pope in poetry, Scott in narration, Jane Austen in fiction and Sainte-Beuve in criticism supplied him with everything he wanted. He hated introspection and shunned emotion.

What interested me most and what I liked best in Arthur Balfour was not his charm or his wits – and not his politics – but his writing and his religion.

Anyone who has read his books with a searching mind will perceive that his faith in God is what has really moved him in life; and no one can say that he has not shown passion here. Religious speculation and contemplation were so much more to him than anything else that he felt justified in treating politics and society with a certain levity.

His mother, Lady Blanche Balfour, was a sister of the late Lord Salisbury and a woman of influence. I was deeply impressed by her character as described in a short private life of her written by the late minister of Whittingehame, Mr Robertson. I should be curious to know, if it were possible, how many men and women of mark in this generation have had religious mothers. I think much fewer than in mine. My husband's mother, Mr McKenna's and Lord Haldane's were all profoundly religious.

This is part of one of Lady Blanche Balfour's prayers, written at the age of twenty-six:

'From the dangers of metaphysical subtleties and from profitless speculation on the origin of evil – Good Lord deliver me.'

*   *   *

Of the other two Prime Ministers I cannot write, though no one knows them better than I do. By no device of mine could I conceal my feelings; both their names will live with lustre, without my conscience being chargeable with frigid impartiality or fervent partisanship; and no one will deny that all of us should be allowed some 'private property in thought'.

X · *The Souls*

No one ever knew how it came about that I and my particular friends were called 'the Souls'. The origin of our grouping together I have already explained: we saw more of one another than we should probably have done had my sister Laura Lyttelton lived, because we were in mourning and did not care to go out in general society; but why we were called 'Souls' I do not know.

The fashionable – what was called the 'smart set' – of those days centred round the Prince of Wales, afterwards King Edward VII, and had Newmarket for its headquarters. As far as I could see, there was more exclusiveness in the racing world than I had ever observed among the Souls; and the first and only time I went to Newmarket the welcome extended to me by the shrewd and select company there made me feel exactly like an alien.

We did not play bridge or baccarat and our rather intellectual and literary after-dinner games were looked upon as pretentious.

Mr Balfour – the most distinguished of the Souls and idolized by every set in society – was the person who drew the enemy's fire. He had been well known before he came among us and it was considered an impertinence on our part to make him play pencil-games, or be our intellectual guide and critic. Nearly all the young men in my circle were clever and became famous; and the women, although not more intelligent, were less worldly than their fashionable contemporaries and many of them both good to be with and distinguished to look at.

What interests me most on looking back now at those ten years is the loyalty, devotion and fidelity which we showed to one another and the pleasure which we derived from friendships that could not have survived a week had they been accompanied by gossip, mocking or any personal pettiness. Most of us had a depth of feeling and moral and religious ambition which are entirely lacking in the clever young men and women of today. Our after-dinner games were healthier and more inspiring than theirs. 'Breaking the news,' for instance, was an entertainment that had a certain vogue among the younger generation before the war. It consisted of two people acting together and conveying to their audience various ways in which they would receive the news of the sudden death of a friend or a relation and was considered extraordinarily funny; it would never have amused any of the Souls. The modern habit of pursuing, detecting and exposing what was ridiculous in simple people and the unkind and irreverent manner in which slips were made material for epigram were unbearable to me. This school of thought – which the young group called 'anticant' – encouraged hard sayings and light doings which would have profoundly shocked the most frivolous among us. Brilliance of a certain kind may bring people together for amusement, but it will not keep them together for long; and the young, hard pre-war group that I am thinking of was short-lived.

The present Lord Curzon[1] also drew the enemy's fire and was probably more directly responsible for the name of the Souls than anyone.

He was a conspicuous young man of ability, with a ready pen, a ready tongue, an excellent sense of humour in private life and intrepid social boldness. He had appearance more than looks, a keen, lively face and an expression of enamelled self-assurance. Like every young man of exceptional promise, he was called a prig. The word was so misapplied in those days that, had I been a clever young man, I should have felt no confidence in myself till the world had called me a prig. He was a remarkably intelligent person in an exceptional generation. He had ambition and – what he claimed for himself in a brilliant description – 'middle class-method'; and he added to a kindly feeling for other people a warm corner for himself. Some of my friends thought his contemporaries in the House of Commons, George Wyndham and Harry Cust, would go farther, as the former was more suggestive and the latter was a finer scholar, but I always said – and have a record of it in my earliest diaries –

[1] Earl Curzon of Kedleston.

that George Curzon would outstrip his rivals. He had two incalculable advantages over them: he was chronically industrious and self-sufficing; and, though Oriental in his ideas of colour and ceremony, with a poor sense of proportion and a childish love of fine people, he was never self-indulgent. He neither ate, drank nor smoked too much and left nothing to chance.

No one could turn with more elasticity from work to play than George Curzon; he was a first-class host and boon companion and showed me and mine a steady and sympathetic love over a long period of years. Even now, if I died, although he belongs to the more conventional and does not allow himself to mix with people of opposite political parties, he would write my obituary notice.

At the time of which I am telling, he was threatened with lung-trouble and was ordered to Switzerland by his doctors. We were very unhappy and assembled at a farewell banquet, to which he entertained us in the Bachelors' Club, on the 10th July 1889. We found a poem welcoming us on our chairs, when we sat down to dinner, in which we were all honourably and categorically mentioned. Some of our critics called us 'the Gang' – to which allusion is made here – but we were ultimately known as the Souls.

This famous dinner and George's poem caused a lot of fun and friction, jealousy, curiosity and endless discussion. It was followed two years later by another dinner given by the same host to the same guests and in the same place, on the 9th July 1891.

The repetition of this dinner was more than the West End of London could stand; and I was the object of much obloquy. I remember dining with Sir Stanley and Lady Clarke to meet King Edward – then Prince of Wales – when my hostess said to me in a loud voice, across the table:

'There were some clever people in the world, you know, before you were born, Miss Tennant!'

Feeling rather nettled, I replied:

'Please don't pick me out, Lady Clarke, as if I alone were responsible for the stupid ones among whom we find ourselves today.'

Having no suspicion of other people, I was seldom on the defensive and did not mean to be rude, but I was young and intolerant.

This was George Curzon's poem:

10th July 1889

Ho! list to a lay
Of that company gay,
Compounded of gallants and graces,
Who gathered to dine,
In the year '89,
In a haunt that in Hamilton Place is.

There, there where they met,
And the banquet was set
At the bidding of GEORGIUS CURZON;
Brave youth! 'tis his pride,
When he errs, that the side
Of respectable licence he errs on.

Around that night –
Was there e'er such a sight?
Souls sparkled and spirits expanded;
For of them critics sang,
That tho' christened the Gang,
By a spiritual link they were banded.

Souls and spirits, no doubt,
But neither without
Fair visible temples to dwell in!
E'en your image divine
Must be girt with a shrine,
For the pious to linger a spell in.

There was seen at that feast
Of this band, the High Priest,
The heart that to all hearts is nearest;
Him may nobody steal
From the true Common weal,
Tho' to each is dear ARTHUR[1] *the dearest.*

[1] The Right Hon. Arthur James Balfour.

America lends,
Nay, she gives when she sends
Such treasures as HARRY[1] *and* DAISY[1];
Tho' many may yearn,
None but HARRY *can turn*
That sweet little head of hers crazy.

There was much-envied STRATH[2]
With the lady[2] *who hath*
Taught us all what may life be at twenty;
Of pleasure a taste,
Of duty no waste,
Of gentle philosophy plenty.

KITTY DRUMMOND[3] *was there –*
Where was LAWRENCE,[3] *oh! where? –*
And my Lord[4] *and my Lady* GRANBY[4];
Is there one of the Gang
Has not wept at the pang
That he never can VIOLET'S *man be?*

From WILTON, *whose streams*
Murmur sweet in our dreams,
Come the Earl[5] *and his Countess*[5] *together.*
In her spirit's proud flights
We are whirled to the heights,
He sweetens our stay in the nether.

Dear EVAN[6] *was there,*
The first choice of the fair,
To all but himself very gentle!
And ASHRIDGE'S *lord*
Most insufferably bored
With manners and modes Oriental.

[1] Mr and Mrs White.
[2] Millicent, Duchess of Sutherland and her husband, the Duke.
[3] Col. and Mrs Lawrence Drummond.
[4] Now the Duke and Duchess of Rutland.
[5] The late Earl and Countess of Pembroke.
[6] The Hon. Evan Charteris.

The Shah, I would bet,
In the East never met
Such a couple as him and his consort.[1]
If the HORNERS[2] *you add,*
Then a man must be mad
Who complains that the Gang is a wrong sort.

From kindred essay
LADY MARY[3] *to-day*
Should have beamed on a world that adores her.
Of her spouse[3] *debonair*
No woman has e'er
Been able to say that he bores her.

Next Bingy[4] *escorts*
His dear wife,[4] *to our thoughts*
Never lost, though withdrawn from our vision,
While of late she has shown
That of spirit alone
Was not fashioned that fair composition.

No, if humour we count,
The original fount
Must to HUGO *be ceded in freehold,*
Tho' of equal supplies
In more subtle disguise
Old GODFREY[5] *has far from a wee hold!*

MRS EDDY[6] *has come*
And we all shall be dumb
When we hear what a lovely voice Emmy's is;
SPENCER,[7] *too, would show what*
He can do, were it not
For that cursed laryngeal Nemesis.

[1] Earl and Countess Brownlow.   [2] Sir John and Lady Horner.
[3] Lord and Lady Elcho.   [4] Lord and Lady Wenlock.
[5] Mr Godfrey Webb.   [6] The Hon. Mrs Edward Bourke.
[7] The Hon. Spencer Lyttelton.

At no distance away
Behold ALAN[1] *display*
That smile that is found so upsetting;
And EDGAR[2] *in bower*
In statecraft, in power,
The favourite first in the betting.

Here a trio we meet,
Whom you never will beat,
Tho' wide you may wander and far go;
From what wonderful art
Of that Gallant Old Bart.,
Sprang CHARTY *and* LUCY *and* MARGOT?

To LUCY[3] *he gave*
The wiles that enslave,
Heart and tongue of an angel to CHARTY[4];
To MARGOT[5] *the wit*
And the wielding of it,
That make her the joy of a party.

LORD TOMMY[6] *is proud*
That to CHARTY *he vowed*
The graces and gifts of a true man.
And proud are the friends
Of ALFRED,[7] *who blends*
The athlete, the hero, the woman!

From the Gosford preserves
Old ST. JOHN[8] *deserves*
Great praise for a bag such as HILDA[8];
True worth she esteemed,
Overpowering he deemed
The subtle enchantment that filled her.

[1] The Hon. Alan Charteris.
[2] Sir Edgar Vincent (later Lord D'Abernon).
[3] Mrs Graham Smith.   [4] Lady Ribblesdale.   [5] Mrs Asquith.
[6] Lord Ribblesdale.   [7] The late Hon. Alfred Lyttelton.
[8] The Hon. St John Brodrick (afterwards Earl of Midleton) and Lady Hilda Brodrick.

Very dear are the pair[1],
He so strong, she so fair,
Renowned as the TAPLOVITE WINNIES;
Ah! he roamed far and wide,
Till in ETTY *he spied*
A treasure more golden than guineas.

Here is DOLL[2] *who has taught*
Us that 'words conceal thought'
In his case is a fallacy silly;
HARRY CUST[3] could display,
Scalps as many, I lay,
From Paris as in Piccadilly.

But some there were too –
Thank the Lord they were few!
Who were bidden to come and who could not:
Was there one of the lot,
Ah! I hope there was not,
Looked askance at the bidding and would not?

The brave LITTLE EARL[4]
Is away, and his pearl-
Laden spouse, the imperial GLADYS[4];
By that odious gout
Is LORD COWPER[5] *knocked out,*
And the wife,[5] who his comfort and aid is.

MISS BETTY'S[6] engaged,
And we all are enraged
That the illness of SIBELL'S[7] *not over;*
GEORGE WYNDHAM[8] can't sit
At our banquet of wit,
Because he is standing at Dover.

[1] Mr and Mrs Willy Grenfell (later Lord and Lady Desborough).
[2] Mr A. G. C. Liddell.   [3] Mr Harry Cust.
[4] Earl and Countess de Grey.   [5] Earl and Countess Cowper.
[6] Miss Ponsonby (later Mrs Montgomery).
[7] Countess Grosvenor.
[8] The late Right Hon. George Wyndham.

But we ill can afford
To dispense with the Lord
Of WADDESDON,[1] *and ill* HARRY CHAPLIN[2];
Were he here, we might shout
As again he rushed out
From the back of that 'd—d big sapling.'

We have lost LADY GAY [3] –
'Tis a price hard to pay
For that Shah and his appetite greedy;
And alas! we have lost! –
At what ruinous cost! –
The charms of the brilliant MISS D.D.[4]

But we've got in their place,
For a gift of true grace,
VIRGINIA'S *marvellous daughter.*[5]
Having conquered the States,
She's been blown by the Fates
To conquer us over the water.

Now this is the sum
Of all those who have come
Or ought to have come to that banquet.
Then call for the bowl,
Flow spirit and soul,
Till midnight not one of you can quit!

And blest by the Gang
Be the rhymester who sang
Their praises in doggerel appalling;
More now were a sin –
Ho, waiters, begin!
Each soul for consommé is calling!

* * *

[1] Baron Ferdinand de Rothschild.   [2] Viscount Chaplin.
[3] Lady Windsor (later Marchioness of Plymouth).
[4] Miss Edith Balfour (wife of the Hon. Alfred Lyttelton).
[5] Mrs Chanler, the American novelist (later Princess Troubetzkoy).

For my own and my children's interest I shall try, however imperfectly, to make a descriptive inventory of some of the Souls mentioned in this poem and of some of my friends who were not.

Gladstone's secretary, Sir Algernon West,[1] and Mr Godfrey Webb had both loved Laura and corresponded with her till she died; and they spent all their holidays at Glen. I never remember the time when Algy West was not getting old and did not say he wanted to die; but, although he is nearly ninety, he is still young, good-looking and – what is even more remarkable – a strong Liberal. He was never one of the Souls, but he was a faithful and loving early friend of ours.

Godfrey Webb was the *doyen* of the Souls. He was as intimate with my brothers and parents as he was with my sisters and self. Godfrey – or Webber, as some called him – was not only a man of parts but he had a peculiar flavour of his own. He had acute observation and his comments were both sly and tender.

For hours together he would poke about the country with a dog, a gun and a cigar, perfectly independent and self-sufficing, whether engaged in sport, repartee or literature. He wrote and published for private circulation a small book of poems and made the Souls famous by his proficiency at all our pencil games. Only a George Meredith can sustain a preface boasting of his heroine's wit, and it would be unwise to quote epigram or verse that depends much on environment and occasion, but I will risk one example of Godfrey's quickness. He took up a newspaper one morning in the dining-room at Glen and, reading that a Mr Pickering Phipps had broken his leg on rising from his knees at prayer, he immediately wrote this stanza:

> On bended knees, with fervent lips,
> Wrestled with Satan Pickering Phipps;
> But when for aid he ceased to beg
> The wily devil broke his leg!

He spent his holidays at Glen and I do not think he ever missed being with us on the anniversary of Laura's death, whether I was

[1] The Right Hon. Sir Algernon West.

at home or abroad. He was a man in a million, the last of the wits, and I miss him every day of my life.

*   *   *

Lord Midleton[1] – better known as St John Brodrick – was my first friend of interest; I knew him two years before I met Arthur Balfour or any of the Souls. He came over to Glen while he was staying with neighbours of ours.

I wired to him not long ago to congratulate him on being made an Earl and asked him in what year it was that he first came to Glen; this is his answer:

'JANUARY 12TH, 1920

'Dearest Margot,

'I valued your telegram of congratulation the more that I know you and Henry (who has given so many and refused all) attach little value to titular distinctions. Indeed, it is the only truly democratic trait about *you*, except a general love of Humanity, which has always put you on the side of the feeble. I am relieved to hear you have chosen such a reliable man as Crewe – with his literary gifts – to be the only person to read your autobiography.

'My visit to Glen in R——y's company was October, 1880, when you were sixteen. You and Laura flashed like meteors on to a dreary scene of empty seats at the luncheon table (the shooting party didn't come in) and filled the room with light, electrified the conversation and made old R——y falter over his marriage vows within ten minutes. From then onwards, you have always been the most loyal and indulgent of friends, forgetting no one as you rapidly climbed to fame, and were raffled for by all parties – from Sandringham to the crossing-sweeper.

'Your early years will sell the book.

'Bless you.

                                        'ST. JOHN.'

St. John Midleton was one of the rare people who tell the truth. Some people do not lie, but have no truth to tell; others are too agreeable – or too frightened – and lie; but the majority are in-

[1] The Right Hon. the Earl of Midleton, of Peper Harow, Godalming.

different: they are the spectators of life and feel no responsibility either towards themselves or their neighbour.

He was fundamentally humble and one of the few people I know who are loyal and who would risk telling me, or anyone he loved, before confiding to an inner circle faults which both he and I think might be overcome. I have had a long experience of inner circles and am constantly reminded of the Spanish proverb, 'Remember your friend has a friend'. I think you should either leave the room when those you love are abused or be prepared to warn them of what they are doing and other people are thinking. This is, as I know to my cost, an unpopular view of friendship, but neither St John nor I would think it loyal to join in the laughter or censure of a friend's folly.

Arthur Balfour himself – the most persistent of friends – remarked laughingly:

'St John pursues us with his malignant[1] fidelity.'

This was only a coloured way of saying that Midleton had none of the detachment commonly found among friends; but, as long as we are not merely responsible for our actions to the police, so long must I believe in trying to help those we love.

St John has the same high spirits and keenness now that he had then and the same sweetness and simplicity. There are only a few women whose friendships have remained as loving and true to me since my girlhood as his – Lady Horner, Miss Tomlinson[2], Lady Desborough, Mrs Montgomery, Lady Wemyss and Lady Bridges[3] – but ever since we met in 1880 he has taken an interest in all that concerns me. He was much maligned when he was Secretary of State for War and bore it without blame or bitterness. He had infinite patience, intrepid courage and a high sense of duty; and these combined to give him a better place in the hearts of men than in the fame of newspapers.

His first marriage was into a family who were incapable of appreciating his particular quality and flavour; even his mother-in-

---

[1] The word 'malignant' was obviously meant in the French sense – *malin*.
[2] Miss May Tomlinson, of Rye.
[3] Lady Bridges, wife of General Sir Tom Bridges.

law – a dear friend of mine – never understood him and was amazed when I told her that her son-in-law was worth all of her children put together, because he had more nature and more enterprise. I have tested St John now for many years and never found him wanting.

*   *   *

Lord Pembroke[1] and George Wyndham were the handsomest of the Souls. Pembroke was the son of Sidney Herbert, famous as Secretary of State for War during the Crimea. I met him first the year before I came out. Lord Kitchener's friend, Lady Waterford – sister to the present Duke of Beaufort – wrote to my mother asking if Laura could dine with her, as she had been thrown over at the last minute. My sister was in the country and my mother sent me. I sat next to Mr Balfour; Lord Pembroke was on the other side, round the corner of the table; and I remember being intoxicated with my own conversation and the manner in which I succeeded in making Arthur Balfour and George Pembroke join in. I had no idea who the splendid stranger was. He told me several years later that he had sent round a note in the middle of that dinner to Blanchie Waterford, asking her what the name of the girl with the red heels was, and that, when he read her answer, 'Margot Tennant', it conveyed nothing to him. This occurred in 1881 and was for me an eventful evening. Lord Pembroke was one of the four best-looking men I ever saw: the others, as I have already said, were the late Earl of Wemyss, Mr Wilfrid Blunt – whose memoirs have been recently published – and Lord D'Abernon.[2] He was six feet four, but his face was even more conspicuous than his height; and the beauty of his countenance can never be forgotten. There was Russian blood in the Herbert family and he was the eldest brother of the beautiful Lady Ripon.[3] He married Lady Gertrude Talbot, daughter of the twentieth Earl of Shrewsbury and Talbot, who was nearly as fine to look at as he himself. He told me among other things at that dinner that he had known Disraeli and had been promised some minor post in his government, but had been too ill

[1] George, 13th Earl of Pembroke.
[2] Our Ambassador in Berlin.
[3] The late wife of the 2nd Marquis of Ripon.

at the time to accept it. This developed into a discussion on politics and Peeblesshire, leading up to our county neighbours; he asked me if I knew Lord Elcho, of whose beauty Ruskin had written and who owned property in my county.

'Elcho,' said he, 'always expected to be invited to join the government, but I said to Dizzy, "Elcho is an impossible politician; he has never understood the meaning of party government and looks upon it as dishonest for even three people to attempt to modify their opinions sufficiently to come to an agreement, leave alone a Cabinet! He is an egotist!" To which Disraeli replied, "Worse than that! He is an Elchoist!" '

Although Lord Pembroke's views on all subjects were remarkably wide – as shown by the book he published called *Roots* – he was a Tory and his politics came to nothing. We formed a deep friendship and wrote to one another till he died a few years after my marriage. In one of his letters to me he added this postscript:

'Keep the outer borders of your heart's sweet garden free from garish flowers and wild and careless weeds, so that when your fairy godmother turns the Prince's footsteps your way he may not, distrusting your nature or his own powers, and only half-guessing at the treasure within, tear himself reluctantly away, and pass sadly on, without perhaps your ever knowing that he had been near.'

This, I imagine, gave a correct impression of me as I appeared to some people. 'Garish flowers' and 'wild and careless weeds' described my lack of pruning; but I am glad George Pembroke put them on the 'outer', not the inner, borders of my heart.

In the ninth verse of Curzon's poem, allusion is made to Lady Pembroke's conversation, which, though not consciously pretentious, had a touch of the Alpine peaks and provoked considerable merriment. She 'stumbled upwards into vacuity', to quote my dear friend Sir Walter Raleigh.

There is no one left today at all like George Pembroke. His combination of intellectual temperament, gregariousness, variety of tastes – yachting, art, sport and literature – his beauty of person and hospitality to foreigners made him the distinguished centre of any company. His first present to me was Butcher and Lang's translation of the *Odyssey*, in which he wrote on the fly-leaf, 'To

Margot, who most reminds me of Homeric days, 1884', and his last was his wedding-present, a diamond dagger, which I always wear close to my heart.

* * *

Among the Souls, Milly Sutherland,[1] Lady Windsor[2] and Lady Granby[3] were the women whose looks I admired most. Lady Brownlow,[4] mentioned in verse eleven, was Lady Pembroke's handsome sister and a famous Victorian beauty; Lady Granby – the Violet of verse eight, Gladys Ripon[5] and Lady Windsor (alluded to as Lady Gay in verse twenty-seven), were all women of arresting appearance: Lady Brownlow, a Roman coin; Violet Rutland, a Burne-Jones Medusa; Gladys Ripon, a great court lady; Milly Sutherland, a Scotch ballad; and Gay Windsor, an Italian Primitive. Gay's genius for lighting the hidden, calming the sudden and touching the unknown enshrined her in my heart from the first moment I ever saw her.

The only unmarried woman among us, except Mrs Alfred Lyttelton, was Betty Montgomery. She was a brilliant girl and the daughter of Sir Henry Ponsonby, Queen Victoria's famous private secretary and one of the strongest Liberals I ever met. Her sister Maggie, though socially more uncouth, had a touch of her father's genius; she said of a court prelate to me one day at Windsor Castle:

'There goes God's butler!'

It was through Betty and Maggie Ponsonby that I first met Lady Desborough. Though not as good-looking as the beauties I have catalogued, nor more intellectual than Lady Horner or Lady Wemyss, Lady Desborough was the cleverest of us. Her flavour was more delicate, her social sensibility finer; and she added to chronic presence of mind undisguised effrontery. I do not suppose she was ever unconscious in her life, but she had no self-pity and no egotism. She was not an artist in any way: music, singing, painting and colour left her cold. She was not a game-player nor was she sporting and she never invested in parlour tricks; yet she created more joy for

[1] Later the Duchess of Sutherland.
[2] Later the Countess of Plymouth.
[3] Later the Duchess of Rutland.
[4] Countess Brownlow.
[5] My friend Lady de Grey.

other people than anybody. She was a woman of genius, who, if subtly and accurately described, either in her mode of life, her charm, wits or character, would have made the fortune of any novelist. To an outsider she might – like all over-agreeable *femmes du monde* – give an impression of light metal; but this would be misleading. Etty Desborough was fundamentally sound and the truest friend that ever lived. Possessed of social and moral *sangfroid* of a high order, she was too elegant to fall into the trap of the candid friend, but nevertheless she could, when asked, give both counsel and judgment with the sympathy of a man and the wisdom of a god. She was the first person that I sought and that I would still seek if I were unhappy, because her genius lay in a penetrating understanding of the human heart and a determination to redress the balance of life's unhappiness. She married Willy Grenfell,[1] a man to whom I was much attached and a British gladiator capable of challenging the world in boating and boxing.

Of their soldier sons, Julian and Billy, I cannot write. They and their friends, Edward Horner, Charles Lister and Raymond Asquith all fell in the war. They haunt my heart; I can see them in front of me now, eternal sentinels of youth and manliness.

In spite of a voracious appetite for enjoyment and an expert capacity in entertaining, Etty Desborough was perfectly happy either with her family, or alone with her books, and could endure, with enviable patience, cold ugly country-seats and fashionable people. I said of her when I first knew her that she ought to have lived in the days of the great King's mistresses. I would have gone to her if I were sad, but never if I were guilty. Most of us have asked ourselves at one time or another whom we would go to if we had done a wicked thing; and the interesting part of this question is that in the answer you will get the best possible indication of human nature. Many have said to me, 'I would go to so-and-so, because they would understand my temptation and make allowances for me'; others, 'I would fly to so-and-so, because they would give me comfort'; but the majority would choose the confidante most competent to point to the way of escape. Etty Desborough would be that confidante.

[1] Lord Desborough, of Taplow Court.

She had neither father nor mother, but was brought up by two prominent and distinguished members of the Souls, my life-long friends, Lord and Lady Cowper, now, alas, both dead. Etty had eternal youth and was alive to everything in life except its irony.

If for health or for any other reason I had been separated from my children when they were young, I would as soon have confided them to the love of Etty and Willy Desborough as to any of my friends.

* * *

Mary Wemyss[1] shared with Gay Windsor[2] the greatest feminine distinction among the Souls and was as wise and just as she was truthful, tactful and generous. She might have been a great influence as indeed she was always a great joy, but she was physically and temperamentally badly equipped for the little things of life. Method is needed in minds as much as in habits; and, just as most boudoir writing-tables have handsome inkstands but no paper, or in a litter of untorn notes you find paper but no pens, so, although Mary was often in London, few of us could find her and much of the fine texture of her talk when you did was tangled by explanations and schemes as to where, when and how you could meet her again. Plan-weaving blinds people to a sound sense of proportion and too much time is spent and lost in the ABC of life. I wrote this in my diary many years ago:

'Mary is generally a day behind the fair, and will only hear of my death from the man behind the counter who is struggling to clinch her over a collar for her chow.'

But, if Mary never had enough time for us, she had other qualities in a greater measure than any woman I have ever known. Indeed she is almost the only woman I can think of who is without touchiness or smallness of any kind. Her *juste milieu*, if a trifle becalmed, amounts to genius and I have always been – and still am – more interested in her moral, social and intellectual opinions than in most of my friends'. It might have been written of her: 'She nothing common did nor mean.'

* * *

Lady Horner[3] was more like a sister to me than anyone outside my

---

[1] The Countess of Wemyss. [2] The Countess of Plymouth.
[3] Lady Horner, of Mells, Frome.

own family. I met her when she was Miss Graham and I was fourteen. She was a leader in what was called the high-art, William Morris School and one of the few girls who ever had a salon in London.

I was deeply impressed by her appearance. It was the fashion of the day to wear the autumn dessert in your hair and 'soft shades' of Liberty velveteen; but it was neither the unusualness of her clothes, nor the sight of Burne-Jones at her feet and Ruskin at her elbow that struck me most, but what Charty's little boy, Tommy Lister, called her 'ghost eyes' and the nobility of her countenance.

There may be women as well endowed with heart, head, temper and temperament as Frances Horner, but I have only met a few: Lady de Vesci (whose niece, Cynthia, married our poet-son, Herbert), Lady Betty Balfour[1] and my daughter Elizabeth. With most women the impulse to crab is greater than to praise, and grandeur of character is surprisingly absent from them; but Frances Horner comprises all that is best in my sex.

To illustrate the jealousy and friction which the Souls caused, I must relate a conversational scrap I had at this time with Lady Londonderry, which caused some talk amongst our critics.

She was a beautiful woman, a little before my day, happy, courageous and violent, with a mind which clung firmly to the obvious. Though her nature was impulsive and kind, she was not forgiving. One day she said to me with pride:

'I am a good friend and a bad enemy. No kiss-and-make-friends about me, my dear!'

I have often wondered since, as I did then, what the difference between a good and a bad enemy is.

She was not so well endowed intellectually as her rival Lady de Grey, but she had a stronger will and was of sounder temperament.

There was nothing wistful, reflective or retiring about Lady Londonderry. She was keen and vivid, but crude and impenitent.

We were accused *entre autres* of being conceited and of talking about books which we had not read, a habit which I have never had the temerity to acquire. John Addington Symonds had brought out a book of essays, which were not very good and caused no sensation.

[1] Sister of the Earl of Lytton and wife of the Right Hon. Gerald Balfour.

One night after dinner I was sitting in a circle of fashionable men and women – none of them particularly intimate with me – when Lady Londonderry opened the talk about books. Hardly knowing her, I entered with an innocent zest into the conversation. I was taken in by her mention of Symonds' *Studies in Italy* and thought she must be literary. Launching out upon style, I said there was a good deal of rubbish written about it, but it was essential that people should write simply. At this someone twitted me with our pencil-game of 'Styles' and asked me if I thought I should know the author from hearing a casual passage read out aloud from one of their books. I said that some writers would be easy to recognise – such as Meredith, Carlyle, De Quincey or Browning – but that when it came to others – men like Scott or Froude, for instance – I should not be so sure of myself. At this there was an outcry: Froude, having the finest style in the world, ought surely to be easily recognized! I was quite ready to believe that some of the company had made a complete study of Froude's style, but I had not. I said that I could not be sure, because his writing was too smooth and perfect, and that, when I read him, I felt as if I was swallowing arrowroot. This shocked them profoundly and I added that, unless I were to stumble across a horseman coming over a hill, or something equally fascinating, I should not even be sure of recognising Scott's style. This scandalized the company. Lady Londonderry then asked me if I admired Symonds' writing. I told her I did not, although I liked some of his books. She seemed to think that this was a piece of swagger on my part and, after disagreeing with a lofty shake of her head, said in a challenging manner:

'I should be curious to know, Miss Tennant, what you have read by Symonds!'

Feeling I was being taken on, I replied rather chillily:

'Oh, the usual sort of thing!'

Lady Londonderry, visibly irritated and with the confident air of one who has a little surprise in store for the company, said:

'Have you by any chance looked at *Essays, Suggestive and Speculative?*'

MARGOT: 'Yes, I've read them all.'

LADY LONDONDERRY: 'Really! Do you not approve of them?'

MARGOT: 'Approve? I don't know what you mean.'

LADY LONDONDERRY: 'Do you not think the writing beautiful . . . the style, I mean?'

MARGOT: 'I think they are all very bad, but then I don't admire Symonds' style.'

LADY LONDONDERRY: 'I am afraid you have not read the book.'

This annoyed me; I saw the company were enchanted with their spokeswoman, but I thought it unnecessarily rude and more than foolish.

I looked at her calmly and said:

'I am afraid, Lady Londonderry, you have not read the preface. The book is dedicated to me. Symonds was a friend of mine and I was staying at Davos at the time he was writing those essays. He was rash enough to ask me to read one of them in manuscript and write whatever I thought upon the margin. This I did; but he was offended by something I scribbled. I was so surprised at his minding that I told him he was never to show me any of his unpublished work again, at which he forgave me and dedicated the book to me.'

Lady Londonderry never belonged to the Souls, but her social antagonist, Lady de Grey, was one of its chief ornaments and my friend. Apart from her beauty, she was the last word in refinement, perception and charm; but there was something unsound in her nature and I heard her say one day that the cry of the cuckoo made her feel ill; she was neither lazy nor idle, but nevertheless she did not develop her intellectual powers or sustain herself by any form of study. She was a luxurious woman with perfect manners, a kind disposition and a moderate sense of duty. When anything went wrong with her entertainments – cold plates, a flat *soufflé*, or someone throwing her over for dinner – her sense of proportion was so entirely lacking that she would become almost impotent from agitation and throw herself into a state of mind only excusable if she had received the news of some great public disaster. She and Mr Harry Higgins – a devoted friend of mine – having revived the opera, Bohemian society became her hobby; but a tenor at tea or a dancer on the lawn are not really wanted, and, although she spent endless time over the opera and achieved every success, restlessness devoured her. While receiving much love, she appeared to me to have tried everything to no purpose and, in spite of an experience which queens and actresses, professionals and amateurs might well have envied, she remained embarrassed by herself, fluid, brilliant and uneasy: but the personal nobility with which she worked her hospital in the Great War brought her peace.

One of the less prominent of the Souls was my friend, Lionel Tennyson. He was the second son of the poet and an official in the India Office. He had an untidy appearance, a black beard and no manners. He sang German beer-songs in a lusty voice and wrote good verses.

He sent me many poems, but I think these two are the best. The first was written to me on my twenty-first birthday, before the Souls came into existence:

> *What is a single flower when the world is white with may?*
> *What is a gift to one so rich, a smile to one so gay?*
> *What is a thought to one so rich in the loving thoughts of men?*
> *How should I hope because I sigh that you will sigh again?*
> > *Yet when you see my gift, you may*
> > (Ma bayadère aux yeux de jais)
> > *Think of me once to-day.*

> *Think of me as you will, dear girl, if you will let me be*
> *Somewhere enshrined within the fane of your pure memory;*
> *Think of your poet as of one who only thinks of you,*
> *That you are all his thought, that he were happy if he knew –*
> > *You did receive his gift, and say*
> > (Ma bayadère aux yeux de jais)
> > 'He thinks of me to-day.'

And this is the second:

> *She drew me from my cosy seat*
> *She drew me to her cruel feet,*
> *She whispered, 'Call me Sally';*
> *I lived upon her smile, her sigh,*
> *Alas, you fool, I knew not I*
> > *Was only her* pis-aller!

The jade! she knew her business well,
She made each hour a heaven or hell,
For she could coax and rally;
She was so loving, frank and kind,
That no suspicion crost my mind
    That I was her pis-aller.

My brother says, 'I told you so!
Her conduct was not comme il faut,
But strictly comme il fallait;
She swore that she was fond and true;
No doubt she was, poor girl, but you
    Were only her pis-aller.'

He asked me what I would like him to give me for a birthday present and I said:

'If you want to give me pleasure, take me down to your father's country-house for a Saturday to Monday.'

This Lionel arranged; and he and I went down to Aldworth, Haslemere, together from London.

While we were talking in the train, a distinguished old lady got in. She wore an ample black satin skirt, small black satin slippers in goloshes, a sable tippet and a large, picturesque lace bonnet. She did not appear to be listening to our conversation, because she was reading with an air of concentration; but, on looking at her, I observed her eyes fixed upon me. I wore a scarlet cloak trimmed with cock's feathers and a black, three-cornered hat. When we arrived at our station, the old lady tipped a porter to find out from my luggage who I was; and when she died – several years later – she left me in her will one of my most beautiful jewels. This was Lady Margaret Beaumont; and I made both her acquaintance and friendship before her death.

Lady Tennyson was an invalid; and we were received on our arrival by the poet. Tennyson was a magnificent creature to look at. He had everything: height, figure, carriage, features and expression. Added to this he had what George Meredith called 'the feminine hint to perfection'. He greeted me by saying:

'Well, are you as clever and spurty as your sister Laura?'

I have never heard the word 'spurty' before, nor indeed have I since. To answer this kind of frontal attack one has to be either saucy or servile; so I said nothing memorable. We sat down to tea and he asked me if I wanted him to dress for dinner, adding:

'Your sister said of me that I was both untidy and dirty.'

To which I replied:

'Did you mind this?'

TENNYSON: 'I wondered if it was true. Do you think I'm dirty?'

MARGOT: 'You are very handsome.'

TENNYSON: 'I can see by that remark that you think I am. Very well then, I will dress for dinner. Have you read Jane Welsh Carlyle's letters?'

MARGOT: 'Yes, I have, and I think them excellent. It seems a pity,' I added, with the commonplace that is apt to overcome one in a first conversation with a man of eminence, 'that they were ever married; with anyone but each other, they might have been perfectly happy.'

TENNYSON: 'I totally disagree with you. By any other arrangement four people would have been unhappy instead of two.'

After this I went up to my room. The hours kept at Aldworth were peculiar; we dined early and after dinner the poet went to bed. At ten o'clock he came downstairs and, if asked, would read his poetry to the company till past midnight.

I dressed for dinner with great care that first night and, placing myself next to him when he came down, I asked him to read out loud to me.

TENNYSON: 'What do you want me to read?'

MARGOT: '*Maud.*'

TENNYSON: 'That was the poem I was cursed for writing! When it came out no word was bad enough for me! I was a blackguard, a ruffian and an atheist! You will live to have as great a contempt for literary critics and the public as I have, my child!'

While he was speaking, I found on the floor, among piles of books, a small copy of *Maud*, a shilling volume, bound in blue paper. I put it into his hands and, pulling the lamp nearer him, he began to read.

There is only one man – a poet also – who reads as my host did; and that is my beloved friend, Professor Gilbert Murray. When I first heard him at Oxford, I closed my eyes and felt as if the old poet were with me again.

Tennyson's reading had the lilt, the tenderness and the rhythm that make music in the soul. It was neither singing, nor chanting, nor speaking, but a subtle mixture of the three; and the effect upon me was one of haunting harmonies that left me profoundly moved.

He began, 'Birds in the high Hall-garden,' and, skipping the next four sections, went on to, 'I have led her home, my love, my only friend,' and ended with:

> *There has fallen a splendid tear*
> *From the passion-flower at the gate.*
> *She is coming, my dove, my dear,*
> *She is coming, my life, my fate;*
> *The red rose cries, 'She is near, she is near;'*
> *And the white rose weeps, 'She is late;'*
> *The larkspur listens, 'I hear, I hear;'*
> *And the lily whispers, 'I wait.'*
>
> *She is coming, my own, my sweet;*
> *Were it ever so airy a tread,*
> *My heart would hear her and beat,*
> *Were it earth in an earthy bed;*
> *My dust would hear her and beat,*
> *Had I lain for a century dead;*
> *Would start and tremble under her feet,*
> *And blossom in purple and red.*

When he had finished, he pulled me on to his knee and said:

'Many may have written as well as that, but nothing that ever sounded so well!'

I could not speak.

He then told us that he had had an unfortunate experience with a young lady to whom he was reading *Maud*.

'She was sitting on my knee,' he said, 'as you are doing now, and after reading,

Birds in the high Hall-garden
When twilight was falling,
Maud, Maud, Maud, Maud,
They were crying and calling,

I asked her what bird she thought I meant. She said, "A nightingale."
This made me so angry that I nearly flung her to the ground:
"No, fool! . . . Rook!" said I.'

I got up, feeling rather sorry for the young lady, but was so
afraid he was going to stop reading that I quickly opened *The
Princess* and put it into his hands and he went on.

I still possess the little *Maud*, bound in its blue paper cover, out
of which he read to us, with my name and a line of poetry written
in it by Tennyson.

The morning after my arrival I was invited by our host to go for a
walk with him, which flattered me very much; but after walking at a
great pace over rough ground for two hours I regretted my vanity.
Except my brother Glenconner I never met such an easy mover.
The most characteristic feature left on my mind of that walk was
Tennyson's appreciation of other poets.

*   *   *

Writing of poets, I come to George Wyndham. It would be
superfluous to add anything to what has already been published of
him, but he was among the best-looking and most lovable of our
friends.

He was a young man of nature, endowed with even greater
beauty than his sister, Lady Glenconner, but with less of her literary
talent. Although his name will always be associated with the Irish
Land Act, he was more interested in literature than politics and,
with a little self-discipline, might have been eminent in both.

Mr Harry Cust is the last of the Souls that I intend writing about
and was in some ways the rarest and the most brilliant of them all.
Someone who knew him well wrote truly of him after he died:

'He tossed off the cup of life without fear of it containing any
poison, but like many wilful men he was deficient in will-power.'

The first time I ever saw Harry Cust was in Grosvenor Square,
where he had come to see my sister Laura. A few weeks later I

found her making a sachet, which was an unusual occupation for her, and she told me it was for 'Mr Cust', who was going to Australia for his health.

He remained abroad for over a year and, on the night of the Jubilee, 1887, he walked into our house where we were having supper. He had just returned from Australia and was terribly upset to hear that Laura was dead.

Harry Cust had an untiring enthusiasm for life. At Eton he had been captain of the school and he was a scholar of Trinity. He had as fine a memory as Professor Churton Collins or my husband and an unplumbed sea of knowledge, quoting with equal ease both poetry and prose. He edited the *Pall Mall Gazette* with brilliance for several years. With his youth, brains and looks, he might have done anything in life; but he was fatally self-indulgent. He was a fastidious critic and a faithful friend, fearless, reckless and unforgettable.

He wrote one poem, which appeared anonymously in the *Oxford Book of English Verse:*

> *Not unto us, O Lord,*
> *Not unto us the rapture of the day,*
> *The peace of night, or love's divine surprise,*
> *High heart, high speech, high deeds 'mid honouring eyes;*
> *For at Thy word*
> *All these are taken away.*
>
> *Not unto us, O Lord:*
> *To us Thou givest the scorn, the scourge, the scar,*
> *The ache of life, the loneliness of death,*
> *The insufferable sufficiency of breath;*
> *And with Thy sword*
> *Thou piercest very far.*
>
> *Not unto us, O Lord:*
> *Nay, Lord, but unto her be all things given –*
> *My light and life and earth and sky be blasted –*
> *But let not all that wealth of love be wasted:*
> *Let Hell afford*
> *The pavement of her Heaven!*

I print also a letter in answer to one of mine which he sent me on 20th October 1887:

I came in to-night, made as woeful as worry can,
Heart like a turnip and head like a hurricane,
When lo! on my dull eyes there suddenly leaped a
Bright flash of your writing, du Herzengeliebte;
And I found that the life I was thinking so leavable
Had still something in it made living conceivable;
And that, spite of the sores and the bores and the flaws in
My own, life's the better for small bits of yours in it;
And it's only to tell you just that that I write to you,
And just for the pleasure of saying good night to you:
For I've nothing to tell you and nothing to talk about,
Save that I eat and I sleep and I walk about.
Since three days past does the indolent I bury
Myself in the British Museum Lib'ary,
Trying in writing to get in my hand a bit,
And reaching Dutch books that I don't understand a bit:
But to-day Lady Charty and sweet Mrs Lucy em-
Broidered the dusk of the British Museum,
And made me so happy by talking and laughing on
That I loved them more than the frieze of the Parthenon.
But I'm sleepy I know and don't know if I silly ain't;
Dined to-night with your sisters, where Tommy was brilliant;
And, while I the rest of the company deafened, I
Dallied awhile with your auntlet of seventy,
While one Mr Winsloe, a volume before him,
Regarded us all with a moody decorum.
No, I can't keep awake, and so, bowing and blessing you.
And seeing and loving (while slowly undressing) you,
Take your small hand and kiss, with a drowsed benediction, it
Knowing, as you, I'm your ever affectionate

HARRY C. C.

*   *   *

I had another friend, James Kenneth Stephen, too wayward and lonely to be available for the Souls, but a man of genius. One

143

afternoon he came to see me in Grosvenor Square and, being told by the footman that I was riding in the Row, he asked for tea and, while waiting, wrote the following parody of Myers' *St Paul* and left it on my writing-table with his card:

> *Lo! what the deuce I'm always saying 'Lo!' for*
> *God is aware and leaves me uninformed.*
> *Lo! there is nothing left for me to go for,*
> *Lo! there is naught inadequately formed.*

He ended by signing his name and writing:

> *Souvenez-vous si les vers que je trace*
> *Fussent parfois (je l'avoue!) l'argot,*
> *Si vous trouvez un peu trop d'audace*
> *On ose tout quand on se dit*
> 'MARGOT'

My dear friend J.K.S. was responsible for the aspiration now frequently quoted:

> *When the Rudyards cease from Kipling*
> *And the Haggards ride no more.*

*   *   *

Although I can hardly claim Symonds as a Soul, he was so much interested in our circle that I must write a short account of him.

I was nursing my sister, Pauline Gordon Duff, when I first met John Addington Symonds, in 1885, at Davos.

I climbed up to Am Hof[1] one afternoon with a letter of introduction, which was taken to the family while I was shown into a wooden room full of beauty. As no one came near me, I presumed everyone was out, so I settled down peacefully among the books, prepared to wait. In a little time I heard a shuffle of slippered feet and someone pausing at the open door.

[1] J. A. Symonds' house.

'Has she gone?' was the querulous question that came from behind the screen.

And in a moment the thin, curious face of John Addington Symonds was peering at me round the corner.

There was nothing for it but to answer:

'No, I am afraid she is still here!'

Being the most courteous of men, he smiled and took my hand; and we went up to his library together. He smoked a very small cigar, the size of a cigarette, and we discussed his friend Robert Louis Stevenson. He said that Stevenson and his wife were a curious *ménage*, being the most unconventional people in the world; that he was an enchanting companion, brave as a lion and perfectly independent of what the world thought of him. He asked me if I knew him. I said I did not but that I knew his great friend Sidney Colvin and would try to get him to let us meet each other. I now possess Stevenson's manuscript of part of 'Across the Plains', given to me by Sir Sidney Colvin; it is among my most precious belongings.

Symonds and I became very great friends.

After putting my sister to bed at 9.30, I climbed every night by starlight to Am Hof, where we talked and read out loud till one and often two in the morning. I learnt more in those winter nights at Davos than I had ever learnt in my life. We read the Plato dialogues together; Swift, Voltaire, Browning, Walt Whitman, Edgar Poe and Symonds' own *Renaissance*, besides passages from every author and poet, which he would turn up feverishly to illustrate what he wanted me to understand.

I shall always think of Lord Morley as the best talker I ever heard and after him I should place Symonds, Birrell and Bergson. George Meredith was too much of a *prima donna* and was very deaf and uninterruptible when I knew him, but he was an amazingly good talker. Alfred Austin was a friend of his and had just been made Poet Laureate by Lord Salisbury, when Admiral Maxse took me down to the country to see Meredith for the first time. Feeling more than usually stupid, I said to him:

'Well, Mr Meredith, I wonder what your friend Alfred Austin thinks of his appointment?'

Shaking his beautiful head he replied:

'It is very hard to say what a bantam is thinking when it is crowing.'

Symonds' conversation is described in Stevenson's essay on *Talks and Talkers*, but no one could ever really give the fancy, the epigram, the swiftness and earnestness with which he not only expressed himself but engaged you in conversation. This and his affection combined to make him an enchanting companion.

The Swiss postmen and woodmen constantly joined us at midnight and drank Italian wines out of beautiful glass which our host had brought from Venice; they were our only interruptions when Mrs Symonds and the handsome girls went to bed. I have many memories of seeing our peasant friends off from Symonds' front door and standing by his side in the dark, listening to the crack of their whips and their yodels yelled far down the snow roads into the starry skies.

When I first left him and returned to England, Mrs Symonds told me he sat up all night, filling a blank book with his own poems and translations, which he posted to me in the early morning. We corresponded till he died; and I have kept every letter that he ever wrote to me.

He was the first person who besought me to write. If only he were alive now, I would show him this manuscript and, if anyone could make anything of it by counsel, sympathy and encouragement, my autobiography might become famous! but alas! he is dead.

'You have *l'oreille juste*,' he would say, 'and I value your literary judgment.'

I will here insert some of his letters, beginning with the one he sent down to our villa at Davos *à propos* of the essays over which Lady Londonderry and I had our little breeze:

'I am at work upon a volume of essays in art and criticism, puzzling to my brain and not easy to write. I think I shall ask you to read them.

'I want an intelligent audience before I publish them. I want to "try them on" somebody's mind – like a dress – to see how they fit. Only you must promise to write observations and, most killing remark of all, to say when the tedium of reading them begins to overweigh the profit of my philosophy.

'I think you could help me.'

After the publication he wrote:

'I am sorry that the Essays I dedicated to you have been a failure – as I think they have been – to judge by the opinions of the Press. I wanted, when I wrote them, only to say the simple truth of what I thought and felt in the very simplest language I could find.

'What the critics say is that I have uttered truisms in the baldest, least attractive diction.

'Here I find myself to be judged, and not unjustly. In the pursuit of truth, I said what I had to say bluntly – and it seems I had nothing but commonplaces to give forth. In the search for sincerity of style, I reduced every proposition to its barest form of language. And that abnegation of rhetoric has revealed the nudity of my commonplaces.

'I know that I have no wand, that I cannot conjure, that I cannot draw the ears of men to listen to my words.

'So, when I finally withdraw from further appeals to the public, as I mean to do, I cannot pose as a Prospero who breaks his staff. I am only a somewhat sturdy, highly nervous varlet in the sphere of art, who has sought to wear the robe of the magician – and being now disrobed, takes his place quietly where God appointed him, and means to hold his tongue in future, since his proper function has been shown him.

'Thus it is with me. And I should not, my dear friend, have inflicted so much of myself upon you, if I had not, unluckily, and in gross miscalculation of my powers, connected your name with the book which proves my incompetence.

'Yes, the Master[1] is right: make as much of your life as you can: use it to the best and noblest purpose: do not, when you are old and broken like me, sit in the middle of the ruins of Carthage you have vainly conquered, as I am doing now.

'Now good-bye. Keep any of my letters which seem to you worth keeping. This will make me write better. I keep a great many of yours. You will never lose a warm corner in the centre of the heart of your friend,

'J. A. SYMONDS.

[1] Dr Jowett, Master of Balliol.

'P.S. Live well. Live happy. Do not forget me. I like to think of you in plenitude of life and activity. I should not be sorry for you if you broke your neck on the hunting field. But, like the Master, I want you to make sure of the young, powerful life you have – before the inevitable, dolorous, long, dark night draws nigh.'

Later on, *à propos* of his translation of the Autobiography of Benvenuto Cellini, he wrote:

'I am so glad that you like my Cellini. The book has been a success; and I am pleased, though I am not interested in its sale. The publisher paid me £210 for my work, which I thought very good wages.'

'My dear Margot,

'I wrote to you in a great hurry yesterday, and with some bothering thoughts in the background of my head.

'So I did not tell you how much I appreciated your critical insight into the points of my Introduction to Cellini. I do not rate that piece of writing quite as highly as you do. But you "spotted" the best thing in it – the syllogism describing Cellini's state of mind as to Bourbon's death.

'It is true, I think, what you say: that I have been getting more nervous and less elaborate in style of late years. This is very natural. One starts in life with sensuous susceptibilities to beauty, with a strong feeling for colour and for melodious cadence, and also with an impulsive enthusiastic way of expressing oneself. This causes young work to seem decorated and laboured, whereas it very often is really spontaneous and hasty, more instinctive and straightforward than the work of middle life. I write now with much more trouble and more slowly, and with much less interest in my subject than I used to do. This gives me more command over the vehicle, language, than I used to have. I write what pleases myself less, but what probably strikes other people more.

'This is a long discourse; but not so much about myself as appears. I was struck with your insight, and I wanted to tell you how I analyze the change of style which you point out, and which results, I think, from colder, more laborious, duller effort as one grows in years.

'The artist ought never to be commanded by his subject, or his vehicle of expression. But until he ceases to love both with a blind passion, he will probably be so commanded. And then his style will appear decorative, florid, mixed, unequal, laboured. It is the sobriety of a satiated or blunted enthusiasm which makes the literary artist. He ought to remember his dithyrambic moods, but not to be subject to them any longer, nor to yearn after them.

'Do you know that I have only just now found the time, during my long days and nights in bed with influenza and bronchitis, to read Marie Bashkirtseff? (Did ever name so puzzling grow upon the Ygdrasil of even Russian life?)

'By this time you must be quite tired of hearing from your friends how much Marie Bashkirtseff reminds them of you.

'I cannot help it. I must say it once again. I am such a fossil that I permit myself the most antediluvian remarks – if I think they have a grain of truth in them. Of course, the dissimilarities are quite as striking as the likenesses. No two leaves on one linden are really the same. But you and she, detached from the forest of life, seem to me like leaves plucked from the same sort of tree.

'It is a very wonderful book. If only *messieurs les romanciers* could photograph experience in their fiction as she has done in some of her pages! The episode of Pachay, short as that is, is masterly – above the reach of Balzac; how far above the laborious beetle-flight of Henry James! Above even George Meredith. It is what James would give his right hand to do once. The episode of Antonelli is very good, too, but not so exquisite as the other.

'There is something pathetic about both "Asolando" and "Demeter", those shrivelled blossoms from the stout old laurels touched with frost of winter and old age. But I find little to dwell upon in either of them. Browning has more sap of life – Tennyson more ripe and mellow mastery. Each is here in the main reproducing his mannerism.

'I am writing to you, you see, just as if I had not been silent for so long. I take you at your word, and expect Margot to be always the same to a comrade.

'If you were only here! Keats said that "heard melodies are sweet, but those unheard are sweeter". How false!

Yes, thus it is: somewhere by me
Unheard, by me unfelt, unknown,
The laughing, rippling notes of thee
Are sounding still; while I alone
Am left to sit and sigh and say –
Music unheard is sweet as they.

'This is no momentary mood, and no light bubble-breath of improvisatory verse. It expresses what I often feel, when, after a long night's work, I light my candle and take a look before I go to bed at your portrait in the corner of my stove.

'I have been labouring intensely at my autobiography. It is blocked out, and certain parts of it are written for good. But a thing of this sort ought to be a master's final piece of work – and it is very exhausting to produce.'

'AM HOF,
DAVOS PLATZ,
SWITZERLAND.
'SEPT. 27TH, 1891

'My dear Margot,

'I am sending you back your two typewritten records. They are both very interesting, the one as autobiographical and a study of your family, the other as a vivid and, I think, justly critical picture of Gladstone. It will have a great literary value some time. I do not quite feel with Jowett, who told you, did he not? that you had made him *understand* Gladstone. But I feel that you have offered an extremely powerful and brilliant conception, which is impressive and convincing because of your obvious sincerity and breadth of view. The purely biographical and literary value of this bit of work seems to me very great, and makes me keenly wish that you would record all your interesting experiences, and your first-hand studies of exceptional personalities in the same way.

'Gradually, by doing this, you would accumulate material of real importance; much better than novels or stories, and more valuable than the passionate utterances of personal emotion.

'Did I ever show you the record I privately printed of an evening passed by me at Woolner, the sculptor's, when Gladstone met

Tennyson for the first time? If I had been able to enjoy more of such incidents, I should also have made documents. But my opportunities have been limited. For future historians, the illuminative value of such writing will be incomparable.

'I suppose I must send the two pieces back to Glen. Which I will do, together with this letter. Let me see what you write. I think you have a very penetrative glimpse into character, which comes from perfect disengagement and sympathy controlled by a critical sense. The absence of egotism is a great point.'

*　　*　　*

When Symonds died I lost my best intellectual tutor as well as one of my dearest friends. I wish I had taken his advice and seriously tried to write years ago, but, except for a few magazine sketches, I have never, before this, written a line for publication in my life. I have only kept a careful and accurate diary;[1] and here, in the interests of my publishers and at the risk of being thought egotistical, it is not inappropriate that I should publish the following letter in connection with these diaries and my writing:

'21 Carlyle Mansions,
Cheyne Walk, S.W.
'April 9th 1915

'My dear Margot Asquith,

'By what felicity of divination were you inspired to send me a few days ago that wonderful diary under its lock and key? – feeling so rightly certain, I mean, of the peculiar degree and particular *pang* of interest that I should find in it? I don't wonder, indeed, at your general presumption to that effect, but the mood, the moment, and the resolution itself conspired together for me, and I have absorbed every word of every page with the liveliest appreciation, and I think I may say intelligence. I have read the thing intimately, and I take off my hat to you as the very Balzac of diarists. It is full of life and force and colour, of a remarkable instinct for getting close to your people and things and for squeezing, in the case of the

---

[1] Out of all my diaries I have hardly been able to quote fifty pages, for on re-reading them I find they are not only full of political matters but jerky, disjointed and dull.

resolute portraits of certain of your eminent characters especially, the last drop of truth and sense out of them – at least as the originals affected your singularly searching vision. Happy, then, those who had, of this essence, the fewest secrets or crooked lives to yield up to you – for the more complicated and unimaginable some of them appear, the more you seem to me to have caught and mastered them. Then I have found myself hanging on your impression in each case with the liveliest suspense and wonder, so thrillingly does the expression keep abreast of it and really translate it. This and your extraordinary fullness of opportunity, make of the record a most valuable English document, a rare revelation of the human inwardness of political life in this country, and a picture of manners and personal characters as "creditable" on the whole (to the country) as it is frank and acute. The beauty is that you write with such authority, that you've seen so much and lived and moved so much, and that having so the chance to observe and feel and discriminate in the light of so much high pressure, you haven't been in the least afraid, but have faced and assimilated and represented for all you're worth.

'I have lived, you see, wholly out of the inner circle of political life, and yet more or less in wondering sight, for years, of many of its outer appearances, and in superficial contact – though this, indeed, pretty anciently now – with various actors and figures, standing off from them on my quite different ground and neither able nor wanting to be of the craft or mystery (preferring, so to speak, my own poor, private ones, such as they have been) and yet with all sorts of unsatisfied curiosities and yearnings and imaginings in your general, your fearful direction. Well, you take me by the hand and lead me back and in, and still in, and make things beautifully up to me – *all* my losses and misses and exclusions and privation – and do it by having taken all the right notes, apprehended all the right values and enjoyed all the right reactions – meaning by the right ones, those that must have ministered most to interest and emotion; those that I dimly made you out as getting while I flattened my nose against the shop window and you were there within, eating the tarts, shall I say, or handing them over the counter? It's to-day as if you had taken all the trouble for me and left me at last all the unearned increment of fine psychological gain!

I have hovered about two or three of your distinguished persons a bit longingly (in the past); but you open up the abysses, or such like, that I really missed, and the torch you play over them is often luridly illuminating. I find my experience, therefore, the experience of simply reading you (you having had all t'other) veritably romantic. But I want so to go on that I deplore your apparent arrest – Saint Simon is in forty volumes – why should Margot be put in one? Your own portrait is an extraordinary patient and detached and touch-upon-touch thing; but the book itself really constitutes an image of you by its strength of feeling and living individual tone. An admirable portrait of a lady, with no end of finish and style, is thereby projected, and if I don't stop now, I shall be calling it a regular masterpiece. Please believe how truly touched I am by your confidence in your faithful, though old, friend,

'HENRY JAMES.'

To return to my triumphant youth: I will end this chapter with a note which my friend, Lady Frances Balfour – one of the few women of outstanding intellect that I have known – sent me from her father, the late Duke of Argyll, the wonderful orator of whom it was said that he was like a cannon being fired off by a canary.

Frances asked me to meet him at a dinner in her house and placed me next to him. In the course of our conversation, he quoted these words that he had heard in a sermon preached by Dr Caird:

'Oh, for the time when Church and State shall no longer be the watchword of opposing hosts, when every man shall be a priest and every priest shall be a king, as priest clothed with righteousness, as king with power!'

I made him write them down for me and we discussed religion, preachers and politics at some length before I went home.

The next morning he wrote to his daughter:

'ARGYLL LODGE,
KENSINGTON.

'Dear Frances,
'How dare you ask me to meet a *syren*.

'Your affectionate,
'A.'

XI · *General Booth and Peter Flower*

—◦◎◦—

My friendship with Lord and Lady Manners, of Avon Tyrrell,[1] probably made more difference to the course of my life than anything that had happened in it.

Riding was what I knew and cared most about; and I dreamt of High Leicestershire. I had hunted in Cheshire, where you killed three foxes a day and found yourself either clattering among cottages and clothes-lines or blocked by carriages and crowds; I knew the stiff plough and fine horses of Yorkshire and the rotten grass in the Bicester; I had struggled over the large fences and small enclosures of the Grafton and been a heroine in the select fields and large becks with the Burton; and the Beaufort had seen the dawn of my foxhunting; but Melton was a name which brought the Hon. Crasher before me and opened a vista on my future of all that was fast, furious and fashionable.

When I was told that I was going to sit next to the Master of the Quorn at dinner, my excitement knew no bounds.

Gordon Cunard – whose brother Bache owned the famous hounds in Market Harborough – had insisted on my joining him at a country-house party given for a ball. On getting the invitation I had refused, as I hardly knew our hostess – the pretty Mrs Farnham – but after receiving a spirited telegram from my new admirer – one of the best men to hounds in Leicestershire – I changed my mind. In consequence of this decision a double event took place. I fell in love with Peter Flower – a brother of the late Lord Battersea – and formed an attachment with a couple whose devotion and goodness to me for more than twenty years encouraged and embellished my glorious youth.

[1] Avon Tyrrell, Christchurch, Hants. Lady Manners was a Miss Fane.

Lord Manners, or 'Hoppy' as we called him, was one of the few men I ever met whom the word 'single-minded' described. His sense of honour was only equalled by his sense of humour; and a more original, tender, uncynical, real being never existed. He was a fine sportsman and had won the Grand Military when he was in the Grenadiers, riding one of his own hunters; he was also the second gentleman in England to win the Grand National in 1882, on a thoroughbred called Seaman, who was by no means everyone's horse. For other people he cared nothing. '*Décidément je n'aime pas les autres,*' he would have said, to quote my son-in-law, Antoine Bibesco.

His wife often said that, but for her, he would not have asked a creature inside the house; be this as it may, no host and hostess could have been more socially susceptible or given their guests a warmer welcome than Con and Hoppy Manners.

What I loved and admired in him was his keenness and his impeccable unworldliness. He was perfectly independent of public opinion and as free from rancour as he was from fear, malice or acerbity. He never said a stupid thing. Some people would say that this is not a compliment, but the amount of silly things that I have heard clever people say makes me often wonder what is left for the stupid.

His wife was very different, though quite as free from rhetoric.

Under a becalmed exterior Con Manners was a little brittle and found it difficult to say she was in the wrong; this impenitence caused some of her lovers a suffering of which she was unconscious: it is a minor failing which strikes a dumb note in me, but which I have since discovered is not only common but almost universal. I often warned people of Con's dangerous smile when I observed them blundering along; but, though she was uneven in her powers of forgiveness, the serious quarrel of her life was made up ultimately without reserve. Lady Manners was clever, gracious and understanding; she was more worldly, more adventurous and less deprecating than her husband; people meant a great deal to her; and the whole of London was at her feet, except those lonely men and women who specialise in collecting the famous as men collect centipedes.

To digress here, I asked my friend Mr Birrell once how the *juste milieu* was to be found – for an enterprising person – between running after the great men of the day and missing them; and he said:

'I would advise you to live among your superiors, Margot, but to be of them.'

My dear friend, Mrs Hamlyn, was the châtelaine of the famous Clovelly, in Devonshire, and was Con's sister. She had that spirit of eternal youth and was full of breathless admiration. I hardly ever met anyone who derived so much pleasure and surprise out of ordinary life. She was as uncritical and tolerant of those she loved as she was narrow and vehement over those who had unaccountably offended her. She had an ebullient and voracious sense of humour and was baffled and *éblouie* by titled people, however vulgar and ridiculous they might be. By this I do not mean she was a snob: on the contrary she made and kept friends among the frumps and the obscure, to whom she showed faithful hospitality; but she was old-fashioned and thought that all duchesses were ladies.

Christine Hamlyn was a character-part; but, if the machinery was not invented by which you could remove her prejudices, no tank could turn her from her friends.

It was through the Souls and these friends whom I have endeavoured to describe that I entered into a new phase of my existence.

*   *   *

Before concluding the story of my girlhood, I must write of an incident which brought a new friend into my life.[1]

I opened my eyes at eight o'clock on a bright morning in June and found them fixed on my ball-dress. I looked at the clock: I saw I had exactly one hour in which to bathe, dress, breakfast and get to Paddington.

Out of bed in an instant, I shouted for my maid. She had not been eight years with me for nothing. My riding-habit, long coat, buff waistcoat, hat, boots, gloves, etc., were all put out. I munched toast while she brushed my hair.

I always find the double tie is the toilette-trap in dressing for

[1] This incident is reprinted, by kind permission, from the *Cornhill Magazine*.

riding. Pulling up the centre under the chin, pinning down the sides – while keeping a straight line at the top of the turn-over – is touch and go. It was June, however – a month in which no one hunts but young ladies in fiction – and I need hardly say my tie was perfect. I pushed my arms into a covert-coat and, rushing downstairs, jumped into a hansom.

Hansoms are as extinct as duelling or garrotting. No one can deny that they had every fault: you caught your dress getting in, you fell on your head getting out; if it rained you were soaked, or if the window was down and the horse slipped your head went through the glass. But they were highly becoming conveyances and generally went along quickly; unfortunately for me, this cab went painfully slow. I delayed it by poking my whip through the trap-door and shouting:

'Hurry up! I will give you five shillings more.'

I gave this up as the lash of the eager driver tingled over my face (another danger to which a hansom exposed you); and full of grim determination – as the Ulsterman said in 1914 – I made up my mind I should have to race for the train.

I was going to a famous horse-dealer in Swindon, to try hunters for myself, Ribblesdale and other members of the family. Elaborate arrangements had been made for me to join my sister, Mrs Graham Smith, later in the afternoon; and to lose this train would not only have put the family about, but cheated me of riding strange horses over strange fences, an amusement that made my spirits rise.

I ran into the station. My train was moving slowly out, a porter was standing in an open doorway of one of the compartments, I jumped on to the step, caught hold of his coat, shouted 'Don't shut the door!' and, as he stepped off, I stepped in.

My gratitude knew no bounds. I threw the man ten shillings: if he had shut the door or shown any fear, I should have been done. Trains move off with great dignity and if travellers would move on instead of crawling like rolling-stock, fewer trains would be missed.

Out of breath but full of gladness, I looked at my top-boots and wondered how many of my friends wore loose boots with thick soles to them. Everyone has a different sort of vanity; mine went

to my head not to my feet: two pairs of stockings and loose boots
were essential to my comfort out hunting.

A propos of this, I must digress a little. The present Duke of
Beaufort's father scolded me for wearing tight boots. We were
riding back to Badminton with the hounds on a cold evening. I
assured him they were so loose that, if one of the hunt servants
would pick up my boot, I could kick it into the road. He challenged
me. I kicked my boot off with the greatest ease.

It was not my boots, but my hats from Mr Lock in St James's
Street that I fancied. From the hoop to the hobble is not a more
violent change than from the riding hats of 1894 to the riding hats of
1917. I see young ladies riding in the Row with very wide flat brims
and no crowns to their hats. Rotten Row has always had a good many
loose horses with riders on them, so perhaps it is not fair to judge
from this. I daresay if I went back to Melton I should see men and
women with crowns to their hats. But I must return to my train. . . .

After arranging a pillow at my back, I looked at my fellow-
travellers. A beautiful old man in a roomy blue overcoat sat reading
near the window with his hat off. He had a beard of black and silver
and curling black and silver hair, a fine studio-head with onyx eyes
and a thin, large, aquiline nose. An unworldly-looking youth sat
next to him, arranging papers and letters in elastic bands. The
empty seat on his other side was piled up with letters, newspaper-
cuttings and documents of every description. The young man was
in great awe of the old gentleman. His head dropped and his chin
retreated whenever he handed the wrong packet. I began to look
about me and for the first time I noticed labels on the windows at
each side of the carriage. I said to myself, 'Hullo! I am not in my
right place. I must apologise for having thrust myself into this
reserved carriage.' How had I best begin? In my youth I called men
'sir', this was peculiar to myself and by no means a fashion. (I was
born at a later period than *The Fairchild Family*) I fidgeted about,
with an occasional glance at the old man. Suddenly I caught his
lively eye fixed on me and said:

'I am sorry, sir, that I hurled myself into this carriage; I see it
has been reserved for you, but missing this train would have been
a serious matter to me.'

THE OLD GENTLEMAN: 'You need not apologise. I do not mind at all. I was afraid you might hurt yourself. What you did was very dangerous; but you must never do it again. Why would it have been serious for you to have missed this train?'

He said these words in a grave tone and added, threateningly: 'What are you going to do?'

MARGOT: 'I am going to try horses for myself and my brother-in-law. What are you going to do?'

HE (*very deliberately*): 'I am going to save souls.'

MARGOT: 'You are sanguine!'

HE: 'Don't you believe in saving souls?'

I confess I thought it a poignant pretension, but he was so bold and good-looking that I did not want to appear unsympathetic.

MARGOT (*thoughtfully*): 'I think I know what you mean, although I have never seen the process. I have often heard of conversion and there was a great deal of excitement in our village when the postmistress' daughter was converted by an American, but I think there is something morally vulgar in trying to get too familiar with men's souls.'

HE (*indignantly*): 'When you are dealing with the drunken and the depraved, you must not be morally aristocratic. You know nothing of real life: I have only to look at you to see that you are not only very young but extremely inexperienced. Look at me, young lady, and tell me truly: when have *you* seen souls flickering out for want of a little light? What do *you* know of the depravity that devastates whole districts? The world you know is not the real world at all! What sort of a world is yours? I do not suppose you have ever seen a pauper! Have you ever been to a workhouse? I don't suppose you have ever seen a lunatic. Have you ever been to an asylum? I don't suppose you have ever seen a convict. Have you ever been in a prison? Have you ever been into a public-house and seen men – yes and women too – grappling and fighting in the sight of God, before the eyes of man, stiff with drink? . . .'

He paused and, after a reproachful look at me, continued:

'What do *you* know about drink? You have probably never seen drunkenness in your life.'

MARGOT: 'Oh, haven't I just! I am Scotch.'

HE (*not listening*): 'Fighting, not with their fists, young woman, but with their souls. The morally aristocratic won't help us much here! What is wanted are work-men and work-women: I am thinking of the next world, you are thinking of this. I can see you are fond of this world and its amusements: perhaps you are fashionable?'

MARGOT: 'Oh dear no!'

HE: 'Who is your brother-in-law?'

MARGOT: 'Ribblesdale.'

HE: 'What is your name?'

MARGOT: 'It won't convey anything to you. I am quite uninteresting.'

HE: 'On the contrary, you interest me. Do you believe in hell?'

MARGOT (*decidedly*): 'No, nor do you.'

Much surprised at this remark, he took off his coat and, leaning forward, I saw 'Salvation Army' embroidered on his blue jersey. So this was General Booth! I had heard much of him and Mrs Booth; I had had close personal experience of their work in my districts (Whitechapel and Wapping), but I did not want our conversation to be interrupted by any autobiography, so I went on rapidly:

'You *think* you do, but you *don't*. Holding hell over the heads of the drunken and depraved is playing down to the lowest side even of these poor people. This is the weak part of your teaching: you excite fear and a sort of spiritual fever.'

GENERAL BOOTH: 'If you were not a rich, idle, self-indulgent young lady, you would see that what you call spiritual fever *I* call spiritual hunger; this does not belong to the lowest side of humanity, but the highest: spiritual torpor *is* hell.'

MARGOT: 'If this is the kind of hell you mean, I *do* believe in it. I have always thought hell is within us, just as I think heaven is and as certainly as I think God is above us.'

GENERAL BOOTH: 'There is a great deal of nonsense in that kind of talk. Good is good, evil is evil, God is God. Heaven is heaven and hell is hell. Don't be equivocal and ecclesiastical, but be frank with your faith. Do not be sly like the High Churchmen. I believe in hell and I believe in heaven. You say heaven lies within us: does it only lie within us? Is there no destination, only the route?'

MARGOT: 'I did not mean that! You might as well say a corridor and Calvary were the same. Of course no one would go on walking or fighting if there were no goal, unless they were fools or saints! But fear of hell is not a good incentive. Threats would have no effect upon me. I would much rather feel that my nature responded to love than to fear. Why worry about hell? Heaven is the light to hold before your flickering souls. I can't argue on theology; I feel like the child who was flying its kite on a misty day. When they said, "Do you enjoy flying your kite when you can't see it?" the child said, "Oh, yes; I always feel it tugging at me." '

The old man liked this story. He said:

'I was not talking of theology, I was only defending myself when you were saying my army does not appeal to the highest in human beings. I say it does. If you had what I call spiritual hunger and you call spiritual fever, you would not be wasting your time in trying horses for your brother-in-law.'

Relieved at this departure from theology and noticing a slight twinkling of his eye, I said I saw no great harm in trying horses for my brother-in-law.

GENERAL BOOTH: 'What sort of a man is Lord Ribblesdale?'

MARGOT: 'He's a fine rider and great judge of a horse.'

GENERAL BOOTH: 'Is he a *good* man?'

MARGOT: 'One of the best! Now, General, what you want to know is how much field for conversion you can find in me and my family and how to start about it. Conversion is extremely risky: it is like the practical joke; you can never know if the end is satisfactory. It is not a good topic: it is ultimately dull, as it means different things to different men. Don't let us talk about conversion. I want to know about your wife and your society.'

GENERAL BOOTH: 'My wife was the most wonderful woman God ever made. This society was entirely her idea: it was her creation, not mine.'

He spoke of her with deep feeling, of her amazing oratory and true goodness. I could only say what I had heard about her and how much I admired him, his family and his work. He was not very forthcoming, which disappointed me. I longed to know more about himself and how the idea of the Salvation Army started, etc., but he never pursued any subject for long; he was a restless listener. I asked him if his wife believed in hell.

GENERAL BOOTH (*guardedly*): 'I think she would have agreed with you about hell. What is the name of your father?'

MARGOT: 'My father is called Charles Tennant. He makes chemicals in Glasgow and gold in the Mysore mines in India.'

GENERAL BOOTH: 'You are Margot Tennant. I know all about you.' (I felt inclined to say, 'Oh, do you!') 'Your father refused to give our army any money.'

MARGOT: 'I don't think my father ever refused to give money to anyone in his life. He knows the value of money too well not to give. He is a very happy man and suffers none of the apprehension, suspicion, and low temperature of the rich. My father would never understand your army and hates noise.'

GENERAL BOOTH: 'Noise?'

MARGOT: 'Yes; you know your lassies thrum tea-trays for hours in the streets and shout even on grass slopes where people play golf. The seventeenth hole at St Andrews – on the road where your people parade – is a very ticklish hole; my father is irritable and highly-strung.'

GENERAL BOOTH: 'Are you?'

MARGOT: '*Very!* Noise is physical pain to me. It does not take much to put you out when you are putting.'

GENERAL BOOTH (*not listening, but watching me attentively*): 'Do you say your prayers?'

MARGOT: 'Always.'

GENERAL BOOTH: 'Would you like to pray now in this carriage?'

MARGOT (*gravely*): 'Certainly, if you would like to.'

General Booth was unprepared for this answer. He had made up his mind that I was a fearless, frivolous female. He had been baulked in his scheme of conversion by a conversational digression and was anxious to return to the charge. For a moment neither of us spoke; then, with a courteous movement of his hand to me, he said:

'Let us kneel and pray.'

The young lieutenant, myself and the general knelt down in a row with our elbows on the opposite seats of the carriage. He opened by exhortation: would God 'bless and be near this our sister'. He was not censorious, but I noticed he emphasized the word *quietness* in quoting Isaiah ('In quietness and confidence lies our strength').

He prayed erect upon his knees with an upright head, throwing his long hair back. I shall never forget this prayer. I found myself not merely conforming but acquiescing and praying. He was perfectly unselfconscious: humble, without being self-centred; grateful, without being complacent; original and uneccentric; full of ideas, without being jumpy; reverent, imaginative and to me deeply moving.

He finished; and we all got up.

I took his hand, pressed it with both of mine and thanked him. I told him how much I had liked his prayer. We sat down in silence. He asked me what I had got in my writing-case. I took out books and a few photographs and trifles and showed them to him: none of these interested him at all. I always travel with a little leather commonplace-book in which I have copied from the writings of many authors quotations upon death and prayer. He took up the book and asked me to lend it to him. I did not want to do this. I have never had success in lending books, even to friends. There were a few empty pages and I said to him:

'You write something in my book for me. I cannot lend it to you; I have never shown this to anyone.'

He did not give me back the book, but held it in his hand.

GENERAL BOOTH: 'I suppose when you get home you will make a good story of your talk and journey today?'

MARGOT: 'If you regret it I will tell no one, but otherwise I shall certainly tell my sister.'

GENERAL BOOTH (*smiling*): 'And the brother-in-law?'

MARGOT: 'Yes, *all of them*; but I don't know what you mean by "a good story". If you mean *I* think it funny to pray, you are completely out in your calculations.'

GENERAL BOOTH: 'You haven't often knelt down in a train before and prayed, have you?'

MARGOT: 'No, never. I generally say my prayers to myself, but I have often prayed out loud with my factory-girls and never observed any of them take it amiss.'

GENERAL BOOTH: 'Shall I ever see you again? Will you ride down Rotten Row in one of my Salvation bonnets?'

MARGOT: 'Never! I think they are hideous! I can see your converts have been very conventional people. You take it for granted that I am vain and worldly and you want to startle me into loving God. I have always believed in the Salvation Army and given money to it, but I don't see that riding in your bonnet would bring in more souls or more subscriptions.'

GENERAL BOOTH: 'It would be an advertisement.'

MARGOT: 'It would cover you, me and your soldiers with ridicule.'

GENERAL BOOTH: 'Christ did not mind being ridiculed.'

MARGOT: 'He would not have liked being advertised. Just write in my book, will you? I will give you my address so that you won't forget me.'

He wrote in silence. We were nearing Swindon station. I felt very sorry to part with my dear old new friend.

He gave me back the book. I read what he had written:

'What is life for but to walk in harmony with God, to secure that disposition and character which will fit us for the enjoyments and employments and companionships of Heaven – and to spend and be spent for the temporal and eternal weal of this suffering world?

'WILLIAM BOOTH.'

I shut my little book and put it in my bag.

GENERAL BOOTH: 'I am very glad to have met you. We will pray for each other and meet soon.'

He took my hand in both of his.

I told him I had loved his prayer and would never forget him, that he must come and see me, or if he wanted me I would go and see him. We said goodbye; we remained friends till he died.

*　　　*　　　*

The first time I ever saw Peter Flower was at Ranelagh, where he had taken my sister Charty Ribblesdale to watch a polo match. They were sitting together at an iron table, under a cedar-tree, eating ices. I was wearing a grey muslin dress with a black sash and a black hat, with coral beads round my throat, and heard him say as I came up to them:

'Nineteen? Not possible! I should have said fifteen! Is that the one that rides so well?'

After shaking hands I sat down and looked around me.

I always notice what men wear; and Peter Flower was the best-dressed man I had ever seen. I do not know who could have worn his clothes when they were new; but certainly he never did. After his clothes, what I was most struck by was his peculiar, almost animal grace, powerful sloping shoulders, fascinating laugh and infectious vitality.

Laurence Oliphant once said to me, 'I divide the world into life-givers and life-takers'; and I have often had reason to feel the truth of this, being as I am acutely sensitive to high spirits. On looking back along the gallery of my acquaintance, I can find not more than three or four people as tenacious of life as Peter was: Lady Desborough, Lady Cunard, my son Anthony and myself. There are various kinds of high spirits: some so crude and rough-tongued that they vitiate what they touch and estrange everyone of sensibility and some so insistent that they tire and suffocate you; but Peter's vitality revived and restored everyone he came in contact with; and, when I said goodbye to him that day at Ranelagh, although I cannot remember a single sentence of any interest spoken by him or by me, my mind was absorbed in thinking of when and how I could meet him again.

In the winter of that same year I went with the Ribblesdales to stay with Peter's brother, Lord Battersea, to have a hunt. I took with me the best of hats and habits and two leggy and faded hirelings, hoping to pick up a mount. Charty twisted her knee the day after we arrived; this enabled me to ride the horse on which Peter was to have mounted her; and full of spirits we all went off to the meet of the Bicester hounds. I had hardly spoken three words to my bene-factor, but Ribblesdale had rather unwisely told him that I was one of the best riders to hounds in England.

At the meet I examined my mount closely while the man was lengthening my stirrup. Havoc, as he was called, was a dark chestnut, 16.1, with a coat like the back of a violin and a spiteful little head. He had an enormous bit on; and I was glad to see a leather strap under the curb-chain.

When I was mounted, Peter kept close to my side and said:

'You're on a topper! Take him where you like, but ride your own line.'

To which I replied:

'Why? Does he rush? I had thought of following you.'

PETER: 'Not at all, but he may pull you a bit, so keep away from the field; the fence isn't made that he can't jump; and as for water he's a swallow! I wish I could say the same of mine! We've got a brook round about here with rotten banks, which will catch the best! But, if we are near each other, you must come alongside and go first and mine will very likely follow you. I don't want to spend the night swimming.'

It was a good scenting day, and we did not take long to find. I stuck to Peter Flower while the Bicester hounds raced across the heavy grass towards a nairy-looking double. In spite of the iron-monger's shop in Havoc's mouth, I had not the faintest control over him, so I said to Peter:

'You know, Mr Flower, I can't stop your horse!'

He looked at me with a charming smile and said:

'But why should you? Hounds are running!'

MARGOT: 'But I can't turn him!'

PETER: 'It doesn't matter! They are running straight. Hullo! Look out! Look out for Hydy!'

We were going great guns. I saw a man in front of me slowing up to the double, so shouted at him:

'Get out of my way! Get out of my way!'

I was certain that at the pace he was going he would take a heavy fall and I should be on the top of him. While in the act of turning round to see who it was that was shouting, his willing horse paused and I shot past him, taking away his spur in my habit skirt. I heard a volley of oaths as I jumped into the jungle. Havoc, however, did not like the brambles and, steadying himself as he landed, arched with the activity of a cat over a high rail on the other side of the double; I turned round and saw Peter's horse close behind me hit the rail and peck heavily upon landing, at which Peter gave him one down the shoulder and looked furious.

I had no illusions. I was on a horse that nothing could stop! Seeing a line of willows in front of me, I shouted to Peter to come along, as I thought if the brook was ahead I could not possibly keep close to him, going at that pace. To my surprise and delight, as we approached the willows Peter passed me and the water widened out in front of us; I saw by his set face that it was neck or nothing with him. Havoc was going well within himself, but his stable-companion was precipitate and flurried; and before I knew what had happened Peter was in the middle of the brook and I was jumping over his head. On landing I made a large circle round the field away from hounds, trying to pull up; and when I could turn round I found myself facing the brook again, with Peter dripping on the bank nearest to me. Havoc pricked his ears, passed him like a flash and jumped the brook again; but the bank on landing was boggy and while we were floundering I got a pull at him by putting the curb-rein under my pommel and, exhausted and distressed, I jumped off. Peter burst out laughing.

'We seem to be separated for life,' he said. 'Do look at my damned horse!'

I looked down the water and saw the animal standing knee-deep nibbling grass and mud off the bank with perfect composure.

MARGOT: 'I really believe Havoc would jump this brook for a third time and then I should be by your side. What luck that you aren't soaked to the skin; hadn't I better look out for the second-horse-men? Hounds by now will be at the sea and I confess I can't ride your horse: does he always pull like this?'

PETER: 'Yes, he catches hold a bit, but what do you mean? You rode him beautifully. Hullo! What is that spur doing in your skirt?'

MARGOT: 'I took it off the man that you call "Hydy", who was going so sticky at the double.'

PETER: 'Poor old Clarendon! I advise you to keep his spur, he'll never guess who took it; and, if I know anything about him, there will be no love lost between you even if you do return it to him!'

I was longing for another horse, as I could not bear the idea of going home. At that moment a single file of second-horse-men came in sight; and Peter's well-trained servant, on a thoroughbred grey, rode up to us at the conventional trot. Peter lit a cigar and, pointing to the brook, said to his man:

'Go off and get a rope and hang that brute! Or haul him out, will you? And give me my lunch.'

We were miles away from any human habitation and I felt depressed.

'Perhaps I had better ride home with your man,' said I, looking tentatively at Peter.

'Home! What for?' said he.

MARGOT: 'Are you sure Havoc is not tired?'

PETER: 'I wish to God he was! But I daresay this infernal Bicester grass, which is heavier than anything I saw in Yorkshire, has steadied him a bit; you'll see he'll go far better with you this afternoon. I'm awfully sorry and would put you on my second horse, but it isn't mine and I'm told its got a bit of a temper; if you go through that gate we'll have our lunch together. . . . Have a cigarette?'

I smiled and shook my head; my mouth was as dry as a Japanese toy and I felt shattered with fatigue. The ground on which I was standing was deep and I was afraid of walking in case I should leave my boots in it, so I tapped the back of Havoc's fetlocks till I got him stretched and mounted myself. This filled Peter with admiration; and, lifting his hat, he said:

'Well! You are the very first woman I ever saw mount herself without two men and a boy hanging on to the horse's head.'

I rode towards the gate and Peter joined me a few minutes later on his second horse. He praised my riding and promised he would mount me any day in the week if I could only get someone to ask me down to Brackley where he kept his horses; he said the Grafton was the country to hunt in and that, though Tom Firr, the huntsman of the Quorn, was the greatest man in England, Frank Beers was hard to beat. I felt pleased at his praise, but I knew Havoc had not turned a hair and that, if I went on, I should kill either myself, Peter or someone else.

'Aren't you nervous when you see a helpless woman on one of your horses?' I said.

PETER: 'No, I'm only afraid she'll hurt my horse! I take her off
pretty quick, I can tell you, if I think she's going to spoil my sale;
but I never mount a woman. Your sister is a magnificent rider, or I
wouldn't have put her on that horse. Now come along and with any
luck you will be alone with hounds this afternoon and Havoc will
be knocked down at Tattersall's for five hundred guineas.'

MARGOT: 'You are sure you want me to go on?'

PETER: 'You think I want you to go home? Very well! If you
go . . . *I* go!'

I longed to have the courage to say, 'Let us both go home', but
I knew he would think that I was funking and it was still early in
the day. He looked at me steadily and said:

'I will do exactly what you like.'

I looked at him, but at that moment the hounds came in sight and
my last chance was gone. We shogged along to the next cover,
Havoc as mild as milk. I was amazed at Peter's nerve: if any horse
of mine had taken such complete charge of its rider, I should have
been in a state of anguish till I had separated them; but he was riding
along, talking and laughing in front of me in the highest of spirits.
This lack of sensitiveness irritated me and my heart sank. Before
reaching the cover, Peter came up to me and suggested that we
should change Havoc's bit. I then perceived he was not quite so
happy as I thought; and this determined me to stick it out. I thanked
him demurely and added, with a slight and smiling shrug:

'I fear no bit can save me today, thank you.'

At which Peter said with visible irritability:

'Oh, for God's sake then don't let us go on! If you hate my horse
I vote we stop!'

'What a cross man!' I said to myself, seeing him flushed and snappy;
but a ringing 'Holloa!' brought our deliberations to an abrupt end.

Havoc and I shot down the road, passing the blustering field;
and, hopping over a gap, we found ourselves close to the hounds,
who were running hell-for-leather towards a handsome country-
seat perched upon a hill. A park is what I hate most out hunting:
hounds invariably lose the line, the field loses its way and I lose
my temper.

I looked round to see if my benefactor was near me, but he was nowhere to be seen. Eight or ten hard riders were behind me; they shouted:

'Don't go into the wood! Turn to your left! Don't go into the wood!'

I saw a fancy gate of yellow polished oak in front of me, at the end of one of the grass rides in the wood, and what looked like lawns beyond. I was unable to turn to the left with my companions, but plunged into the trees where the hounds paused: not so Havoc, who, in spite of the deep ground, was still going great guns. A lady behind me, guessing what had happened, left her companions and managed somehow or other to pass me in the ride; and, as I approached the yellow gate, she was holding it open for me. I shouted my thanks to her and she shouted back:

'Get off when you stop!'

This was my fixed determination, as I had observed that Havoc's tongue was over the bit and he was not aware that anyone was on his back, nor was he the least tired and no doubt would have jumped the yellow gate with ease.

After leaving my saviour I was joined by my former companions. The hounds had picked up again and we left the gate, the wood and the country-seat behind us. Still going very strong, we all turned into a chalk field with a white road sunk between two high banks leading down to a ford. I kept on the top of the bank as I was afraid of splashing people in the water, if not knocking them down. Two men were standing by the fence ahead, which separated me from what appeared to be a river; and I knew there must be a considerable drop in front of me. They held their hands up in warning as I came galloping up; I took my foot out of the stirrup and dropping my reins gave myself up for lost, but in spite of Havoc slowing up he was going too fast to stop or turn. He made a magnificent effort, but I saw the water twinkling below me; and after that I knew no more.

When I came to, I was lying on a box-bed in a cottage, with Peter and the lady who had held the yellow gate kneeling by my side.

'I think you are mad to put anyone on that horse!' I heard her say indignantly. 'You know how often it has changed hands; and you yourself can hardly ride it.'

Havoc had tried to scramble down the bank, which luckily for me had not been immediately under the fence, but it could not be done, so we took a somersault into the brook most alarming for the people in the ford to see. However, as the water where I landed was deep, I was not hurt, but had fainted from fear and exhaustion.

Peter's misery was profound; ice-white and in an agony of fear he was warming my feet with both his hands while I watched him quietly. I was taken home in a brougham by my kind friend, who turned out to be Mrs Bunbury, a sister of John Watson the Master of the Meath Hounds and daughter of old Mr Watson the Master of the Carlow, and the finest rider to hounds in England.

This was how Peter and I first came really to know each other; and after that it was only a question of time when our friendship developed into a serious love-affair. I stayed with Mrs Bunbury in the Grafton country that winter for several weeks and was mounted by everyone.

As Peter was a kind of hero in the hunting-field and had never been known to mount a woman, I was the object of some jealousy. The first scene in my life occurred at Brackley, where he and a friend of his, called Hatfield Harter, shared a hunting-box together.

There was a lady of charm and beauty in the vicinity who went by the name of Mrs Bo. They said she had gone well to hounds in her youth, but I had never observed her jump a twig. She often joined us when Peter and I were changing horses and once or twice had ridden home with us. Peter did not appear to like her much, but I was too busy to notice this one way or the other. One day I said to him I thought he was rather snubby to her and added:

'After all, she must have been a very pretty woman when she was young and I don't think it's nice of you to show such irritation when she joins us.'

PETER: 'Do you call her old?'

MARGOT: 'Well, oldish I should say. She must be over thirty, isn't she?'

PETER: 'Do you call that old?'

MARGOT: 'I don't know! How old are you, Peter?'

PETER: 'I shan't tell you.'

One day I rode back from hunting, having got wet to the skin. I had left the Bunbury brougham in Peter's stables, but did not like to go back in wet clothes; so, after seeing my horse comfortably gruelled, I walked up to the charming lady's house to borrow dry clothes. She was out, but her maid gave me a coat and skirt which – though much too big – served my purpose.

After having tea with Peter, who was ill in bed, I drove up to thank the lady for her clothes. She was lying on a thickly pillowed couch, smoking a cigarette in a boudoir that smelt of violets. She greeted me coldly; and I was about to leave when she threw her cigarette into the fire and, suddenly sitting very erect said:

'Wait! I have something to say to you.'

I saw by the expression on her face that I had no chance of getting away, though I was tired and felt at a strange disadvantage in my flowing skirts.

MRS BO: 'Does it not strike you that going to tea with a man who is in bed is a thing no one can do?'

MARGOT: 'Going to see a man who is ill? No, certainly not!'

MRS BO: 'Well, then let me tell you for your own information how it will strike other people. I am a much older woman than you and I warn you, you can't go on doing this sort of thing! Why should you come down here, among all of us who are friends, and make mischief and create talk?'

I felt chilled to the bone and, getting up, said:

'I think I had better leave you now, as I am tired and you are angry.'

MRS BO (*standing up and coming very close to me*): 'Do you not know that I would nurse Peter Flower through yellow fever! But, though I have lived next door to him these last three years, I would never dream of doing what you have done today.'

The expression on her face was so intense that I felt sorry for her and said as gently as I could:

'I do not see why you shouldn't! Especially if you are all such friends down here as you say you are. However, everyone has a different idea of what is right and wrong. . . . I must go now!'

I was determined not to stay a moment longer and walked to the door, but she had lost her head and said in a hard, bitter voice:

'You say everyone has a different idea of right and wrong, but I should say you have none!'

At this I left the room.

When I told Mrs Bunbury what had happened, all she said was:

'Cat! She's jealous! Before you came down here, Peter Flower was in love with her.'

This was a great shock to me and I determined I would leave the Grafton country, as I had already been away far too long from my parents; so I wrote to Peter saying I was sorry not to say goodbye to him, but that I had to go home. The next day was Sunday. I got my usual love-letter from Peter – who, whether I saw him or not, wrote daily – telling me that his temperature had gone up again and that he would give me his two best horses on Monday, as he was not allowed to leave his room. After we had finished lunch, Peter turned up looking ill. Mrs Bunbury greeted him sweetly and said:

'You ought to be in bed, you know; but, since you *are* here, I'll leave Margot to look after you while Jacky and I go round the stables.'

When we were left to ourselves, Peter, looking at me, said:

'Well! I've got your letter! What is all this about? Don't you know there are two horses coming over from Ireland this week which I want you particularly to ride for me?'

I saw that he was thoroughly upset and told him that I was going home, as I had been already too long away.

'Have your people written to you?' he said.

MARGOT: 'They always write. . . .'

PETER (*seeing the evasion*): 'What's wrong?'

MARGOT: 'What do you mean?'

PETER: 'You know quite well that no one has asked you to go home. Something has happened; someone has said something to you; you've been put out. After all it was only yesterday that we were discussing every meet, and you promised to give me a lurcher. What has happened since to change you?'

MARGOT: 'Oh, what does it matter? I can always come down here again later on.'

PETER: 'How wanting in candour you are! You are not a bit like what I thought you were!'

MARGOT (*sweetly*): 'No? . . .'

PETER: 'Not a bit! You are a regular woman. I thought differently of you somehow!'

MARGOT: 'You thought I was a dog-fancier or a rough-rider, did you, with a good thick skin?'

PETER: 'I fail to understand you! Are you alluding to the manners of my horses?'

MARGOT: 'No, to your friends.'

PETER: 'Ah! Ah! *Nous y sommes!* . . . How can you be so childish! What did Mrs Bo say to you?'

MARGOT: 'Oh, spare me from going into your friends' affairs!'

PETER (*flushed with temper, but trying to control himself*): 'What does it matter what an old woman says whose nose has been put out of joint in the hunting-field?'

MARGOT: 'You told me she was young.'

PETER: 'What an awful lie! You said she was pretty and I disagreed with you.' (*Silence.*) 'What did she say to you? I tell you she is jealous of you in the hunting-field!'

MARGOT: 'No she's not; she's jealous of me in your bedroom and says I don't know right from wrong.'

PETER (*startled at first and then bursting out laughing*): 'There's nothing very original about that!'

MARGOT (*indignantly*): 'Do you mean to say that it's a platitude? And that I *don't* know right from wrong?'

PETER (*taking my hands and kissing them with a sigh of relief*): 'I wonder!'

MARGOT (*getting up*): 'Well, after that, nothing will induce me to stay down here or ride any of your horses ever again! No regiment of soldiers will keep me!'

PETER: 'Really, darling, how can you be so foolish! Who would ever think it wrong to go and see a poor devil ill in bed! You had to ride my horse back to its stable and it was your duty to come and ask after me and thank me for all my kindness to you and the good horses I've put you on!'

MARGOT: 'Evidently in this country I am not wanted. Mrs Bo said so; and you ought to have warned me you were in love with her. You said I was not the woman you thought I was: well, I can say the same of you!'

At this Peter got up and his laughter disappeared.

'Do you mean what you say? Is this the impression you got from talking to Mrs Bo?'

MARGOT: 'Yes.'

PETER: 'In that case I will go and see her and ask her which of the two of you is lying! If it's you, you needn't bother yourself to leave this country, for I shall sell my horses. . . . I wish to God I had never met you!'

I felt very uncomfortable and unhappy, as in my heart I knew that Mrs Bo had never said Peter was in love with her; she had not alluded to his feelings for her at all. I got up to stop him leaving the room and put myself in front of the door.

MARGOT: 'Really, why make scenes! There is nothing so tiring; and you know quite well you are ill and ought to go to bed. Is there any object in going round the country discussing me?'

PETER: 'Just go away, will you? I'm ill and want to get off.'

I did not move; I saw he was white with rage. The idea of going round the country talking about me was more than he could bear; so I said, trying to mollify him:

'If you want to discuss me, I am always willing to listen; there is nothing I enjoy so much as talking about myself.'

It was too late. All he said to me was:

'Do you mind leaving that door? You tire me and it's getting dark.'

MARGOT: 'I will let you go, but promise me you won't go to Mrs Bo today; or, if you *do*, tell me what you are going to say to her first.'

PETER: 'You've never told me yet what she said to you, except that I was in love with her, so why should I tell you what I propose saying to her! For once you cannot have it all your own way. You are *so* spoilt since you've been down here that . . .'

I flung the door wide open and, before he could finish his sentence, ran up to my room.

*　　　*　　　*

Peter was curiously upsetting to the feminine sense; he wanted to conceal it and to expose it at the same time, under the impression it might arouse my jealousy. He was specially angry with me for dancing with King Edward, then the Prince of Wales. I told him that if he would learn to waltz instead of prance I would dance with

him, but till he did I should choose my own partners. Over this
we had a great row; and, after sitting out two dances with the Prince,
I put on my cloak and walked round to 40 Grosvenor Square
without saying good-night to Peter. I was in my dressing-gown,
with my hair standing out round my head, when I heard a noise
in the street and, looking down, I saw Peter standing on the wall of
our porch gazing across an angle of the area into the open window
of our library, contemplating, I presumed, jumping into it; I raced
downstairs to stop this dangerous folly, but I was too late and, as I
opened the library-door, he had given a cat-like spring, knocking a
flower-pot into the area, and was by my side. I lit two candles on
the writing-table and scolded him for his recklessness. He told me
he had made a great deal of money by jumping from a stand on to
tables and things and once he had won £500 by jumping on to a
mantelpiece when the fire was burning. As we were talking, I
heard voices in the area; Peter, with the instinct of a burglar,
instantly lay flat on the ground behind the sofa, his head under the
valance of the chintz, and I remained at the writing-table, smoking
my cigarette. The door opened; I looked round and was blinded by
the blaze of a bull's-eye lantern. When it was removed from my face,
I saw two policemen, an inspector and my father's servant. I got
up slowly and, with my head in the air, sat upon the arm of the sofa,
blocking the only possibility of Peter's full length being seen.

MARGOT (*with great dignity*): 'Is this a practical joke?'

INSPECTOR (*coolly*): 'Not at all, madam, but it is only right to
tell you a hansom-cabman informed us that, as he was passing this
house a few minutes ago, he saw a man jump into that window.'

He walked away from me and, holding his lantern over the area,
peered down and saw the broken flower-pot. I knew lying was
more than useless and, as the truth had always served me well, I
said, giving my father's servant, who looked sleepy, a heavy kick
on the instep:

'This is quite true; a friend of mine *did* jump in at that window,
about a quarter of an hour ago; but' (*looking down with a sweet and
modest smile*) 'he was not a burglar. . . .'

HENRY HILL (*my father's servant*): 'How often I've told you,
miss, that as long as Master Edward loses his latch-keys, there is

nothing to be done and something is bound to happen! One day he will not only lose the latch-key but his life.'

INSPECTOR: 'I'm sorry to have frightened you, madam, I will now take down your names. . . .'

MARGOT (*anxiously*): 'Oh, I see, you have to report it in the police-news, have you? Has the cabman given you his name? He ought to be rewarded, he might have been the means of saving us from a horrible burglary.'

I felt that I could have strangled the cabman, but, collecting myself, took one candle off the writing-table and, blowing the other out, led the way to the library-door, saying slowly:

'Margaret . . . Emma . . . Alice Tennant. Do I have to add my occupation?'

INSPECTOR (*busily writing in a small note-book*): 'No, thank you.' (*Turning to Hill.*) 'Your name, please.'

My father's servant was thoroughly roused and I regretted my kick when in a voice of thunder he said:

'Henry Hastings Appleby Hill.'

I felt quite sure that my father would appear over the top of the stair and then all would be over; but, by the fortune that follows the brave, perfect silence reigned throughout the house. I walked slowly away, while Hill led the three policeman into the hall. When the front door had been barred and bolted, I ran down the back stairs and said, smiling brightly:

'I shall tell my father all about this! You did very well; good night, Hill.'

When the coast was clear, I returned to the library with my heart beating and shut the door. Peter had disentangled himself from the sofa and was taking fluff off his coat with an air of happy disengagement; I told him with emphasis that I was done for, that my name would be ringing in the police-news next day and that I was quite sure by the inspector's face that he knew exactly what had happened; that all this came from Peter's infernal temper, idiotic jealousy and complete want of self-control. Agitated and eloquent, I was good for another ten minutes' abuse; but he interrupted me by saying, in his most caressing manner:

'The inspector is all right, my dear! He is a friend of mine! I wouldn't have missed this for the whole world: you were magnificent! Which shall we reward, the policeman, the cabman, or Hill?'

MARGOT: 'Don't be ridiculous! What do you propose doing?'

PETER (*trying to kiss my hands, which I had purposely put behind my back*): 'I propose having a chat with Inspector Wood and then with Hastings Appleby.'

MARGOT: 'How do you know Inspector Wood, as you call him?'

PETER: 'He did a friend of mine a very good turn once.'

MARGOT: 'What sort of turn?'

PETER: 'Sugar Candy insulted me at the Turf and I was knocking him into a jelly in Brick Street, when Wood intervened and saved his life. I can assure you he would do anything in the world for me and I'll make it all right. He shall have a handsome present.'

MARGOT: 'How vulgar! Having a brawl in Brick Street! How did you come to be in the East End?'

PETER: 'East End! Why, it's next to Down Street, out of Piccadilly!'

MARGOT: 'It's very wrong to bribe the police, Peter!'

PETER: 'I'm not going to bribe him, governess. I'm going to give him my Airedale terrier.'

MARGOT: 'What! That brute that killed the lady's lap-dog?'

PETER: 'The very same!'

MARGOT: 'God help poor Wood!'

Peter was so elated with this shattering escapade that a week after – on the occasion of another row, in which I pointed out that he was the most selfish man in the world – I heard him whistling under my bedroom window at midnight. Afraid lest he should wake my parents, I ran down to open the front door, but nothing would induce the chain to move. It was a newly-acquired habit of the servants started by Henry Hill from the night he had barred out the police. Being a hopeless mechanic and particularly weak in my fingers, I gave it up and went to the open window in the library. I begged him to go away, as nothing would induce me to forgive him, and I told him that my papa had only just retired to bed.

Peter, unmoved, ordered me to take the flower-pots off the window-sill, or he would knock them down and make a horrible noise, which would wake the whole house. After I had refused to do this, he said he would very likely break his neck when he jumped, as clearing the pots would mean hitting his head against the window frame. Fearing an explosion of temper, I weakly removed the flower-pots and watched his acrobatic feat with delight.

We had not been talking on the sofa for more than five minutes when I heard a shuffle of feet outside the library door. I got up with lightning rapidity and put out the two candles on the writing-table with the palms of my hands, returning noiselessly to Peter's side on the sofa, where we sat in black darkness. The door opened and my father came in holding a bedroom candle in his hand; he proceeded to walk stealthily round the room, looking at his pictures. The sofa on which we were sitting was in the window and had nothing behind it but the curtains. He held his candle high and close to every picture in turn and, putting his head forward, scanned them with tenderness and love. I saw Peter's idiotic hat and stick under the Gainsborough and could not resist nudging him as 'The Ladies Erne and Dillon' were slowly approached. A candle held near one's face is the most blinding of all things, and, after inspecting the sloping shoulders and anæmic features of the Gainsborough ladies, my father, quietly humming to himself, returned to his bed.

*   *   *

Things did not always go so smoothly with us. One night Peter suggested that I should walk away with him from the ball and try an American trotter which had been lent to him by a friend. As there was a glorious moon, I thought it might be rather fun, so we walked down Grosvenor Street into Park Lane; and there under a lamp stood the buggy. American trotters always appear to be mis-shapen; they are like coloured prints that are not quite in drawing and have never attracted me.

After we had placed ourselves firmly in the rickety buggy, Peter said to the man as he took the reins:

'Let him go, please!'

And go he did, with a curious rapid, swaying waddle. There was no traffic and we turned into the Edgware Road towards Hendon at a great pace, but Peter was a bad driver and after a little time said his arms ached and he thought it was time the damned horse was made to stop.

179

'I'm told the only way to stop an American trotter,' he said, 'is to hit him over the head.'

At this I took the whip out of the socket and threw it into the road.

Peter, maddened by my action, shoved the reins into my hands, saying he would jump out. I did not take the smallest notice of this threat, but slackened the reins, after which we went quite slowly. I need hardly say Peter did not jump out but suggested with solemnity that we should go back and look for the whip.

This was the last thing I intended to do, so when we turned I leant back in my seat and tugged at the trotter with all my might and we flew home without uttering a single word.

I was a fair whip, but that night had taxed all my powers and, when we pulled up at the corner of Grosvenor Square, I ached in every limb. We were not in the habit of arriving together at the front door; and after he had handed me down to the pavement I felt rather awkward. I had no desire to break the silence, but neither did I want to take away Peter's coat, which I was wearing, so I said tentatively:

'Shall I give you your covert-coat?'

PETER: 'Don't be childish! How can you walk back to the front door in your ball-dress? If anyone happened to be looking out of the window, what would they think?'

This was really more than I could bear. I wrenched off his coat and, placing it firmly on his arm, said:

'Most people, if they are sensible, are asleep at this time of night, but I thank you all the same for your consideration.'

We turned away from each other and I walked home alone. When I reached our front door my father opened it and, seeing me in my white tulle dress, was beside himself with rage. He asked me if I would kindly explain what I was doing, walking in the streets in my ball-dress at two in the morning. I told him exactly what had happened and warned him soothingly never to buy an American trotter; he told me that my reputation was ruined, that his was also and that my behaviour would kill my mother; I put my arms round his neck, told him soothingly that I had not really enjoyed myself *at all* and promised him that I would never do it again.

By this time my mother had come out of her bedroom and was leaning over the staircase in her dressing-gown. She said in a pleading voice:

' Pray do not agitate yourself, Charlie. You've done a very wrong action, Margot! You really ought to have more consideration for your father: no one knows how impressionable he is. . . . Please tell Mr Flower that we do not approve of him at all! . . .'

MARGOT: 'You are absolutely right, dear mama, and that is exactly what I have said to him more than once. But you need not worry, for no one saw us. Let's go to bed, darling, I'm dog-tired!'

*   *   *

Peter was thoroughly inconsequent about money and a great gambler; he told me one day in sorrow that his only chance of economising was to sell his horses and go to India to shoot big game, incidentally escaping his creditors.

When Peter went to India I was very unhappy, but to please my people I told them I would say goodbye and not write to him for a year, a promise which was faithfully kept.

While he was away, a young man of fortune fell in love with me out hunting. He never proposed, he only declared himself. I liked him particularly, but his attentions sat lightly on me; this rather nettled him and he told me one day, riding home in the dark, that he was sure I must be in love with somebody else. I said that it did not at all follow and that, if he were wise, he would stop talking about love and go and buy himself some horses for Leicestershire, where I was going in a week to hunt with Lord Manners. We were staying together at Cholmondeley Castle, in Cheshire, with my friend, Winifred Cholmondeley,[1] then Lady Rocksavage.

My new young man took my advice and went up to London, promising he would lend me 'two of the best that money could buy' to take to Melton, where he proposed shortly to follow me.

When he arrived at Tattersalls there were several studs of well-known horses being sold: Jock Trotters', Sir William Eden's and Lord Lonsdale's. Among the latter was a famous hunter, called Jack Madden, which had once belonged to Peter Flower; and my friend determined he would buy it for me. Someone said to him:

[1] The Marchioness of Cholmondeley.

'I don't advise you to buy that horse, as you won't be able to ride it!'

(The fellow who related this to me added, 'As you know, Miss Tennant, this is the only certain way by which you can sell any horse.')

Another man said:

'I don't agree with you, the horse is all right; when it belonged to Flower I saw Miss Margot going like a bird on it. . . .'

MY FRIEND: 'Did Miss Tennant ride Flower's horses?'

At this the fellow said:

'Why, my dear man, where *have* you lived! . . .'

* * *

Some months after I had ridden Jack Madden and my own horses over High Leicestershire, my friend came to see me and asked me to swear on my Bible oath that I would not give him away over a secret which he intended to tell me.

After I had taken my solemn oath he said:

'Your friend Peter Flower who is in India was going to be put in the bankruptcy court and turned out of every club in London; so I went to Sam Lewis and paid his debt, but I don't want him to know about it, and he never need, unless you tell him.'

MARGOT: 'What does he owe? And whom does he owe it to?'

MY FRIEND: 'He owes ten thousand pounds, but I'm not at liberty to tell you who it's to; he is a friend of mine and a very good fellow. I can assure you that he has waited longer than most people would for Flower to pay him.'

MARGOT: 'Is Peter Flower a friend of yours?'

MY FRIEND: 'I don't know him by sight and have never spoken to him in my life, but he's the man you're in love with and that's enough for me.'

* * *

When the year was up and Peter – for all I knew – was still in India, I had made up my mind that, come what might, I would never, under any circumstances, renew my friendship with him.

That winter I was staying with the Manners's, as usual, and finding myself late for a near meet cut across country. Larking is always a stupid thing to do; horses that have never put a foot wrong generally refuse the smallest fence and rather than upset them at the beginning of the day you end by going through the gate, which you had better have done at first.

I had a mare called Molly Bawn given to me by my former fiancé, who was the finest timber-jumper in Leicestershire, and, seeing the people at the meet watching me as I approached, I could not resist, out of pure swagger, jumping an enormous gate. I thought to myself how disgusted Peter would have been at my vulgarity! But at the same time it put me in good spirits. Something, however, made me turn round; I saw a man behind me, jumping the fence beside my gate; and there was Peter Flower! He was in tearing spirits and told me with eagerness how completely he had turned over a new leaf and never intended doing this, that or the other again, as far the most wonderful thing had happened to him that had ever happened to anyone.

'I'm under a lucky star, Margie! By heavens I am! And the joy of seeing you is *so great* that I won't allude to the gate, or Molly Bawn, or you, or anything ugly! Let us enjoy ourselves for once; and for God's sake don't scold. Are you glad to see me? Let me look at you! Which do you love best, Molly Bawn or me? Don't answer but listen.'

He then proceeded to tell me how his debts had been paid by Sam Lewis – the money-lender – through an unknown benefactor and how he had begged Lewis to tell him who it was, but that he had refused, having taken his oath never to reveal the name. My heart beat and I said a remarkably stupid thing:

'How wonderful! But you'll have to pay him back, Peter, won't you?'

PETER: 'Oh, indeed! Then perhaps you can tell me who it is. . . .'

MARGOT: 'How can I?'

PETER: 'Do you know who it is?'

MARGOT: 'I do not.'

I felt the cock ought to have crowed, but I said nothing; and Peter was so busy greeting his friends that I prayed he had not observed my guilty face.

Some days after this there was a race-meeting at Leicester. Lord Lonsdale took a special at Oakham for the occasion and the Manners's,

Peter and I all went to the races. When I walked into the paddock, I saw my new friend – the owner of Jack Madden – talking to the Prince of Wales. When we joined them, the Prince suggested that we should go and see Mrs Langtry's horse, as it was a great rogue and difficult to mount.

As we approached the Langtry horse, the crowd made way for us and I found my friend next to me; on his other side was Peter Flower and then the Prince. The horse had its eyes bandaged and one of its forelegs was being held by a stable-boy. When the jockey was up and the bandage removed, it jumped into the air and gave an extended and violent buck. I was standing so near that I felt the draught of its kick on my hair. At this my friend gave a slight scream and, putting his arm round me, pulled me back towards him. A miss is as good as a mile, so after thanking him for his protection I chatted cheerfully to the Prince of Wales.

There is nothing so tiring as racing and we all sat in perfect silence going home in the special that evening.

Neither at dinner nor after had I any opportunity of speaking to Peter, but I observed a singularly impassive expression on his face. The next day – being Sunday – I asked him to go round the stables with me after church; he refused, so I went alone. After dinner I tried again to talk to him, but he would not answer; he did not look angry, but he appeared to be profoundly sad, which depressed me. He told Hoppy Manners he was not going to hunt that week as he feared he would have to be in London. My heart sank. We all went to our rooms early and Peter remained downstairs reading. As he never read in winter I knew there was something seriously wrong, so I went down in my tea-gown to see him. The room was empty and we were alone. He never looked up.

MARGOT: 'Peter, you've not spoken to me once since the races. What can have happened?'

PETER: 'I would rather you left me, *please*. . . . Pray go back to your room.'

MARGOT (*sitting on the sofa beside him*): 'Won't you speak to me and tell me all about it?'

Peter put down his book and, looking at me steadily, said very slowly:

'I'd rather not speak to a liar!'

I stood up as if I had been shot and said:

'How dare you say such a thing!'

PETER: 'You lied to me.'

MARGOT: 'When?'

PETER: 'You know perfectly well! And you are in love! You know you are. Will you deny it?'

'Oh! It's this that worries you, is it?' said I sweetly. 'What would you say if I told you I was *not*?'

PETER: 'I would say you were lying again.'

MARGOT: 'Have I ever lied to you, Peter?'

PETER: 'How can I tell?' (*shrugging his shoulders*). 'You have lied twice, so I presume since I've been away you've got into the habit of it.'

MARGOT: 'Peter!'

PETER: 'A man doesn't scream and put his arm round a woman, as D——ly did at the races today, unless he is in love. Will you tell me who paid my debt, please?'

MARGOT: 'No, I won't.'

PETER: 'Was it D——ly?'

MARGOT: 'I shan't tell you. I'm not Sam Lewis; and, since I'm such a liar, is it worth while asking me these stupid questions?'

PETER: 'Ah, Margot, this is the worst blow of my life! I see you are deceiving me. I know who paid now.'

MARGOT: 'Then why ask *me*? . . .'

PETER: 'When I went to India I had never spoken to D——ly in my life. Why should he have paid my debts for me? You had much better tell me the simple truth and get it over: it's all settled and you're going to marry him.'

MARGOT: 'Since I've got into the way of lying, you might spare yourself and me these vulgar questions.'

PETER (*seizing my hands in anguish*): 'Say you aren't going to marry him . . . tell me, tell me it's *not* true!'

MARGOT: 'Why should I? He has never asked me to.'

*   *   *

After this the question of matrimony was bound to come up between us. The first time it was talked of, I was filled with anxiety. It seemed to put a finish to the radiance of our friendship and, worse than that, it brought me up against my father, who had often said to me:

'You will never marry Flower, you must marry your superior.'

Peter himself, in a subconscious way, had become aware of the situation. One evening, riding home, he said:

'Margie, do you see that?'

He pointed to the spire of the Melton church and added:

'That is what you are in my life. I am not worth the button on your boot!'

To which I replied:

'You must not say that, but I cannot find goodness for two.'

I was profoundly unhappy. To live for ever with a man who was incapable of loving anyone but himself and me, a man without any kind of moral ambition and chronically indifferent to politics and religion, was a nightmare.

'I will marry you,' I said, 'if you get some serious occupation, Peter, but I won't marry an idle man; you think of nothing but yourself and me.'

PETER: 'What in the name of goodness would you have me think of? Geography?'

MARGOT: 'You know exactly what I mean. Your power lies in love-making, not in loving; you don't love anyone but yourself.'

At this, Peter moved away from me as if I had struck him and said in a low, tense voice:

'I am glad I did not say that. I would not care to have said such a cat-cruel thing; but I pity the man who marries you! He will think – as I did – that you are impulsively warm, kind and gentle; and he will find that he has married a governess and a prig; and a woman whose fire – of which she boasts so much – blasts his soul.'

I listened to a Peter I had never heard before. His face frightened me. It indicated suffering. I put my head against his and said:

'How can I make an honest man of you, my dearest?'

*   *   *

I was getting quite clever about people, as the Mrs Bo episode had taught me a lot.

A short time after this conversation, I observed a dark, good-looking woman pursuing Peter Flower at every ball and party. He told me when I teased him that she failed to arrest his attention and that, for the first time in my life, I flattered him by my jealousy. I persisted and said that I did not know if it was jealousy but that I was convinced she was a bad friend for him.

PETER: 'I've always noticed you think things bad when they don't suit you, but why should I give up my life to you? What do you give me in return? I'm the laughing-stock of London! But, if it is any satisfaction to you, I will tell you I don't care for the black lady, as you call her, and I never see her except at parties.'

I knew Peter as well as a cat knows its way in the dark and I felt the truth of his remark: what did I give him? But I was not in a humour to argue.

The lady often asked me to go and see her, but I shrank from it and had never been inside her house.

One day I told Peter I would meet him at the Soane Collection in Lincoln's Inn Fields. To my surprise he said he had engaged himself to see his sister, who had been ill, and pointed out with a laugh that my governessing was taking root. He added:

'I don't mind giving it up if you can spend the whole afternoon with me.'

I told him I would not have him give up going to see his sister for the world.

Finding myself at a loose end, I thought I would pay a visit to the black lady, as it was unworthy of me to have such a prejudice against someone I did not know. It was a hot London day; pale colours, thin stuffs, naked throats and large hats were strewn about the parks and streets.

When I arrived, the lady's bell was answered by a hall-boy and, hearing the piano, I told him he need not announce me. When I opened the door, I saw Peter and the dark lady sharing the same seat in front of the open piano. She wore a black satin sleeveless tea-gown, cut low at the throat, with a coral ribbon round her waist, and she had stuck a white rose in her rather dishevelled Carmen hair. I stood still, startled by her beauty and stunned by Peter's face. She got up charmed to see me and expressed her joy at the amazing luck which had brought me there that very afternoon, as she had a wonderful Spaniard coming to play to her after tea and she had often been told by Peter how musical I was, etc., etc. She hoped I was not shocked by her appearance, but she had just come back from a studio and it was too hot to expect people to get into decent clothes. She was perfectly at her ease and more than welcoming; before I could answer, she rallied Peter and said she pleaded guilty to having lured him away from the path of duty that afternoon, ending with a slight twinkle:

'From what I'm told, Miss Margot, you would *never* have done anything so wicked? . . .'

I felt ice in my blood and said:

'You needn't believe that! I've lured him away from the path of duty for years, haven't I, Peter?'

There was an uncomfortable silence and I looked about for a means of escape, but it took me some little time to find one. I said goodbye and left the house.

When I was alone, I locked the door, flung myself on my sofa, and was blinded by tears. Peter was right; he had said, 'Why should I give up my life to you?' Why indeed! And yet, after so many years, this seemed a terrible ending to me.

'What do you give me in return?' What indeed? What claim had I to his fidelity? I thought I was giving gold for silver, but the dark lady would have called it copper for gold. Was she prepared to give everything for nothing? Why should I call it nothing? What did I know of Peter's love for her? All I knew was she had taught him to lie; and he must love her very much to do that: he had never lied to me before.

I went to the opera that night with my father and mother. Peter came into our box in a state of intense misery; I could hardly look at him. He put out his hand towards me under the programme and I took it. At that moment the servant brought me a note and asked me to give her the answer. I opened it and this was what I read:

'If you want to do a very kind thing come and see me after the opera tonight. Don't say no.'

I showed it to Peter, and he said, 'Go'. It was from the dark

lady; I asked him what she wanted me for and he said she was
terribly unhappy.

'Ah, Peter,' said I, 'what *have* you done? . . .'

PETER: 'I know . . . it's quite true; but I've broken it off for
ever with her.'

Nothing he could have said then would have lightened my heart.
I scribbled 'Yes' on the same paper and gave it back to the girl.

When I said good night to my mother after the opera, I told her
where I was going. Peter was standing in the front hall and took me
in a hansom to the lady's house, saying he would wait for me.

It was past midnight and I felt overpoweringly tired. My beautiful
rival opened the front door to me and I followed her silently up
to her bedroom. She took off my opera-cloak and we sat down
facing each other. The room was large and dark but for a row of
candles on the mantelpiece and two high church-lights each side of a
silver pier-glass. There was a table near my chair with odds and ends
on it and a general smell of scent and flowers. I looked at her in her
blue satin night-gown and saw that she had been crying.

'It is kind of you to have come,' she said, 'and I daresay you
know why I wanted to see you tonight.'

MARGOT: 'No, I don't; I haven't the faintest idea!'

THE LADY (*looking rather embarrassed, but after a moment's pause*):
'I want you to tell me about yourself.'

I felt this to be a wrong entry: she had sent for me to tell her
about Peter Flower and not myself; but why should I tell her about
either of us? I had never spoken of my love-affairs excepting to my
mother and my three friends – Con Manners, Frances Horner, and
Etty Desborough – and people had ceased speaking to me about
them; why should I sit up with a stranger and discuss myself at this
time of night? I said there was nothing to tell. She answered by
saying she had met so many people who cared for me that she felt
she almost knew me, to which I replied:

'In that case, why talk about me?'

THE LADY: 'But some people care for both of us.'

MARGOT (*rather coldly*): 'I daresay.'

THE LADY: 'Don't be hard, I want to know if you love Peter
Flower. . . . Do you intend to marry him?'

The question had come then: this terrible question which my mother had never asked and which I had always evaded! Had it got to be answered now . . . and to a stranger?

With a determined effort to control myself, I said:

'You mean, am I engaged to be married?'

THE LADY: 'I mean what I say; are you going to marry Peter?'

MARGOT: 'I have never told him I would.'

THE LADY (*very slowly*): 'Remember, my life is bound up in your answer. . . .'

Her words seemed to burn, and I felt a kind of pity for her. She was leaning forward with her eyes fastened on mine and her hands clasped between her knees.

'If you don't love him enough to marry him, why don't you leave him alone?' she said. 'Why do you keep him bound to you? Why don't you set him free?'

MARGOT: 'He is free to love who he likes; I don't keep him, but I won't share him.'

THE LADY: 'You don't love him, but you want to keep him; that is pure selfishness and vanity.'

MARGOT: 'Not at all! I would give him up tomorrow and have told him so a thousand times, if he would marry; but he is not in a position to marry anyone.'

THE LADY: 'How can you say such a thing! His debts have just been paid by God knows who – some woman, I suppose! – and you are rich yourself. What is there to hinder you from marrying him?'

MARGOT: 'That was not what I was thinking about. I don't believe you would understand even if I were to explain it to you.'

THE LADY: 'If you were really in love you could not be so critical and censorious.'

MARGOT: 'Oh yes, I could! You don't know me.'

THE LADY: 'I love him in a way you would never understand. There is nothing in the world I would not do for him! No pain I would not suffer and no sacrifice I would not make.'

MARGOT: 'What could you do for him that would help him?'

THE LADY: 'I would leave my husband and my children and go right away with him.'

I felt as if she had stabbed me.

'Leave your children! And your husband!' I said. 'But how can ruining them and yourself help Peter Flower? I don't believe for a moment he would ever do anything so vile.'

THE LADY: 'You think he loves you too much to run away with me, do you?'

MARGOT (*with indignation*): 'Perhaps I hope he cares too much for *you*.'

THE LADY (*not listening and getting up excitedly*): 'What do you know about love? I have had a hundred lovers, but Peter Flower is the only man I have ever really cared for; and my life is at an end if you will not give him up.'

MARGOT: 'There is no question of my giving him up; he is free, I tell you. . . .'

THE LADY: 'I tell you he is not! He doesn't *consider* himself free, he said as much to me this afternoon . . . when he wanted to break it all off.'

MARGOT: 'What do you wish me to do then? . . .'

THE LADY: 'Tell Peter you don't love him in the right way, that you don't intend to marry him; and then leave him alone.'

MARGOT: 'Do you mean I am to leave him to you? . . . Do *you* love him in the right way?'

THE LADY: 'Don't ask stupid questions. . . . I shall kill myself if he gives me up.'

After this, I felt there was nothing more to be said. I told her that Peter had a perfect right to do what he liked, and that I had neither the will nor the power to influence his decision; that I was going abroad with my sister Lucy to Italy and would in any case not see him for several weeks; but I added that all my influence over him for years had been directed into making him the right sort of man to marry and that all hers would of necessity lie in the opposite direction. Not knowing quite how to say goodbye, I began to finger my cloak; seeing my intention, she said:

'Just wait one moment, will you? I want to know if you are as good as Peter always tells me you are; don't answer till I see your eyes. . . .'

She took two candles off the chimney-piece and placed them on the table near me, a little in front of my face, and then knelt upon the ground; I looked at her wonderful wild eyes and stretched out my hands towards her.

'Nonsense!' I said. 'I am not in the least good! Get up! When I see you kneeling at my feet, I feel sorry for you.'

THE LADY (*getting up abruptly*): 'For God's sake don't pity me!'

*   *   *

Thinking the situation over in the calm of my room, I had no qualms as to either the elopement or the suicide, but I felt a revulsion of feeling towards Peter. His lack of moral indignation and purpose and his incapacity to improve had been cutting a deep though unconscious division between us; and I determined at whatever cost, after this, that I would say goodbye to him.

A few days later, Lord Dufferin came to see me in Grosvenor Square.

'Margot,' he said, 'why don't you marry? You are twenty-seven; and life won't go on treating you so well if you go on treating it like this. As an old friend who loves you, let me give you one word of advice. You should marry in spite of being in love, but never because of it.'

Before I went away to Italy, Peter and I had said goodbye to each other for ever.

The relief of our friends at our parting was so suffocating that I clung to the shelter of a stranger.

XII · *My Husband*

I first met my husband at a dinner given by Peter Flower's brother Cyril[1] in 1891. I had never heard of him, which gives some indication of how much I was wasting my time. When I was not hunting or entertaining or being entertained by my intellectual and social friends I went through a short period of stage fever and was at the feet of Ellen Terry and Irving: I say 'short' advisedly, for then, as now, I found Bohemian society duller than any English wateringplace. Everyone probably has a different idea of hell and few of us connect it with flames, but stage suppers in a mild way have brought me punishment and, with a few classical exceptions – Irving and Ellen Terry, Irene Vanbrugh, Sir Gerald du Maurier and the Beerbohm Tree family – I have seldom met the hero or heroine off the stage that was not ultimately dull.

The dinner where I was introduced to my husband was in the House of Commons and I sat next to him. I was deeply impressed by his conversation and his clear Cromwellian face. I thought then, as I do now, he had a way of putting you not only at your ease but at your best when talking to him which is given to few men of note. He was different to the others and, although unfashionably dressed, had so much personality that I made up my mind at once that this was the man who could help me and who would understand everything.

After dinner we all walked on the Terrace and I was flattered to find my new friend at my side. Lord Battersea chaffed me in his noisy and flamboyant manner, trying to separate us, but with tact and determination his frontal attack was resisted and my new friend

[1] Lord Battersea.

and I retired to the darkest part of the Terrace where, leaning over the parapet, we gazed into the river and talked far into the night.

Our host and his party – thinking that I had gone home and that Mr Asquith had returned to the House when the division bell rang – had disappeared; and when we finished our conversation the Terrace was deserted and the sky light.

It never occurred to me that he was married, nor would that have affected me in any way. I had always been more anxious that Peter Flower should marry than myself, because he was thirteen years older than I was, but matrimony had not been the austere purpose of either of our lives.

Mr Asquith and I met a few days later dining with Sir Algernon West – and after this we saw each other constantly. I found out from something he said to me that he was married and lived at Hampstead and that his days were divided between 1 Paper Buildings and the House of Commons. He told me that he had always been a shy man and in some ways that is true of him even now; but I am glad that I did not observe it at the time, as shy people disconcerted me: I liked modesty, I pitied timidity, but I was embarrassed by shyness.

I cannot truly say, however, that the word shy described my husband at any time: he was a little *gauche* in movement and blushed when he was praised, but I have never seen him nervous or embarrassed by any social dilemma. His unerring instinct into all sorts of people and affairs – quite apart from his intellectual temperament and learning – and his incredible lack of vanity struck me at once. (He retains to this day an incurable modesty.)

When I discovered that he was married, I asked him to bring his wife to dinner, which he did, and directly I saw her I said:

'I do hope, Mrs Asquith, you have not minded your husband dining here without you, but I rather gathered Hampstead was too far away for him to get back to you from the House of Commons. You must always let me know and come with him whenever it suits you.'

*   *   *

My husband's father was Joseph Dixon Asquith, a cloth-merchant in Morley, at the time a small town outside Leeds. He was a man of high character, who held Bible classes for young men. He married a daughter of William Willans, of Huddersfield, who sprang of an old Yorkshire Puritan stock.

He died when he was thirty-five, leaving four children: William Willans, Herbert Henry, Emily Evelyn and Lilian Josephine. They were brought up by their mother, who was a woman of genius. I named my only daughter after Goethe's mother, but was glad when I found out that her grandmother Willans had been called Elizabeth.

William Willans – who is dead – was the eldest of the family and a clever little man. He taught at Clifton College for over thirty years.

Lilian Josephine died when she was a baby; and Evelyn – one of the best of women – is the only near relation of my husband still living.

My husband's mother, old Mrs Asquith, I never knew; my friend Mark Napier told me that she was a brilliantly clever woman but an invalid.

Her delicate lungs obliged her to live on the South coast; and, when her two sons went to the City of London School, they lived alone together in lodgings in Islington. The cost of their education and maintenance in London was generously met by their mother's brothers, the Willanses.

Although Henry's mother was an invalid she had a moral, religious and intellectual influence over her family that cannot be exaggerated. She was a profound reader and a brilliant talker and belonged to what was in those days called orthodox nonconformity, or Congregationalism.

After my husband's first marriage he made money by writing, lecturing and examining at Oxford. When he was called to the Bar success did not come to him at once.

He had no rich patron and no one to push him forward. He had made for himself a great Oxford reputation: he was a fine scholar and lawyer, but socially was not known by many people.

He first came into prominence when he devilled at Lord James of Hereford's request the Bradlaugh case for Mr Gladstone's speech.

In making this profound and attaching friendship with the stranger of that House of Commons dinner, I had placed myself in a difficult position when Helen Asquith died. To be a stepwife and a stepmother was unthinkable, but the moment had arrived when a decision – involving a complete change in my life – had become inevitable. I had written to Peter Flower before we parted every day – with the exception of the months he had spent flying from his creditors in India – and I had prayed for him every night, but it had not brought more than happiness to both of us and when I deliberately said goodbye to him I shut down a page of my life which, even if I had wished to, I could never have reopened. When Henry told me he cared for me, that unstifled inner voice which we all of us hear more or less distinctly told me I would be untrue to myself and quite unworthy of life if, when such a man came knocking at the door, I did not fling it wide open.

The rumour that we were engaged to be married caused alarm amounting to consternation in certain circles. Both Lord Rosebery and Lord Randolph Churchill, without impugning me in any way, deplored the marriage, nor were they alone in thinking such a union might ruin the life of a promising politician. Some of my own friends were equally apprehensive from another point of view: to start my new life charged with a ready-made family of children brought up differently from myself, with a man who played no games and cared for no sport, in London instead of in the country, with no money except what he could make at the Bar, was, they thought, taking too many risks.

My Melton friends said it was a terrible waste that I was not marrying a sporting man and told me afterwards that they nearly signed a round-robin to implore me never to give up hunting, but feared I might think it impertinent.

The rumour of my engagement caused a sensation in the East End of London as well as the West. The following was posted to me by an anonymous well-wisher:

'At the meeting of the "unemployed" held on Tower Hill yesterday afternoon, John E. Williams, the organiser appointed by the Social Democratic Federation, said that on the previous day they had gone through the West End squares and had let the "loafers" living there know that they were alive. On the previous evening he had seen an announcement which, at first sight, had caused tears to run down his face, for he had thought it read, "Mr Asquith going to be murdered". However, it turned out that Mr Asquith was going to be married, and he accordingly proposed that the unemployed, following the example of the people in the West End, should forward the right hon. gentleman a congratulatory message. He moved: "That this mass meeting of the unemployed held on Tower Hill, hearing that Mr Asquith is about to enter the holy bonds of matrimony, and knowing he has no sympathy for the unemployed, and that he has lately used his position in the House of Commons to insult the unemployed, trusts that his partner will be one of the worst tartars it is possible for a man to have, and that his family troubles will compel him to retire from political life, for which he is so unfit." The reader of the resolution was followed by loud laughter and cheers. Mr Crouch (National Union of Boot and Shoe Operatives) seconded the motion, which was supported by a large number of other speakers and adopted.'

I was more afraid of spoiling Henry's life than my own and, what with old ties and bothers and new ties and stepchildren, I deliberated a long time before the final fixing of my wedding-day.

I had never met any of his children except little Violet when I became engaged and he only took me to see them once before we were married, as they lived in the country, at Redhill, under the charge of a kind and careful governess; he never spoke of them except one day when, after my asking him if he thought they would hate me and cataloguing my grave imperfections and moderate qualifications for the part, he stopped me and said that his eldest son, Raymond, was remarkably clever and would be devoted to me, adding thoughtfully:

'I think – and hope – he is ambitious.'

This was a new idea to me: we had always been told what a wicked thing ambition was; but we were a fighting family of high spirits and hot temper, so we had acquiesced, without conforming to the nursery teaching. The remark profoundly impressed me and I pondered it over in my heart. I do not think, by the way, that it turned out to be a true prophecy, but Raymond Asquith had such unusual intellectual gifts that no one could have convicted him of lack of ambition. To win without work, to score without effort and to delight without premeditation is given to few.

One night after our engagement we were dining with Sir Henry and Lady Campbell-Bannerman. While the women were talking and the men drinking, dear old Mrs Gladstone and other political wives took me on as to the duties of the spouse of a possible Prime Minister; they were so eloquent and severe that at the end of it my nerves were racing round like a squirrel in a cage.

When Mr Gladstone came into the drawing-room I felt depressed and, clinging to his arm, I switched him into a corner and said I feared the ladies took me for a jockey or a ballet-girl, as I had been adjured to give up, among other things, dancing, riding and acting. He patted my hand, said he knew no one better fitted to be the wife of a great politician than myself and ended by saying that, while I was entitled to disregard exaggeration in rebuke, it was a great mistake not to take criticism wisely and in a spirit which might turn it to good account.

I have often thought of this when I see how brittle and egotistical people are at the smallest disapprobation. I never get over my surprise, old as I am, at the surly moral manners, the lack of humbleness and the colossal personal vanity that are the bed-rock of people's incapacity to take criticism well. There is no greater test of size than this; but, judged by this test, most of us are dwarfs.

*   *   *

Disapproving of long engagements and wishing to escape the cataract of advice by which my friends thought to secure both my husband's and my own matrimonial bliss, I hurried matters on and, in spite of the anxiety of friends and relations, we were married at St George's, Hanover Square, on 10th May 1894. From Grosvenor Square to St George's is a short distance, but from our front door to the church the pavements were blocked with excited and enthusiastic people.

An old nurse of my sister Charlotte – and later of my own – Jerusha Taylor, told me that a gentleman outside St George's had said to her, 'I will give you £10 for that ticket of yours!' and when she refused he said, 'I will give you *anything you like!* I must see Margot Tennant married!' I asked her what sort of a man he was. She answered:

'Oh, he was a real gentleman, ma'am! I know a gentleman when I see him: he had a gardenia in his buttonhole, but he didn't get my ticket!'

Our register was signed by four Prime Ministers: Mr Gladstone, Lord Rosebery, Mr Balfour and my husband.

We spent the first part of our honeymoon at Mells Park, Frome, lent to us by Sir John and Lady Horner, and the second at Clovelly Court with our friend and hostess, Mrs Hamlyn.

XIII · *The Asquith Family*

———◦◦◦———

I do not think if you had ransacked the world you could have found natures so opposite in temper, temperament and outlook as myself and my stepchildren when I first knew them.

If there was a difference between the Tennants and Lytteltons of laughter, there was a difference between the Tennants and Asquiths of tears. Tennants believed in appealing to the hearts of men, firing their imagination and penetrating and vivifying their inmost lives. They had a little loose love to give to the whole world. The Asquiths – without mental flurry and with perfect self-mastery – believed in the free application of intellect to every human emotion; no event could have given heightened expression to their feelings. Shy, self-engaged, critical and controversial, nothing surprised them and nothing upset them. We were as zealous and vital as they were detached, and as cocky and passionate as they were modest and emotionless.

They rarely looked at you and never got up when anyone came into the room. If you had appeared downstairs in a ball-dress or a bathing-gown they would not have observed it and would certainly never have commented upon it if they had. Whether they were glowing with joy at the sight of you, or thrilled at receiving a friend, their welcome was equally composed. They were devoted to one another and never quarrelled; they were seldom wild and never naughty. Perfectly self-contained, truthful and deliberate, I never saw them lose themselves in my life and I have hardly ever seen the saint or hero that excited their disinterested emotion.

When I thought of the storms of revolt, the rage, the despair, the wild enthusiasms and reckless adventures of our nursery and schoolroom, I was stunned by the steadiness of the Asquith temper.

Let it not be inferred that I am criticizing them as they now are, or that their attitude towards myself was at any time lacking in sympathy. Blindness of heart does not imply hardness; and expression is a matter of temperament or impulse; but it was their attitude towards life that was different from my own. They overvalued brains, which was a strange fault, as they were all remarkably clever.

Hardly any Prime Minister has had famous children, but the Asquiths were all conspicuous in their different ways: Raymond and Violet the most striking, Arthur the most capable, Herbert a poet and Cyril the shyest and the rarest.

*   *   *

Cys Asquith, who was the youngest of the family, combined what was best in all of them morally and intellectually and possessed what was finer than brains.

He was two, when his mother died, and a clumsy, ugly little boy with a certain amount of graceless obstinacy, with which both Tennants and Asquiths were equally endowed. To the casual observer he would have appeared less like me than any of my step-family, but as a matter of fact he and I had the most in common; we shared a certain spiritual foundation and moral aspiration that solder people together through life.

It is not because I took charge of him at an early age that I say he was more my own than the others, but because, although he did not always agree with me, he never misunderstood me. He said at Mürren one day, when he was seventeen and we had been talking together on life and religion:

'It must be curious for you, Margot, seeing all of us laughing at things that make you cry.'

This showed remarkable insight for a schoolboy. When I look at his wonderful face now and think of his appearance at the time of our marriage, I am reminded of the Hans Andersen toad with the jewel in its head, but the toad is no longer there.

I have a friend called Bogie Harris, who told me that, at a ball given by Con and Hoppy Manners, he had seen a young man whose face had struck him so much that he looked about for someone in the room to tell him who it was. That young man was Cyril Asquith.

* * *

My stepdaughter Violet – now Lady Bonham Carter – though intensely feminine, would have made a remarkable man. I do not believe there is any examination she could not have passed either at a public school or university. Born without shyness or trepidation, from her youth upwards she had perfect self-possession and patience. She loved dialectics and could put her case logically, plausibly and eloquently; and, although quite as unemotional as her brothers, she had more enterprise and indignation. In her youth she was delicate and what the French call *trés personnelle*; and this prevented her going through the mill of rivalry and criticism which had been the daily bread of my girlhood.

She had the same penetrating sense of humour as her brother Raymond and quite as much presence of mind in retort. Her gift of expression was amazing and her memory unrivalled. My daughter Elizabeth and she were the only girls except myself that I ever met who were real politicians, not interested merely in the personal side – whether Mr B. or C. spoke well or was likely to get promoted – but in the legislation and administration of Parliament; they followed and knew what was going on at home and abroad and enjoyed friendships with most of the young and famous men of the day. Violet Bonham Carter has, I think, a great political future in the country if not in the Commons. She is a natural speaker, easy, eloquent, witty, short and of imperturbable *sang-froid*.

Life in the House is neither healthy, useful nor appropriate for a woman; and the functions of a mother and a member are not compatible. This was one of the reasons why my husband and I were against giving the franchise to women. Violet is a real mother and feels the problem acutely, but she is a real Liberal also and, with gifts as conspicuous as hers, she must inevitably exercise wide political influence. Her speeches in her father's election at Paisley, in February 1919, brought her before a general as well as intellectual audience from which she can never retire; and, whenever she appears on a platform, the public shout from every part of the hall calling upon her to speak.

*   *   *

Raymond Asquith was born on 6th November 1878, and was killed fighting against the Germans before his regiment had been in action ten minutes, on 15th September 1916.

He was intellectually one of the most distinguished young men of his day and beautiful to look at, added to which he was light in hand, brilliant in answer and interested in affairs. When he went to Balliol he cultivated a kind of cynicism which was an endless source of delight to the young people around him; in a good-humoured way he made a butt of God and smiled at man. If he had been really keen about any one thing – law or literature – he would have made the world ring with his name, but he lacked temperament and a certain sort of imagination and was without ambition of any kind.

His education was started by Miss Case, a clever woman who kept a day-school at Hampstead; from there he took a Winchester scholarship and he became a scholar of Balliol. At Oxford he went from triumph to triumph. He took a first in classical moderations in 1899; first-class *literæ humaniores* in 1901; first class jurisprudence in 1902. He won the Craven, Ireland, Derby and Eldon scholarships. He was President of the Union and became a Fellow of All Souls in 1902; and after he left Oxford he was called to the Bar in 1904.

In spite of this record, a more modest fellow about his own achievements never lived.

One day when he was at home for his holidays and we were all having tea together, to amuse the children I began asking riddles. I told them that I had only guessed one in my life, but it had taken me three days. They asked me what it was, and I said:

'What is it that God has never seen, that kings see seldom and that we see every day?'

Raymond instantly answered:

'A joke.'

I felt that the real answer, which was 'an equal', was very tepid after this.

Raymond was charming and good-tempered from his boyhood

and I only remember him once in his life getting angry with me. He had been urged by both his wife and his father to go into politics and had been invited by the Liberal Association of a northern town to become their candidate. He was saying that standing for Parliament, from what he saw of his friends' constituencies, involved meeting many boring people, although his own promised to be an exception. I told him that I thought closer contact with ordinary people would be the making of him. At this he flared up and made me appear infinitely ridiculous, to the delight of his listeners, who were always stirred to a high pitch of enthusiasm by his arctic analysis of what he called 'cant'. But, in spite of these differences, we never got on each other's nerves and I found myself constantly, if rather wistfully, wondering in what way I could best serve him.

In 1907 he married from 10 Downing Street Katherine Horner, a beautiful creature of character and intellect, as free from illusion as himself. Humble by nature and exalted by love, her life with him and their mutual happiness was a perpetual joy to me; I felt in a vague way that I had contributed to it: Katherine was the daughter of Laura's great friend, my beloved Lady Horner.

Raymond found in both his mother-in-law and Sir John Horner friends capable of appreciating his fine flavour. He wrote with ease both prose and poetry. I will quote two of his poems:

IN PRAISE OF YOUNG GIRLS

Attend, my Muse, and, if you can, approve
While I proclaim the 'speeding' up of Love;
For Love and Commerce hold a common creed –
The scale of business varies with the speed;
For Queen of Beauty or for Sausage King
The Customer is always on the wing –
Then praise the nymph who regularly earns
Small profits (if you please) but quick returns.
Our modish Venus is a bustling minx,
But who can spare the time to woo a Sphinx?
When Mona Lisa posed with rustic guile
The stale enigma of her simple smile,
Her leisured lovers raised a pious cheer

While the slow mischief crept from ear to ear.
Poor listless Lombard, you would ne'er engage
The brisker beaux of our mercurial age
Whose lively mettle can as easy brook
An epic poem as a lingering look –
Our modern maiden smears the twig with lime
For twice as many hearts in half the time.
Long ere the circle of the staid grimace
Has wheeled your weary dimples into place,
Our little Chloe (mark the nimble fiend!)
Has raised a laugh against her bosom friend,
Melted a marquis, mollified a Jew,
Kissed every member of the Eton crew,
Ogled a Bishop, quizzed an aged peer,
Has danced a Tango and has dropped a tear.
Fresh from the schoolroom, pink and plump and pert,
Bedizened, bouncing, artful and alert,
No victim she of vapours and of moods
Though the sky fall she's 'ready with the goods' –
Will suit each client, tickle every taste
Polite or gothic, libertine or chaste,
Supply a waspish tongue, a waspish waist.
Astarte's breast or Atalanta's leg,
Love ready-made or glamour off the peg –
Do you prefer 'a thing of dew and air'?
Or is your type Poppæa or Polaire?
The crystal casket of a maiden's dreams,
Or the last fancy in cosmetic creams?
The dark and tender or the fierce and bright,
Youth's rosy blush or Passion's pearly bite?
You hardly know perhaps; but Chloe knows,
And pours you out the necessary dose,
Meticulously measuring to scale,
The cup of Circe or the Holy Grail –
An actress she at home in every rôle,
Can flout or flatter, bully or cajole,
And on occasion by a stretch of art

Can even speak the language of the heart,
Can lisp and sigh and make confused replies,
With baby lips and complicated eyes,
Indifferently apt to weep or wink,
Primly pursue, provocatively shrink,
Brazen or bashful, as the case require,
Coax the faint baron, curb the bold esquire,
Deride restraint, but deprecate desire,
Unbridled yet unloving, loose but limp,
Voluptuary, virgin, prude and pimp.

LINES TO A YOUNG VISCOUNT, WHO DIED AT OXFORD,
ON THE MORROW OF A BUMP SUPPER

Dear Viscount, in whose ancient blood
        The blueness of the bird of March,
        The vermeil of the tufted larch,
Are fused in one magenta flood.

Dear Viscount – ah! to me how dear,
        Who even in thy frolic mood
        Discerned (or sometimes thought I could)
The pure proud purpose of a peer!

So on the last sad night of all
        Erect among the reeling rout
        You beat your tangled music out
Lofty, aloof, viscontial.

You struck a footbath with a can,
        And with the can you struck the bath.
        There on the yellow gravel path,
As gentleman to gentleman.

We met, we stood, we faced, we talked
        While those of baser birth withdrew;
        I told you of an Earl I knew;
You said you thought the wine was corked;

206

And so we parted – on my lips
    A light farewell, but in my soul
    The image of a perfect whole,
A Viscount to the finger tips –

An image – Yes; but thou art gone;
    For nature red in tooth and claw
    Subsumes under an equal law
Viscount and Iguanodon.

Yet we who know the Larger Love,
    Which separates the sheep and goats
    And segregates Scolecobrots,[1]
Believing where we cannot prove,

Deem that in His mysterious Day
    God puts the Peers upon His right,
    And hides the poor in endless night,
For thou, my Lord, art more than they.

It is a commonplace to say after a man is dead that he could have done anything he liked in life and often an exaggeration; but of Raymond Asquith the phrase would have been true.

His oldest friend was Harold Baker,[1] a man whose academic career was as fine as his own and whose changeless affection and intimacy we have long valued; but Raymond had many friends as well as admirers. His death was the first great sorrow that occurred in my stepchildren's lives after I married and an anguish to his father and me. My husband's natural pride and interest in him had always been intense and we were never tired of discussing him when we were alone: his personal charm and wit, his little faults and above all the success which so certainly awaited him. Henry's grief darkened the waters in Downing Street at a time when, had they been clear, certain events could never have taken place.

When Raymond was dying on the battle-field he gave the doctor

[1] A word from the Greek Testament meaning people who are eaten by worms.
[2] The Right Hon. Harold Baker.

his flask to give to his father; it was placed by the side of his bed and never moved till he left Whitehall.

I had not realized before how powerless a stepwife is when her husband is mourning the death of his child; and not for the first time I profoundly wished that Raymond had been my son.

*   *   *

Our second son, Herbert, began his career as a lawyer. He had a sweet and gentle nature and much originality. He was a poet and wrote the following some years before the Great War of 1914, through which he served from first day to the last:

THE VOLUNTEER[1]

Here lies a clerk who half his life had spent
Toiling at ledgers in a city grey,
Thinking that so his days would drift away
With no lance broken in life's tournament;
Yet ever 'twixt the book and his bright eyes
The gleaming eagles of the legions came,
And horsemen, charging under phantom skies,
Went thundering past beneath the oriflamme.

And now those waiting dreams are satisfied,
From twilight to the halls of dawn he went;
His lance is broken — but he lies content
With that high hour, in which he lived and died.
And falling thus, he wants no recompense
Who found his battle in the last resort,
Nor needs he any hearse to bear him hence
Who goes to join the men at Agincourt.

'Beb', as we called him, married Lady Cynthia Charteris, a lovely niece of Lady de Vesci and daughter of my friend Lady Wemyss.

*   *   *

Our third son, Arthur Asquith, was one of the great soldiers of the war. He married Betty, the daughter of my greatest friend Lady

[1] Reprinted from *The Volunteer and other Poems*, by kind permission of Messrs Sidgwick & Jackson.

Manners – a woman who has never failed me in affection and loyalty.

Arthur Asquith joined the Royal Naval Division on its formation in September 1914, and was attached at first to the 'Anson' and during the greater part of his service to the 'Hood' Battalion. In the early days of October 1914, he took part in the operations at Antwerp and, after further training at home in the camp at Blandford, went in February 1915, with his battalion to the Dardanelles, where they formed part of the Second Naval Brigade. He was in all the fighting on the Gallipoli peninsula and was wounded, but returned to duty and was one of the last to embark on the final evacuation of Helles, in January 1916.

In the following May the Naval Division joined the army in France, becoming the 63rd Division, and the 'Hood' Battalion (now commanded by Commander Freyberg, V.C.) formed part of the 189th Brigade.

In the Battle of the Ancre (February 1917) Arthur Asquith was severely wounded and was awarded the D.S.O.

Arthur Asquith was recommended for the V.C. (in fact, he received a second bar to his D.S.O.).

On 16th December 1917, he was appointed Brigadier to command the 189th Brigade; a few days later, in reconnoitring the position, he was again severely wounded. His leg had to be amputated and he was disabled from further active service in the war.

I never knew Arthur Asquith lose his temper or think of himself in my life.

*   *   *

We were all wonderfully happy together, but, looking back, I think I was far from clever with my stepchildren; and they grew up good and successful independently of me.

In consequence of our unpopularity in Peeblesshire, I had no opportunity of meeting other young people in their homes; and I knew no family except my own. The wealth of art and music, the luxury of flowers and colour, the stretches of wild country both in Scotland and High Leicestershire, which had made up my life till I married, had not qualified me to understand children reared in different circumstances. I would not perhaps have noticed many trifles in my step-family, had I not been so much made of, overloved and independent before my marriage.

Every gardener prunes the roots of a tree before it is transplanted, but no one had ever pruned me. If you have been sunned through and through like an apricot on a wall from your earliest days, you are over-sensitive to any withdrawal of heat. This had been clearly foreseen by my friends and they were genuinely anxious about the happiness of my stepchildren. I do not know which of us had been considered the boldest in our marriage, my husband or myself; and no doubt step-relationships should not be taken in hand unadvisedly, lightly or wantonly, but reverently, discreetly and soberly. In every one of the letters congratulating me there had been a note of warning. Mr Gladstone wrote:

'MAY 5TH, 1894.
'You have a great and noble work to perform. It is a work far beyond human strength. May the strength which is more than human be abundantly granted you.
'Ever yours,
'W. E. G.'

I remember, on receiving this, saying to my friend, Con Manners:
'Gladstone thinks my fitness to be Henry's wife should be prayed for like the clergy: "Almighty and Everlasting God, who alone workest great marvels. . . ." '

*   *   *

If my stepchildren were patient with me, I dare not say what their father was: there are some reservations the boldest biographer has a right to claim; and I shall only write of my husband's character – his loyalty, lack of vanity, freedom from self, warmth and width of sympathy – in connection with politics and not with myself; but since I have touched on this subject I will give one illustration of his nature.

When the full meaning of the disreputable General Election of 1918, with its promises and pretensions and all its silly and false cries, was burnt into me at Paisley in this year of 1920 by our Coalition opponent re-repeating them, I said to Henry:

'Oh, if I had only quietly dropped all my friends of German name when the war broke out and never gone to say goodbye to those poor Lichnowskys, these ridiculous lies propagated entirely for political purposes would never have been told; and this criminal pro-German stunt could not have been started!'

To which he replied:

'God forbid! I would rather ten thousand times be out of public life for ever.'

XIV · *Self-Portrait 1906*

<hr/>

I will finish with a character-sketch of myself copied out of my diary, written nine weeks before the birth of my fifth and last baby (in 1906) and, like everything else that I have quoted, never intended for the public eye:

'I am not pretty and I do not know anything about my expression, although I observe it is this that is particularly dwelt upon if one is sufficiently plain; but I hope, when you feel as kindly towards your fellow-creatures as I do, that some of that warmth may modify an otherwise alert and rather knifey *contour*.

'My figure has remained as it was: slight, well-balanced and active. Being socially courageous, I think I can come into a room as well as many people of more appearance and prestige. I do not propose to treat myself like Mr Bernard Shaw in this account. I shall neither excuse myself from praise nor shield myself from blame, but put down the figures as accurately as I can and leave others to add them up.

'I think I have imagination, born not of fancy but of feeling; a conception of the beautiful, nor merely in poetry, music, art and nature, but in human beings; and I have a clear though distant vision, down dark, long and often divergent avenues, of the ordered meaning of God. I take this opportunity of saying my religion is a reality and never away from me and this is all I shall write upon the subject.

'It is difficult to describe what one means by imagination, but I think it is more than inventiveness or fancy. Discussing the question once with John Addington Symonds and to give him a hasty illustration of what I meant, I said I thought naming a Highland regiment the "Black Watch" showed a *high* degree of imagination. He was pleased with this; and in an early love-letter to me, Henry wrote:

' "Imaginative insight you have more than anyone I have ever met!"

'I think I am deficient in one form of imagination; and Henry will agree with this. I have a great longing to help those I love, which leads me to intrepid personal criticism; and I do not always know what hurts my friends' feelings. I do not think I should mind anything that I have said to others being said to me, but one never can tell; I have taken adverse criticism pretty well all my life and had a lot of it, but by some gap I have not succeeded in making my friends take it well. I am not vain or touchy, and it takes a lot to offend me; but when I am hurt the scar remains. I feel differently about people who have hurt me; my confidence has been shaken; I hope I am not ungenerous, but I fear I am not really forgiving. Worldly people say that explanations are a mistake; but having it out is the only chance anyone can ever have of retaining my love; and those who have neither the candour, generosity or humbleness to say they are wrong are not worth loving. I am not afraid of suffering too much in life, but much more afraid of feeling too little; and all quarrels make me profoundly unhappy. One of my complaints against the shortness of life is that there is not time enough to feel pity and love for enough people. I am infinitely compassionate and moved to my foundations by the misfortunes of others.

'As I said in my 1888 character-sketch, truthfulness with me is hardly a virtue, but I cannot discriminate between truths that need and those that need not be told. Want of courage is what makes so many people lie. It would be difficult for me to say exactly what I am afraid of. Physically and socially, not much; morally, I am afraid of a good many things; reprimanding servants, bargaining in shops; or, to turn to more serious matters, the loss of my health, the children's or Henry's. Against these last possibilities I pray in every recess of my thoughts.

'With becoming modesty I have said that I am imaginative, loving and brave! What then are my faults?

'I am fundamentally nervous, irritable and restless. These may sound slight shortcomings, but they go to the foundation of my nature, crippling activity, lessening my influence and preventing my achieving anything remarkable. I wear myself out in a hundred unnecessary ways, regretting the trifles I have not done, arranging and re-arranging what I have got to do and what everyone else is going to do, till I can hardly eat or sleep. To be in one position for long at a time, or sit through bad plays, to listen to moderate music or moderate conversation is a positive punishment to me. I am energetic and industrious, but I am a little too quick; I am *driven* along by my temperament till I tire myself and everyone else.

'I did not marry till I was thirty. This luckily gave me time to read and if I had had real application – as the Asquiths have – I should by now be a well-educated woman; but this I never had. I am not at all dull and never stale, but I don't seem to be able to grind at uncongenial things. I have a good memory for books and conversations, but bad for poetry and dates; wonderful for faces and pitiful for names.

'Physically I have done pretty well for myself. I ride better than most people and have spent or wasted more time on it than any woman of intellect ought to. I have broken both collar-bones, my nose, my ribs and my knee-cap; dislocated my jaw, fractured my skull, and had five concussions of the brain; but – though my horses are to be sold next week[1] – I have not lost my nerve. I dance, drive and skate well; I don't skate very well, but I dance really well. I have a talent for drawing and am intensely musical, playing the piano with a touch of the real thing, but have neglected both these accomplishments. I may say here in self-defence that marriage and five babies, five stepchildren and a husband in high politics have all contributed to this neglect, but the root of the matter lies deeper: I am restless.

'After riding, what I have enjoyed doing most in my life is writing. I have written a great deal, but do not fancy publishing my exercises. I have always kept a diary and commonplace-books and for many years I wrote criticisms of what I read. It is rather difficult for me to say what I think of my own writing. Arthur Balfour once said that I was a good letter-writer; Henry tells me I write well; and Symonds said I had *l'oreille juste;* but writing of the kind that I like reading I cannot do: it is a long apprenticeship. Possibly, if I had had this apprenticeship forced upon me by circumstances, I should have done it better than anything else. I am a careful critic of all I read

---

[1] My horses were sold at Tattersalls, 11th June 1906.

and I do not take my opinions of books from other people; I have not got "a lending-library mind", as Henry well described that of a friend of ours. I do not take any opinion upon any subject from other people; from this point of view – not a very high one – I might be called original.

'When I read Arthur Balfour's books and essays, I realized before I had heard them discussed in what a beautiful style he wrote. Raymond, whose intellectual taste is as fine as his father's, in a paper for his All Souls Fellowship said that Arthur had the finest style of any living writer; and Raymond and Henry sometimes justify my literary verdicts.

'From my earliest age I have been a collector: not of anything particularly valuable, but of letters, old photographs of the family, famous people and odds and ends. I do not lose things. Our cigarette ash-trays are plates from my dolls' dinner-service; I have got china, books, whips, knives, match-boxes and clocks given me since I was a child. I have kept our early copy-books, with the family signatures in them, and many trifling landmarks of nursery life. I am painfully punctual, tidy and methodical, detesting indecision, change of plans and the egotism that they involve. I am a little severe except with children: for these I have endless elasticity and patience. Many of my faults are physical. If I could have chosen my own life – more in the hills and less in the traffic – I should have slept better and might have been less overwrought and disturbable. But after all I may improve, for I am on a man-of-war now, which is better than being on a pirate-ship.

'Well, I have finished; I have tried to relate of my manners, morals, talents, defects, temptations and appearance as faithfully as I can; and I think there is nothing more to be said. If I had to confess and expose one opinion of myself which might differentiate me a little from other people, I should say it was my power of love with my power of criticism; but what I lack is what Henry possesses above all men: equanimity, moderation, self-control and the authority that comes from a perfect sense of proportion. I can only pray that I am not too old or too stationary to acquire them.

'M. A.

'JUNE 1906.

'P.S. This is my second attempt to write about myself and I am not sure that my old character-sketch of 1888 is not the better of the two – it is more external – but, after all, what can one say of one's inner self that corresponds with what one really is or what one's friends think one is? I am within a few weeks of my baby's birth and am tempted to take a gloomy view. I am inclined to sum up my life in this way:

' "An unfettered childhood and triumphant youth; a lot of love-making and a little abuse; a little fame and more abuse; a real man and great happiness; the love of children and seventh heaven; an early death and a crowded memorial service."

'But perhaps I shall not die, but live to write another volume of this diary and a better description of an improved self.'

PART II

XV · *The Jameson Raid - Mr Cecil Rhodes*

———❦———

Soon after our marriage, in the early part of the year 1896, England was stirred to its foundations by the news of the Jameson Raid – an abortive expedition undertaken by a handful of British soldiers and civilians to frighten President Kruger in South Africa.

With the exception of a few people in Mayfair, everyone combined in 1896 to repudiate an enterprise which covered England with ridicule, and the friends of Mr Rhodes and Mr Chamberlain with confusion.

Lady Warwick[1] – or 'Comrade Warwick' as I ought to call her since she joined the Labour Party – wrote the following letter to the Editor of *The Times*:

'WARWICK CASTLE,
'JAN. 4, 1896

'Sir,

'It passes belief that to-day the English Press is so far forgetful of its bright traditions as to discuss, in cold blood, the prospective shooting or hanging of Englishmen by the Boers. To what is it owing that this nomadic tribe is encamped in the Transvaal at all? It is owing to the determination of our nation that unspeakable indignities perpetrated on the negro race and its traffic in African slaves should no longer be permitted within a colony under the English flag. Are the unrequited wrongs of Kaffirs and Hottentots, are all the outrages which resulted in the "bag and baggage" removal of the Transvaal Boers to be at this date supplemented by the judicial murder of Dr Jameson?

'Sir, would any Englishman worthy of the name and the nation have failed to act exactly as Dr Jameson and his gallant companions have done? He is appealed to by the leading residents of Johannes-

———
[1] The Countess of Warwick.

burg to come to the assistance of their women and children at a moment when a revolution is seen to be inevitable. On his way to succour his countrywomen with a force of mounted police, and after having disclaimed every intention of hostility to the Boers, he is apparently attacked by their armed forces. Further than this we as yet know nothing.

'But, whatever may have been his fate, there is not an English-woman of us all whose heart does not go out in gratitude and sympathy to these brave men. They did their duty, and if they have gone to their death, even in a fair fight, so much the worse for the Boers. But if they have been taken prisoners, to be afterwards done to death in cold blood, then there is no longer room in South Africa for a "Republic" administered by the murderers. Neither German nor French jealousy can weigh in the balance at such a moment.

' "Freebooters" and "Pirates"! Are English gentlemen – person-ally known to many of us – are such as these "land pirates" and "thieves" because when implored by a majority of the respectable residents of an important town they attempt to police that town at a moment of extreme urgency?

'Are we, in short, so stranded in the shallows of diplomacy and of German intrigues that it is a crime for our kinsfolk to succour their kinsfolk in a mining camp in South Africa? Had Dr Jameson, on the contrary, turned a deaf ear to the appeal of these of our race, and had an outbreak of race-hatred placed our kinsfolk in the Transvaal at the mercy of that community, so vividly depicted by the late Lord Randolph Churchill, then, indeed, Dr Jameson had rightly incurred the reprobation of the German Emperor.

'Happily – and this is the one bright light in all this black business – there is a large-minded Englishman in South Africa upon whose resolute personality our hearts and hopes rely.

'I remain, Sir,

'Yours faithfully,

'FRANCES EVELYN WARWICK.'

On 11th January 1896, *The Times* published a poem called 'Jameson's Ride', from a famous contributor to the *Daily Telegraph*, the then Poet Laureate (one of the late Lord Salisbury's rather cynical appointments).

I will quote a few of the verses:

'SWINFORD OLD MANOR,
'JAN. 9TH, 1896

Wrong! Is it wrong? Well, maybe:
But I'm going, boys, all the same.
Do they think me a Burgher's baby,
To be scared by a scolding name?
They may argue and prate, and order;
Go, tell them to save their breath:
Then, over the Transvaal border,
And gallop for life or death!

There are girls in the gold-reef city,
There are mothers and children, too!
And they cry, 'Hurry up! for pity!'
So what can a brave man do?
If even we win, they'll blame us;
If we fail, they will howl and hiss.
But there's many a man lives famous
For daring a wrong like this!

So we forded and galloped forward,
As hard as our beasts could pelt,
First eastward, then trending northward,
Right over the rolling veldt;
Till we came on the Burghers lying
In a hollow with hills behind,
And their bullets came hissing, flying
Like hail on an Arctic wind!

I suppose we were wrong! were madmen:
Still I think at the Judgment Day,
When God sifts the good from the bad men,
There'll be something more to say.
We were wrong, but we aren't half sorry,
And, as one of the baffled band,
I would rather have had that foray
Than the crushings of all the Rand.

'ALFRED AUSTIN.'

A few days after this my husband and I were dining with Lord and Lady Reay. I was introduced to the great South African millionaire, Robinson, of Robinson's Gold Mines, who had taken Dudley House for the London season. He was tall and deaf, and, as he offered me his arm to take me in to dinner, he paused on the stair, looked at me and said in a voice of thunder:

'What is your name?'

To which I replied almost as loud: 'Asquith!'

Still standing in the middle of the staircase and blocking the way to the dining-room, he said:

'Any relation to the famous Asquith?'

At which I shouted: 'Wife!'

He appeared so surprised that I wondered what he thought Henry's wife ought to have looked like. After a short pause during which he seemed puzzled, he conducted me in to dinner and placed me opposite Sir Donald Wallace, who was then foreign editor of *The Times*.

I opened the conversation with my millionaire by asking him to tell me about South Africa, hoping to hear both the details and his opinions of the Jameson Raid. He asked me if I had ever been out there, to which I replied 'No.'

MR ROBINSON: 'Are you rich?' to which I answered no, but that my father was.

MR ROBINSON: 'Who is your Arthur?'

I explained that I had not said 'Arthur' but 'father'.

MR ROBINSON: 'Oh, well, I'll tell you how I made my money, if you'll tell me afterwards how he made his.'

I gave myself up for lost, but soon became absorbed in his story.

He told me that he had started life in a humble way by keeping a little shop. One day a man came to him, with whom he had a slight acquaintance, and said that he was in great difficulties, adding that, if he could be helped with the loan of fifty pounds, his life would be saved: he promised that he would pay everything back, and Mr Robinson lent him the money.

Time passed, but he heard nothing of his debtor. Two years later he received a letter from him, saying that he had been away trekking out of all reach of posts, which accounted for his silence. There was a map attached to the letter, giving a detailed description of a field on a farm which he said would some day be of enormous value: he had prospected it and found gold there. He enclosed his debt; and Robinson started off up country the same day.

The Boer farmer, who owned the field, received him with suspicion. They walked over the estate, and, when they came to the part indicated on the map, Robinson said that it looked an arid kind of place, but that he would like to buy it, as he did not suppose it would be dear, and he wanted to start farming in a mild fashion.

To his surprise the Boer opened his mouth rather wide, asking him £500,[1] to which Robinson demurred. But the farmer was obdurate, so he gave way and bought the field. When the business was over, they returned to lunch in the bosom of the Boer family, a neighbour or two having strayed in to see the foreigner. At the conclusion of the meal, the host, gazing steadily at Mr Robinson, lifted his glass, and said he proposed to drink his health in honour of the day's sale, and with a rapid wink at his son he gulped down the country claret.

Mr Robinson ended the story by telling me that after this he was pursued by all the women and children of the place, offering him dolls, beads and every kind of cheap ornament, as they looked upon him as a zany capable of buying anything.

This was the beginning of the great Robinson Mine.

When he had finished I turned to my other neighbour, feeling that I had perhaps neglected him, and found him in the throes of an argument about the Jameson Raid; he said that Jameson was a hero in spite of his failure, and that he himself was an Imperialist and thought it was high time we fought the Boers. He added in the vernacular of the day that it was only the damned Radicals who criticized Jameson, and they were well-known to love every country but their own. After a little talk I found the young Imperialist's conversation not so new to me as Mr Robinson's, and, fearing lest he should discover I was a 'damned Radical', I turned round and asked Mr Robinson why the girls in the gold-reefed city had sent the famous telegram.

[1] I am not quite sure if this was the exact sum.

'How can you be so green?' he answered: 'That telegram came from London!'

On hearing this, Sir Donald Wallace leant across the table and said that he was the only person in the world who was in a position to contradict this, as the telegram had passed through his hands before being published in *The Times*. Not hearing what he said, Mr Robinson interrupted by giving me a poke with his elbow.

'What is he talking about?' said he. 'Does he say I'm a liar?' To which I answered firmly:

'Yes, Mr Robinson.'

I have often wondered and doubt if we shall ever know what the true history of that telegram was; for, though Sir Donald Wallace was a man of the highest honour, he might have been taken in. Mr Robinson told me nothing further about Dr Jameson, and we all got up from the table.

In connection with South Africa and Sir Starr Jameson, Lord Kitchener, on his return from the Boer War, came to see me before he went to India. In the course of our talk he told me that the two best people he had ever met in his life were Dr Jameson and Lady Waterford,[1] and added that his experience of the so-called Loyalists in South Africa had not been a happy one, they were people of no sort of judgment, far too fond of money, he had never known them right on any question of politics – and ended by saying:

'Doctor Jim was the only one of the lot who could have made a fortune, but never owned a shilling! He was a really fine fellow.'

Lord Kitchener was right. Sir Starr Jameson was an uncommon person and had great beauty and simplicity of nature; I heard an equally high testimony paid to him many years later by General Botha.

My husband and I met the Doctor first – a week or ten days before his trial and sentence – at Georgiana Lady Dudley's house: and the night before he went to prison he dined with us alone in Cavendish Square.

Dr Jim had personal magnetism, and could do what he liked with my sex. He was one of those men who, if he had been a quack, could have made a vast fortune, either as a doctor, a thought-reader,

[1] The sister of the Duke of Beaufort.

a faith-healer or a medium; but he was without quackery of any kind. I never thought him a fine judge of people, but here I may be wrong. If his brains had been as good as his nature, he would have had a commanding position in any country. The reason that convinced me that they were not was when he told us of the great scheme that had failed: which was to kidnap President Kruger and carry him off in person. This somewhat jejune intention was happily frustrated. The Doctor was tried for 'fitting out a warlike expedition against a friendly State in breach of the Foreign Enlistment Act' before Lord Chief Justice Russell, and on 20th July 1896, he was condemned.

In connection with this trial my husband had a bet with a famous Irish Member of Parliament. This is what he wrote:

'HOUSE OF COMMONS

'Bet lost to Mr Asquith ref. the trial of Dr Jameson.

'Bet being a sixpenny stamp to a twopence-halfpenny one that the prisoners would be convicted.

'The penalty of the wager enclosed.

'MICHAEL DAVITT.'

The responsibility for the Raid could not, however, be confined to Dr Jameson. Both Mr Cecil Rhodes' and Mr Joseph Chamberlain's reputations were involved, and everyone was stirred.

Admirers of Mr Rhodes went about saying that, if his name was struck off the list of Privy Councillors, they would show Joe up; and admirers of Mr Chamberlain were going to show someone else up; and a Government Committee was appointed to show everyone up. The secret history of this affair may or may never be written: but it would be of interest to learn how much those in authority knew of the intentions at the time of the South African Raiders.

I remember opening the front door of 20 Cavendish Square to Mr Chamberlain one morning about that time, and showing him into my husband's library. At the end of a long visit I went into the room and said:

'What did Joe want, Henry?' To which he answered:

'He asked me if I would serve on the Committee of Inquiry into the responsibility of the Jameson Raid – they call it "the Rhodes Commission" – and I refused.'

I asked him why he had refused, to which he answered:

'Do you take me for a fool?'

I never spoke to Mr Cecil Rhodes in my life, but I met him once at a party in Downing Street, when Mr Balfour was leader of the House of Commons.

It was early in 1899 when South Africa was in a state of suppressed turmoil. Sir Alfred Milner – the then Lord High Commissioner – was writing letters from Cape Town, warning us of the exact situation, but the Government turned a deaf ear to all his warnings.

Mr Balfour had been told that if you listen to the man on the spot you cannot go wrong, and that Cecil Rhodes – the great hero of South Africa – was the proper person to consult about the Boer problems over which Milner and so many of us were exercised.

Mr Rhodes had a name that was famous all the world over. Men and women trembled before him. A phrase much in vogue at the time – 'Think Imperially' – was attributed to him; also the poignant epigram, quoted by the more enlightened Tariff Reformers, that it was not the Article but the Art that ought to be encouraged in British trade. It is perhaps hardly fair to credit him with both these sayings, but it is certain that his lightest word carried weight. Lord Fisher, writing to me from the Admiralty, quoted a talk he had had with Cecil Rhodes which impressed him deeply; his letter ended with:

'Rhodes is a wonderful fellow! I will finish this long letter by quoting a clever thing he said to me to-day:

' "I have found one thing, and that is, if you have an idea and it is a good idea, if you will only stick to it, you will come out all right."

'Your affectionate

'FISHER.'

On arriving at Mr Balfour's party in Downing Street, where I was to meet Mr Rhodes, I took my host aside and asked him if 'the man on the spot' – generally a favourite with the stupid – had given him his views on South Africa, to which he replied:

'Yes: he doesn't think there is the slightest chance of war; he says, not only that the Boers *won't* fight, but that they *can't*.'

'Thinking Imperially' had made us confident that, after an experience of twenty years, Rhodes must know his South Africa, and we all took comfort together.

I looked round me at No. 10 but saw no one I wanted to talk to, so I penetrated into the next room. There, for the first time, I saw Burne-Jones' *Legend of the Briar Rose* hanging on the high panels put up by Disraeli in the Downing Street dining-room; but more striking than this was the circle of fashionable ladies crouching at Cecil Rhodes' feet. He sat like a great bronze gong among them: and I had not the spirit to disturb their worship.

XVI · *The General Election 1906*

━━━━◦◉◦━━━━

I do not propose going into details of old political controversy, which are certain to be ably dealt with in the coming biographies of Sir William Harcourt and Sir Henry Campbell-Bannerman; but as the events of 1905 and 1906 killed the Conservative Party, and not only brought the Liberals into power with the largest majority ever seen, but led to my husband becoming Prime Minister, I shall quote passages from diaries in which I chronicled with great fidelity the happenings of every day.

*Survey of the year 1903, written in November 1904.

━━━━━━━

In May 1903, the Unionist Government was in a good position. They had finished the Boer War and had won their Khaki Election, but the Commission set up following upon the war had disclosed serious blunders of organization in many Departments. Mr Brodrick's[1] new army scheme was a failure; the Budget was criticized, and the Education Bill was unpopular; the general expenses were enormous, and a universal feeling of lack of efficiency was abroad: the excuse given by the Government for this was that they had been too long in Office and were all completely exhausted. They talked fluently of being ready and willing to give up but nevertheless clung comfortably on.

On the morning of the 16th of May, 1903, my husband came into my bedroom at 20 Cavendish Square with *The Times* in his hand.

'Wonderful news today', he said, 'and it is only a question of time when we shall sweep this country.'

* From my diary, November 1904.   [1] The Earl of Midleton.

Sitting upon my bed he showed me the report of a speech made at Birmingham the night before by Mr Chamberlain.[1]

Joseph Chamberlain at that time stood in the eyes of his fellow-countrymen as the Business man; the great Imperialist and the Strong Fighter. The sort of praise one was always hearing of him was: 'No shilly-shallying about Joe! He hits straight from the shoulder! He'll give it 'em! A pity there aren't a few more Joes!' etc.

Political bruising, perfect speaking, artistic self-advertisement, audacity and courage combine to make Mr Chamberlain today the most conspicuous politician since Gladstone.

On the 15th of May, 1903, before the Whitsuntide recess he delivered a speech to his constituents at Birmingham which, as my husband said, had transformed the position of every political party. It advocated for the first time a policy of naked Protection, and woke up the barely controlled hopes of the whole Tory Party. This caught on like wildfire with the semi-clever, moderately educated, the Imperialists, Dukes, Journalists, and Fighting Forces; incidentally bringing unity to the Liberals and chaos into the Government ranks.

The Prime Minister[2] had one opportunity if he did not agree with his Colleagues, and we wondered if he would take it.

On the adjournment of the House of Commons on the 28th of May, 1903, I went to the Speaker's Gallery full of excitement to hear the debate, and, meeting Mr Balfour's secretary, Mr Saunders, I seized him by the hand and said: 'Tell Arthur Balfour this is a *most* important occasion and do not let him think he can slip out of it.'

'Don't be anxious, Mrs Asquith, Joe is not going to speak today and all will be well', he said, smiling sweetly at me, with the sympathy of one who thinks he scents an unconscious love affair.

Mr Chamberlain, however, did speak; Arthur Balfour did not repudiate him, the fat was in the fire, and it has been bubbling and boiling over ever since; this fire cannot be put out, and at the present moment the Government majority has diminished by half.

On September the 9th, 1903, Mr Chamberlain resigned. He ended his letter to the Prime Minister by saying he thought he could promote the cause of Protection which he had at heart better if he were

[1] The Right Hon. Joseph Chamberlain, Colonial Secretary.
[2] The Right Hon. Arthur Balfour.

outside the Cabinet than in. His resignation was followed by several other members of the Cabinet, and when Arthur Balfour filled their places with avowed Protectionists people began to grope about for the Prime Minister's convictions.

The methods by which Mr Balfour contrived to rid himself both of the Free Traders and Mr Chamberlain in his Government was a matter of speculation at the time, upon which I shall pronounce no judgment. He wound up a speech of importance at Sheffield on October the 1st by saying:

'My request therefore to you tonight is that the people of this country should give to the Government, from whatever party that Government may be drawn, that freedom of negotiation of which we have been deprived, not by the force of circumstances, not by the action of over-mastering forces, not by the pressure of foreign Powers, but by something which I can only describe as our own pedantry and our own self-conceit.'

Upon this speech *The Times* (October the 3rd, 1903) wrote: 'What is the net result of the proceedings at Sheffield? It is that the Prime Minister has directly challenged and condemned a fiscal system which has held undisputed sway in this country for two generations, and in doing so has received the absolutely undivided support of the most authoritative gathering of Conservative representatives that it is possible to convene. People who think that nothing should be done must be singularly ignorant of the political history of their country. We do not hesitate to tell them that it is a great deal more than they had any right to expect, and a striking testimony to the political sagacity and admirable leadership alike of Mr Balfour and of Mr Chamberlain. It is a perfectly astonishing thing that it seems to have been left only to the more clear-sighted opponents of these two men to perceive that they are playing the game with the perfect mutual understanding and the consummate skill of accomplished whist players.'

Poor Arthur Balfour! In his anxiety to build a bridge upon which his colleagues can stand, he calls himself a Retaliator and says that he is *against Protection*. Free Traders are ousted from the Government and the Liberal Unionists have captured the Party Machine. In the by-elections the Tory candidate is blessed by both Balfour and Chamberlain, and though the Government profess absolute loyalty to the Prime Minister not a member of the front bench knows what to say or how to say it.

What the Prime Minister enjoys doing with his subtle, detached and dissenting intellect, the rest of his followers perspire over in a labyrinth of confused platitudes and contradictory figures.

I have come to the conclusion that the imagination that can work out and foresee the definite results of any policy proposed is rarer than the imagination that creates nymphs, moons, or passions.

A group of young Tory dissentients led by Lord Hugh Cecil called themselves Free-Fooders. These young gentlemen were either going to break with the Unionist Party and join us or compel the Prime Minister to break with Mr Chamberlain; but I never much believed in them, and the result of it all is that they have broken with one another.

A small party which included Sir Edgar Vincent,[1] Sir John Poynder,[2] Mr Winston Churchill, and others, joined us.

In June 1903, Sir Michael Hicks Beach said to me: 'Of the two policies, Chamberlain's or Balfour's, I prefer the former; if retaliation were carried it would be infinitely more dangerous, but luckily it is impossible; it can never be a policy, rarely a remedy, and at best a bad expedient.'

I saw little of Sir Michael this summer of 1904, but last year he was a frequent caller; he is handsome and agreeable, though a trifle uncertain. Henry, who likes him and thinks him an admirable speaker, said that people mistook for courage in him what was very often temper.

There will be a great redivision of parties in the future and we want new blood. Gladstone smashed us over Home Rule, and the Boer War divided us again, but now I believe the future is with us.

The Chamberlain men get more annoyed with Arthur Balfour as his followers woo and draw him away from Protection, and the baffled and irritated Joeites hope against hope. The dividing line between the two is a tax upon food.

Mr Chamberlain is booked to address several meetings, and, the oftener he speaks, the better for us. Henry has followed him in all his fiscal orations.

[1] Lord D'Abernon.   [2] Lord Islington.

The flaws of the shallow Protectionist mind are just his subjects; a large grasp of accurate figures and the imaginative insight that is needed to expose the moral and commercial consequences of Protection show him at his best, and his arguments have neither been met nor answered. He has unswerving industry, a persistent and precise memory, and real judgment. The stand he has made against the fallacies and light reasoning of his opponents has been appreciated by both divisions in our Party – the C.B.ites and the Imperialists, and I doubt if he has ever stood higher than he does today.

*   *   *

1905

*On the 2nd of January, 1905, the fall of Port Arthur brought the Russo-Japanese war to an end. It needed no witch to foretell the outcome of this conflict.

The internal condition of Russia had been horrifying thoughtful people for months past, nor can it be said that Peace as understood by the present Russian Government[1] is much better, if you can apply such a word to the indifference and active hatred shown in that melancholy country today. Docile Russians are dying in thousands, not for making extravagant demands, but merely for asking for a little happiness, and the Czar, who was their Father and their God, counts for nothing.

Any form of Government that continued for years against the will of the governed must degenerate into barbarity, as force has never been a remedy.[2]

On the 22nd of January, 1905, a body of peaceful unarmed men went to the Palace with a deputation from the strikers to ask for decent treatment and a chance of life, but the Czar hid and would not

---

* From my diary, 1905.

[1] On 28th October 1905, Arthur Balfour said to me at dinner at Whittinghame: 'It is ridiculous and boring to draw parallels, but really the French Revolution was not much worse than what is going on in Russia today.'

[2] I remember the same futile remark 'Law and Order first' being made about Russia then as is made about Ireland today. Belief in Force is what will always differentiate the Unionist Party from ours.

see them, and the soldiers fired and killed the men, women and children.

There will be no necessity for Anarchists now for the Czar has multiplied them; he will not be forgiven, and there are thousands of Russians today ready to kill and be killed for their country.

Admiral Togo has annihilated the Fleet, which is a crushing blow, and there is only one disaster left for Russia to suffer now, which is a well-organized, complete, and bloody internal Revolution.

*   *   *

We were dining at Windsor Castle in November 1905, two months before the General Election. After dinner Lord Farquhar, my husband, Mr Chamberlain and General Oliphant went into the smoking-room, where they discussed the whole political situation. Henry told me about this talk; he said he had questioned the wisdom of the Government going for a General Election when everyone was saying the result would be defeat. At this Chamberlain said that, although we were sure to win, we could not last as our majority would not be independent of the Irish and that then his policy would triumph throughout the country.

This appeared to Henry as it does to me an astonishing forecast. He was amazed and said:

'Well, my dear Chamberlain, I am not a betting man, but I am prepared to make you a small bet.'[1] At that moment Lord Farquhar rushed into the room and said:

'Come along quick! The King!' General Oliphant uttered an irreverent epithet, and they joined us in the tapestry room, where we had been standing first upon one leg and then upon the other ever since dinner.

On the 8th (March 1905) Winston Churchill brought in a private member's motion that 'This House was against Protective taxes on food as not promoting the unity of the Empire'.

The Whips were in a wild state of fear lest the Government should be turned out as their majority had dwindled to 70.

We dined in the House that night with Mr Ernest Beckett;[2] our

[1] This is the remark Mr Chamberlain alludes to in his letter on page 245.
[2] Later Lord Grimthorpe.

fellow-guests were Herbert Gladstone, John Morley, Harry Cust and Jack Poynder. Winston made an admirable, short and telling speech after dinner.

Chamberlain's fire seems to have gone and his speech was dull. The House got impatient and shouted 'time! time!' as they wanted to hear Lord Hugh Cecil, Henry, and Arthur Balfour. I should think this has never happened before to Mr Chamberlain.

I wrote to Winston Churchill congratulating him on his speech and saying I was surprised that 12 of the Free Fooders had had the courage to vote with us; and this is his answer:

'MARCH 9TH, 1905

'Dear Mrs Asquith,

'Your letter is very kind and I am delighted to hear you were pleased.

'You are wrong about the Free Fooders. No other similar body of men would have displayed such constancy amid such conflicting strains. I have always considered Edgar V quite consistent in his line – tho I do not agree with that line and quite understand that it does not commend itself to the Liberal party.

'The world is not made up of heroes and heroines – luckily or where would you and I find our backgrounds!

'Yours very sincerely,

'WINSTON S. C.'

*On the 30th of March I lunched at 10 Downing Street; Evelyn Rayleigh, Arthur Balfour, Alfred Lyttelton and Gerald Balfour were there. They looked profoundly harassed, and I wished I had not accepted Evelyn's invitation. Not wanting to mention politics I talked of Chesterton's new book on Watts (the artist). Arthur Balfour asked me absently if I meant Dr Watts the hymn writer or the steam man, adding: 'By the way, he is Watt, I think.'

We then got on to biography; Arthur said that Mommsen, Stubbs and Creighton thought Macaulay the greatest historian that had ever lived; I said that perhaps he was, but that he was a noisy writer, to which Arthur answered:

* From my diary, March 1905.

234

'If great knowledge and accuracy welded into a picturesque whole is the function of History, Macaulay can well lay claim to being the greatest.' Alfred Lyttelton quoted John Morley's remark about brass instruments, but that 'he missed the mystery of the strings'.

Walter Long, who had taken no part in the conversation, got up saying that he had to go to the House of Commons and the party scattered.

*   *   *

There has been a keen correspondence on the late Lord Salisbury's views upon Protection. On March the 30th Mr Chamberlain wrote to *The Times*, Lord Hugh Cecil, Sir Michael Hicks Beach, Henry and others following him.

I am a witness of Sir Michael Hicks Beach's account of his last talk to Lord Salisbury. He came to tea with me at 20 Cavendish Square, and said:

'You will never guess where I have been all this afternoon.' As I was unable to guess, he told me he had been at Hatfield saying farewell to his chief. Not knowing that Lord Salisbury was fatally ill I expressed my distress and asked how he was, to which Sir Michael replied:

'I never heard him talk better and nothing you can say, Mrs Asquith, against the Chamberlain policy or methods is as strong as what Lord Salisbury said to me this afternoon. He told me he had at one time been rather bitten with Protection, but that he had come out on the other side. I said to him: "My dear Chief, you need not tell me this!" for I can assure you, Mrs Asquith, that I had been very anxious at that time over Lord Salisbury's marked want of orthodoxy, and I told him so.'

*The Unionist majority was getting shakier every day and the political situation developed rapidly. On Monday the 13th of November Henry came into my bedroom at Cavendish Square, where I was having my hair washed, and told me that he had seen Sir Henry Campbell-Bannerman.

Hearing this I could not wait, but tying a shawl round my head ran down to the library, where I sat down on one of the leather arm-

* From my diary, November 1905.

chairs. Henry walked up and down the room and told me all he could remember of his talk with C.B.

He found him in his library in Belgrave Square looking at a newspaper called *The Week's Survey*, which he asked Henry if he had heard of.

Henry replied that he had not. They then proceeded to discuss Russia and Germany. Henry was glad to find him sound on Germany. He dislikes the Kaiser and thinks him a dangerous, restless, mischief-making man.

Suddenly he said that he thought things looked like coming to a head politically, and that any day after Parliament met we might expect a General Election. He gathered that he would probably be the man the King would send for, in which case he would make no phrases but would consent to form a Government.

Henry said: 'C.B. then looked at me and said: "I do not think we have ever spoken of the future Liberal Government, Asquith? What would you like? The Exchequer, I suppose?" – I said nothing – "or the Home Office?" I said, "Certainly not." At which he said: "Of course, if you want legal promotion what about the Woolsack? No? Well then, it comes back to the Exchequer. I hear that it has been suggested by that ingenious person, Richard Burdon Haldane,[1] that I should go to the House of Lords, a place for which I have neither liking, training nor ambition. In this case you would lead the House of Commons. While Lord Spencer was well and among us, nothing under Heaven would have made me do this! Nothing except at the point of the bayonet. Spencer and I talked it over, and he was quite willing that I should go to the House of Lords." '

C.B. then went on to say what a generous fine old fellow Lord Spencer was, but that he feared he would never again be able to take office; should he, however, recover sufficiently, he might be in the Cabinet without a portfolio and asked Henry what he thought of the idea.

I could see that the impression left upon Henry's mind while he was telling me of this conversation was that it would be with reluctance and even repugnance that Campbell-Bannerman would ever go to the House of Lords.

[1] Viscount Haldane of Cloan.

C.B. then asked my husband who he thought best fitted for the Home Office; to which Henry replied that that depended upon who would have the Woolsack, and added:

'For that, my dear C.B., there are only two possible people, Haldane or Reid',[1] and went on to say that Reid had told him in past days that he did not fancy leaving the House of Commons; 'in which case', said Henry, 'why not give him the Home Office and Haldane the Woolsack?'

C.B. answered, 'Why not *vice versa*?'

When Henry told me this – knowing as I do that Haldane had set his heart on being Lord Chancellor, I was reminded of George Eliot's remark, 'When a man wants a peach it is no good offering him the largest vegetable marrow', but I merely said that I hoped Haldane would not stand out if Reid desired the Woolsack. He went on to tell me that C.B. had then said:

'There are two more delicate offices we've not mentioned, Asquith – the Colonial and the Foreign Office.'

Henry said he thought Edward Grey[2] should have the Foreign Office; C.B. answered that he had considered Lord Elgin for this, but Henry was very strong upon Grey. He said that he was the *only* man, and that it was clear in his mind that Grey's appointment as Foreign Minister would be popular all over Europe. He expatiated at great length and convincingly on Grey's peculiar fitness for a post of such delicacy.

C.B. said he wanted him for the War Office, but Henry told me – having been unshakable upon this point – he felt pretty sure that he had made an impression, as C.B. ultimately agreed that Lord Elgin would do well in the Colonial Office.

Henry ended our talk by saying to me:

'I could see that C.B. had never before realized how urgently Grey is needed at the Foreign Office and I feel pretty sure that he will offer it to him.'

I said Grey could fill with equal success at least six places in the Government, including a noble appearance as Viceroy of India.*

Although possessed of many of the qualities for which he was

[1] Lord Loreburn.   [2] Viscount Grey of Fallodon.
* End of my diary quotation.

deservedly popular, Sir Henry Campbell-Bannerman differed fundamentally from the public conception of him, and he was fortunate in having Mr Balfour as a political foil; they not only fought with very different weapons, but, with the exception of fine manners, two men of more different type, temper, and training could not have been imagined.

'C.B.' (as he was called) was as much stimulated as Mr Balfour was irritated by his opponent, and, considering the inequality of their intellect, they made a fair duel. Sir Henry's patent sincerity constantly pierced the armour of Mr Balfour's insolent detachment, and the Tories who took him to be a guileless person found themselves confronted by an unforeseen combination of pawkiness and courage.

No one can become Prime Minister of this country without having exceptional qualities; and, in spite of being easy-going to the point of laziness, Sir Henry had neither lethargy nor indifference. He recoiled from what was not straight, and had a swift and unerring insight into his fellow-men.

A certain lack of dignity prevented him from ever carrying much authority in the House of Commons, and he was always nervous about his health; but his modesty and good humour endeared him to all, and he was both loved and trusted.

As the principal characters concerned in the events that took place after the fall of the Balfour Ministry – Lord Grey, Lord Haldane and my husband – are alive, I cannot write freely about them, but it is well known that Lord Grey and Lord Haldane wanted Sir Henry Campbell-Bannerman to be Prime Minister in the House of Lords, and my husband to lead the Commons, and were loth to accept office under any other arrangement, so I shall be betraying no secrets by writing of the discussions which took place over the matter.

It is difficult to imagine any of the prominent politicians of the present day showing the same qualities of straightness or simplicity that were shown by Sir Henry Campbell-Bannerman, Edward Grey, and my husband in these transactions. Their behaviour would have been remarkable at any period; but writing as I am in the autumn of 1921, when there is a lack of straightness, statesmanship and manners in high places, it appears to me that those negotiations mark the end of the great political traditions of the nineteenth century.

On 4th December 1905, the night before Sir Henry Campbell-Bannerman kissed hands with King Edward, he had an interview with Sir Edward Grey, in which the latter had put his own situation with painful fidelity before him, and on the morning of the 5th C.B. sent for Henry to talk things over before he went to the Palace.

I will here quote from my diary:

*On the 5th December, 1905, C.B. and Henry had a moving interview. *No* one could have been straighter and nicer than Campbell-Bannerman was to him. He told him of the talk he had had the night before with Sir Edward Grey. He spoke well of him, but said he was a regular Grey and had all the defects of his qualities. He added that he (C.B.) was well aware that Henry was better equipped to lead the House of Commons than he was; that he easily recognized this; but that, after standing all the stress and strain of the last few years, he did not wish people to say that he had run away when the pinch came – he could not bear the idea that anyone should think he was a coward.

Henry answered that the position was almost too delicate and personal for them to discuss; but C.B. pressed him to say frankly everything that was in his mind. Henry pointed out what a fearful labour C.B. would find the combination of leading the House and being Prime Minister, as they were practically two men's work; that no one could possibly accuse him of being a coward; that the House of Lords was without a leader, and that it was placing him (Henry) in a cruel and impossible position if under the circumstances Edward Grey refused to take Office; he was his dearest friend as well as supporter, and to join a Government without such a friend would be personal pain to him, as they had never worked apart from one another.

Henry left after this as the King was to see Sir Henry at a quarter to eleven; he said he would return when C.B. had kissed hands.

When they met after the interview C.B. told him His Majesty had been most amiable and expressed himself delighted at hearing he would undertake to form a Government. He warned him, however, by saying that being Prime Minister and leading the Commons at the same time would be heavy work, and added:

* From my diary, 5th December 1905.

'We are not as young as we were, Sir Henry!'

He suggested he should go to the House of Lords, to which C.B. seems to have answered that no doubt he would ultimately be obliged to do this, but that he would prefer starting in the Commons if only for a short time. The King, instead of pushing the matter – which was what I would have liked – seemed to fall in very pleasantly with the idea and shook him warmly by the hand. Knowing that he ought to kneel and kiss hands, C.B. advanced and waited, but the King interrupted by some commonplace remark; when he had finished speaking, C.B. again advanced meaning to kneel, but the King only wrung his hand, at which he felt the interview was over, as to have had another try would have been grotesque. He retired from the presence of His Majesty to Lord Knollys's room and told him he feared he had never kissed hands at all, to which Lord Knollys replied that it did not matter, as he would see that it was properly published and in the right quarter the next day.

When Henry had finished telling me all this I could see by his face how profoundly anxious he was. He had left C.B. saying that as the matter was one of vital importance to him personally it could not be settled in a day, and that he must be given time to think things over.

On December the 6th, Violet and I went to Hatfield in the afternoon, and Henry arrived later on the same day. He went straight to his room, where I joined him, and we talked for an hour before dressing for dinner. He told me that he had seen John Morley that day who had been wonderfully nice and clever throughout the troubles; that C.B. had spoken to him (Morley) at great length about Edward Grey, of his character and of their interview, and that Morley had ended by saying:

'C.B. is not a big man; he should either have ordered Grey out of the room after this, as Mr Gladstone would have done, or accepted Grey's alternative suggestion.' C.B. had told John Morley how touched he had been at Henry's wonderful delicacy in presenting the case for him (C.B.) to go to the House of Lords.

In this connection I may say Henry is always considerate; of course, this could hardly be a test case as he could not very well have asserted his superior qualities for the leadership, but Henry has sensibility for other people's feelings to a greater degree than anyone that I have ever known. He realizes what will make for peace, and, having no vanity or wish to give his enemy a pat, he can deal with the most subtle situations as if they were of no personal interest to him. Edward Grey is not only perfectly fearless but prides himself upon his own characteristics. He wants nothing for himself but would like Henry to lead the House of Commons and Haldane to be Lord Chancellor.

Henry ended by telling me he had gone himself to see Grey after his conversation with Morley and had found him in an uncompromising three-cornered humour.

That night at dinner at Hatfield, my husband looked worn out, and I admired him more than I could say for throwing himself into the social atmosphere of a fancy ball, with his usual simplicity and unselfcentredness.

On Wednesday (the 6th of December) we motored to London. Henry went at once to see C.B. and Herbert Gladstone came to talk over the whole situation with me. Herbert told me that he himself had urged C.B. to go to the House of Lords and thus remove all difficulties; that he had impressed upon him how hard his father had found combining the Office of Prime Minister and Leader of the House; but C.B. had answered that his wife was to arrive from Scotland at seven that night and that she would be the final arbiter; at which Herbert had left him to come to me, feeling pretty sure that he *would* go to the Lords. Hearing that Herbert had been given the Admiralty I congratulated him and asked him if there would be any objection to Haldane going to the War Office since the Woolsack was disposed of by Reid's acceptance.

I said that every soldier I had seen was keen upon his appointment. He did not answer this, but said he had heard nothing definite about the Admiralty for himself; and after this he left me.

Herbert Gladstone is not only the oldest of my friends but one of the best, straightest and most loyal of men.

I returned to Hatfield that evening where Henry joined me. He was much moved in relating what had occurred during the day. In view of Edward Grey's difficulty in joining the Government he had done what he never thought possible – he had been to C.B. and made a great personal appeal to him.

HENRY (to me): 'I said, "It is no use going over the ground again, my dear C.B. I make a personal appeal to you, which I've never done before; I urge you to go to the House of Lords and solve this difficulty." I could see that C.B. was moved, but he repeated what you tell me he said to Herbert Gladstone about the arrival of his wife, and that he wished her to be the final arbiter; with which our interview ended.'

The next evening at Hatfield (7th of December) when Henry arrived I saw at a glance that it was all up. He told me that C.B. had said to his secretary, Sinclair,[1] that morning at breakfast that he had had a talk with his lady the night before, and that she had said:

'*No surrender.*'

'I don't often make up my mind, Sinclair, but I've done it now – I shan't go to the Lords.'

After Sinclair had told him this Henry went to see C.B.

HENRY (to me): 'He looked white and upset and began like a man who, having taken the plunge, meant to make the best of it. He spoke in a rapid, rather cheerful and determined manner: "I'm going to stick to the Commons, Asquith, so will you go and tell Grey he may have the Foreign Office and Haldane the War Office." '

*We left Hatfield the next day, and, opening *The Times* in the train, read that Sir Edward Grey had definitely refused to join the Government.

On arriving at 20 Cavendish Square we seized our letters.

Henry had a line from Haldane:

'7TH DECEMBER, 1905

My dear A.,

'I have talked the question over with E.G. and have induced him to reconsider his position as regards taking the F.O. He is to see C.B. in the morning.

'My decision will follow his after he has seen C.B.

'Ever yours affectly,

'R. B. H.'

After reading this Henry left me and went to see Lord Haldane.

[1] Lord Pentland.
* From my diary, 8th December 1905.

At 12 o'clock Herbert Gladstone came into my boudoir, his face shining with happiness; he opened his arms and said:

'It's all right, Margot!'

'Not possible!' I exclaimed.

HERBERT: 'Yes – Grey and Haldane are both in and the two men that deserve gold medals are Spender[1] and Acland.'[2]

Herbert could hardly speak of Henry's conduct throughout the whole anxious week without emotion, and ended by saying:

'You have done nobly throughout, Margot, and I've been much struck by your wisdom and generosity.' At which I burst into tears.

So we were all in, and not *one* of us had got what we wanted! I sent a telegram to Louis Malet[3] at the Foreign Office, which I had promised to do:

'Settled Maria'; and this is his answer:

'Thank you and God. Suspense awful. Malet.'

The Foreign Office adore Edward Grey and were in a state of trembling anxiety lest he should stand out. Both Reggie Lister[4] and Louis Malet had made me promise to wire to them the moment I knew of Grey's final decision. I suggested that 'Maria' would be a wiser signature than 'Margot'.

This is what Grey wrote in answer to a line from me:

'FALLODON,
'DECEMBER 11TH, 1905

'Dear Mrs Asquith,

'My bolt is shot. . . . As to the Government, the only declarations of Policy which count are those of the Prime Minister; having entered his Government my statements will be in line with his as long as I am in it.

'There is no difficulty about this, for my views as to what should be done in the next Parliament are not different from his, but he must state them in his own way.

'Yours sincerely,
'E. GREY.'

---

[1] Mr Alfred Spender, Editor of the *Westminster Gazette*.
[2] Mr Arthur Acland, Minister of Education.
[3] Sir Louis Malet.
[4] The Hon. Reginald Lister.

*On the 11th of December our new Ministry was published in all the papers. I looked down the list and my eye rested upon:

'*Chancellor of the Exchequer, Mr Asquith.*'

On the 12th I went to see my father and found him far from well, which filled me with sadness. He asked me how I liked the idea of going to 11 Downing Street and letting my own house. I told him that I would either have to farm out my own, or my stepchildren, as there was no room for both a nursery and a schoolroom at No. 11.

He was most dear and generous and said that he would pay us the rent which we hoped to get for 20 Cavendish Square to enable us to live there, and in consequence we have lent 11 Downing Street to the Herbert Gladstones, who have no London house.

On the 21st of December I received a letter from Lord Hugh Cecil, in which he says:

'The new Government makes a good show, better than the late one; the weak spot in this Government is the Prime Minister, in the last it was the one strong point. I don't think you have lost much by taking Office. My guess is that your party will come back 230 – giving you a majority of about 40 over us and the Irish together.'

*   *   *

†On January the 8th, 1906, Sir Henry Campbell-Bannerman's election address was published in the papers. It was quite good, but not as striking as Robespierre's, which I read the other day:

'Our purpose is to substitute morality for egoism, honesty for honour, principles for usages, duties for properties, the empire of reason for the tyranny of fashion; dignity for insolence, nobleness for vanity, love of glory for the love of lucre, good people for good society, merit for intrigue, genius for brilliance, the charm of contentment for the satiety of pleasure, the majesty of man for noble lineage, a magnanimous, powerful and happy people for an amiable, frivolous and wretched people: that is to say every virtue of a Republic that will replace the vices and absurdities of a Monarchy.'

On Sunday the 14th we heard that Arthur Balfour's seat and all the others at Manchester had been won by Liberals, and after that I knew that we were safe.

* From my diary, 11th December 1905.
† From my diary, 8th January 1906.

The results of the General Election were that the Liberals had an immense majority – Liberals 379 – Labour 51 – Nationalists 83 – and the Unionists 155.

I won £150 in bets that I had taken with Edgar Vincent, Jack Poynder and others the week of Chamberlain's first speech on Protection, made on the 15th of May, 1903, as I prophesied that the whole country would revolt against any such folly.

I congratulated Mr Chamberlain on his gains in Birmingham, and he answered me in this letter:

'JAN. 23. 06

'My dear Mrs Asquith,

'You at least have the magnanimity the absence of which I thought I detected in our great Prime Minister. Many thanks for your congratulations. We have done well to-day in Handsworth and in Austin's division, and altogether we are rather pleased with ourselves here.

'But what a smash! For once I was quite out in my estimate and it was only the information of Horace Farquhar at Windsor that has saved me sixpence when I was about to bet with your husband against his having a majority over the Irish.

'Well, we shall see what we shall see. Your Coach has about 12 horses and will require skilful driving.

'You are quite right in saying that I agreed with you that every week we stayed in after the end of 1903 cost us many votes – but even then I did not anticipate the labour earthquake.

'It is all very interesting.

'Believe me,
'Yours very truly,
'J. CHAMBERLAIN.'

When the final figures of the Elections were published everyone was stunned, and it certainly looks as if it were the end of the great Tory Party as we have known it.

In discussing the results of this amazing General Election with Henry, I said that Balfour's and Chamberlain's minds were too different ever to work well together, and that it had been an unfortunate alliance. He answered: 'Joe drives further, but Arthur beats him at the short game.'

'It ought to have been the strongest of combinations,' I said; to which he replied:

'Unfortunately they have both been in a bunker for the last three years.'

*   *   *

*On the 3rd of June we were staying at Littlestone-on-Sea when I received a letter from my father written from Broadoaks, Weybridge, and on the 6th I heard of his death.

He was buried in Traquair Kirk on the 8th and we all travelled up from London the night before for the funeral.

We arrived at Innerleithen Station on a characteristic Peeblesshire morning – misty, pearly and windless, and followed the coffin at a foot's pace in covered carriages along the winding road leading to Traquair. My mother, Jack's wife, Helen, Laura and her little son, and all of us are buried in Traquair. I have knelt many times in the dark and said my prayers without disturbing the lambs huddled against the cross of Laura's grave and I love the churchyard. It is away from the noise of life, guarded by the Yarrow and the Tweed, and surrounded by the beckoning hills. I wondered as we stood by the open tomb that morning which of us would die next, and whether I would be buried in Traquair.†

* From my diary, June, 1906.
† End of diary quotation.

XVII · *10 Downing Street*

—◦◎◦—

*On the 27th of March, 1908, Henry came into my room at 7.30 p.m. and told me that Sir Henry Campbell-Bannerman had sent for him that day to tell him that he was dying. They had talked for over an hour, and Henry's voice shook as he repeated their conversation to me.

C.B. began by telling him the text he had chosen out of the Psalms to put on his grave, and the manner of his funeral. He was resigned and even cheerful, but after a little while, with his strong immovability, he turned the subject deliberately on to material things, flimsy matters – such as patronage, titles and bishops, etc.

Henry was deeply moved when he went on to tell me that Campbell-Bannerman had thanked him for being a wonderful colleague.

'So loyal, so disinterested and so able.'

Sir Henry Campbell-Bannerman's resignation having been accepted we expected to hear at any moment from the King.

† At five o'clock in the evening of Sunday, the 6th of April, 1908, my husband received a letter from King Edward, and he left the same night for Biarritz.

Not feeling well enough to go to the station we parted on the doorstep and he waved to me out of the motor as it disappeared round the corner of the Square. On the 8th I received a wire from Biarritz:

'Have just kissed hands; back Friday, ask Grey to dinner. Bless you. H.' On the same day he wrote to me:

'8 APRIL 08

'Darling – only time for a line. I saw Reggie Lister for a few minutes in Paris and then came on here by a train which got in about

* From my diary, March 1908.   † From my diary, April 1908.

¼ past 10 last night. Fritz Ponsonby met me at the station and I am comfortably lodged in the King's hotel.

'This morning I put on a frock coat, and escorted by Fritz and old Stanley Clarke went to the King who was similarly attired. I presented him with a written resignation of the office of Chr. of the Exr. and he then said "I appoint you P.M. and 1st Lord of the Treasury" whereupon I knelt down and kissed his hand. *Voilà tout!*

'He then asked me to come into the next room and breakfast with him. We were quite alone for an hour and I went over all the appointments with him. He made no objection to any of them and discussed the various men very freely and with a good deal of shrewdness.

'I am going to dine in his company at Mrs Cassel's villa to-night. The weather here is vile beyond description, pouring rain and plenty of wind. I leave at 12 noon to-morrow (Thursday) and arrive Charing Cross 5.12 Friday afternoon. You will no doubt arrange about dinner that evening – Love.'

And on the 10th I met him at Charing Cross.

There was a dense crowd outside the station, and a large one on the platform. I shook hands with a few waiting friends, and observed a thousand Pressmen taking notes. When at last the train came in and room was made for me by the officials, I greeted Henry, and arm in arm we walked to our open motor, bowing through the crush of people all mad with enthusiasm, some even throwing flowers at us.

We drove to 10 Downing Street, and I waited outside while Henry went in to enquire after Campbell-Bannerman.

The street was empty, and but for the footfall of a few policemen there was not a sound to be heard.

I looked at the dingy exterior of No. 10 and wondered how long we should live in it.

Leaning back I watched the evening sky reflected in the diamond panes of the Foreign Office windows, and caught a glimpse of green trees. The door opened and the Archbishop came out.

The final scene in a drama of Life was being performed in that quiet by-street. The doctor[1] going in and the priest coming out; and as I reflected on the dying Prime Minister I could only hope that no

[1] Sir Thomas Barlow.

sound had reached him of the crowd that had cheered his successor.*

*   *   *

When we moved into 10 Downing Street on the 5th of May, I could not help a feeling of sadness as I am faithful to a fault, and sensitively sentimental about my home. All the colour, furniture, grates, curtains, and every chair, table, and rug in Cavendish Square I had chosen myself. Houses like people should be individual; and though it is better to talk of a Queen Anne, Elizabethan, Jacobean or Georgian house than Sindlay, Lenygon, or Maple, I want people who come into a room to say this is 'Frances Horner', 'Annie Tennant', 'Margot Asquith' or any of the people of taste.

Rich men's houses are seldom beautiful, rarely comfortable, and never original. It is a constant source of surprise to people of moderate means to observe how little a big fortune contributes to Beauty.

You may go to a house in which all that you are shown is priceless. You spend your day with fellow-guests in a chorus of praise touring till you are tired looking at pictures that are numbered, books that are autographed, furniture which is dated, and bronzes that are signed. Your host swallows with complacency in a circular smile all that is said, while punctuating the pauses with complaints of his own poverty.

'God knows!' he will say with a smile and a shrug, 'how long any of us will be able to keep anything.'

And the company is shocked when you suggest that the contents if sold of a single vitrine would square his bank-book.

You risk bursting a blood-vessel after dinner if you pull up a tapestry chair, and the beauty of the brocade is scant consolation when you retire to bed, for bells that bring no one, and lights by which you cannot read. It is a sure sign of lack of imagination if you do not make your guests comfortable, and money has never yet bought imagination.

It is the general atmosphere, colour and arrangement that makes a house beautiful, and there was little of this to console me in my new home.

* End of diary quotation.

10 Downing Street ought to be as well known in London as the Marble Arch or the Albert Memorial, but it is not. Although I lived there from April 1908, till December 1916, I nearly always had to tell my driver the way. I was taken to Down Street, Piccadilly, when I was sleepy or unobservant; or there was a risk of the children and umbrellas being thrown into the streets by the taxi-man opening the door suddenly from his seat and asking me where Downing Street was.

This historic house is in a quiet cul-de-sac off Whitehall and of such diffident architecture that the most ardent tourist would scarcely recognize it again.

Knowing as it did every Cabinet secret, and what was going on all over the world, I could not but admire the reserve with which 10 Downing Street treated the public. Even the Press while trying to penetrate the Prime Minister's heart was unable to divulge the secret of his home.

Liver-coloured and squalid, the outside of No. 10 gives but little idea to the man in the street of what it is really like.

Having been intimate with four Prime Ministers – Gladstone, Rosebery, Balfour and Campbell-Bannerman – I thought I knew what in the 'sixties was called 'the Prime Minister's lodgings' pretty well; but when we went to live there I found I was wrong.

It is an inconvenient house with three poor staircases, and after living there a few weeks I made up my mind that owing to the impossibility of circulation I could only entertain my Liberal friends at dinner or at garden parties.

Having no bump of locality, soon after our arrival I left the drawing-room by one of the five doors and found myself in the garden instead of the hall. By the help of mildly lit telephones and one of the many messengers, I retraced my steps through a long and sepulchral basement, but I began to regret the light and air of my deserted home in Cavendish Square.

I will quote a sentence that I wrote in my diary about Number 10:

*I never knew what prevented anyone coming into this house at any moment: some would say atter lunching with us that nothing had. There was a hall porter who looked after our interests when

* From my diary.

visitors arrived, but he was over-anxious and appeared flurried when spoken to. Poor man, he was never alone; he sat in his hooded chair, snatching pieces of cold mutton at odd hours; tired chauffeurs shared his picture paper, and strange people – not important enough to be noticed by a secretary or a messenger – sat watching him on hard sills in the windows; or, if he were left for a moment, the baize doors would fly open and he would find himself faced by me, seeing a parson, a publican or a protectionist out of the house.

But our porter was not a strong man, and any determined Baronet with hopes of favours to come about the time of the King's birthday could have penetrated into Number 10.*

Things started well for us in Parliament, and Henry's colleagues were a perpetual study. Their moral and intellectual stature, as well as their appearances, manners and habits became extremely familiar to me, nor can I say I was far out in any of the predictions I made then upon their characters.

When John Morley heard that Winston Churchill was reading the lives of Napoleon he said:

'He would do better to study the drab heroes of life. Framing oneself upon Napoleon has proved a danger to many a man before him.'

He said this to me in a memorable talk soon after my husband became Prime Minister.

We were sitting in the garden at Flowermead discussing men and things. He spoke of his youth and how he had met Mrs Morley first at a students' ball. We spoke of his early intellectual heroes – John Stuart Mill, Meredith and Carlyle.

'One day', he said, 'I asked Carlyle what Mrs John Stuart Mill had been really like, to which he answered: "She was full of unwise intellect, asking and re-asking stupid questions." '

We then got on to the different gods that men worship and I told him that Arthur Balfour once said to me:

'If there is no future life this world is a bad joke; and whose joke?'

Although he is neither humble nor penitent, John Morley is a religious man who does not finish God in a phrase. He fights, gropes and aspires; he is never dry or smug but always tender, humorous

* End of diary quotation.

and understanding, and there is nothing fine that does not appeal to his feeling mind. I was glad that his peerage had made no stir. It is a far cry from 'Honest John' to 'Viscount Morley of Blackburn', but it excited no criticism. He is not only the most distinguished living Englishman, but a natural aristocrat. My husband called him a man of moods, but he is also a man of courage, sensitive to a fault, and responsive as a woman. An artist in conversation he can talk about himself without being self-centred. He is never obvious or predictable, and although easily flattered is an encouraging companion, as he can quote what you have said in former conversations if it has struck him as sound, and always responds to what is new or witty. I can truly say I would rather talk to him than to anyone I have ever met.

*   *   *

I paid my first visit to Windsor Castle that year (20th June 1908), for though Henry had already been there and I had attended the big banquets I had never stayed in the Castle before.

You must be rather stupid or easily bewildered if you do not enjoy staying at Windsor Castle. There is something there for every taste; fine food and drinks, fine pictures, fine china, fine books, comfort and company.

I will quote what I wrote in my diary of this visit:

*On the 20th of June, 1908, we motored Violet[1] to the garden party at Windsor, and after sending her back to London we walked up to the Castle. We turned in at the Lancastrian archway and were greeted by Sir Charles Frederick. Before going to rest, having been told that dinner was at 15 to 9, I examined the Prime Minister's apartments. They consist of two bedrooms, with marble baths attached to each; and a small sitting-room with large windows looking out upon the park. Hanging on a shiny grey and white wallpaper are indifferent portraits of Gladstone, Peel, Lord Cross, Melbourne and Disraeli. We found flowers on the tables and every kind of newspaper laid out for us to read.

I wore a Parma-violet satin dress for dinner with long silver sashes

---

* From my diary, Windsor Castle, 20th June 1908.
[1] Lady Bonham Carter.

and a kind of loose netting over the skirt; and at twenty minutes to nine Henry and I walked along the circular corridor gazing at the pictures as we passed the vermilion servants.

I was taken in to dinner by my friend the Marquis de Soveral, the cleverest foreigner I have ever met, and I may say a remarkable man in any country.

We assembled in a large uninteresting room – the ladies standing upon one side and the men upon the other while we awaited the entrance of the King.[1]

The Castle party consisted of Gladys de Grey,[2] Alice Keppel,[3] Lady Savile, Lady Lowther and her husband, the Turkish Ambassador, John Morley, Edward Grey and Count Mensdorff.[4]

The King and Queen were in high spirits and more than gracious to us. She looked divine in a raven's wing dress, contrasting with the beautiful blue of the Garter ribbon and her little head a blaze of diamonds.

She chaffed me about the Suffragettes who had been pursuing us with true feminine and monotonous malignity.

After dinner we played bridge – Grey and I, Mensdorff and Sir Gerald Lowther – while Henry played with the Queen; and the King made a four with Alice Keppel, Lady Savile and the Turkish Ambassador.

I am always happy with Sir Edward Grey and have a deep affection for him. His reality, thoughtfulness, and freedom from pettiness give him true distinction. He is unchangeable and there is something lonely, lofty and even pathetic about him which I could not easily explain.

On Sunday the 21st I had hoped to have gone to St George's Chapel, but the service was held in the Castle. After carefully pinning on a black hat, our page – a Dane of 75 or 80, who sits guarding our apartments on a chair in the passage – told me I was not to wear a hat, so I wrenched it off and fearing I should be late hastily joined the others in the gallery.

We heard a fine sermon upon men who justify their actions; have

[1] Edward VII.   [2] The Marchioness of Ripon.
[3] Mrs George Keppel.   [4] The Austrian Ambassador.

no self-knowledge, and never face life squarely; but I do not think many people listened to it.

The King and Queen and Princess Victoria sat in a box above our heads and were faced by the Prince of Wales with his eldest boy and girl in the gallery opposite.[1]

Gladys looked handsome, but seemed over-anxious. No one appeared to me to be quite at their ease in the presence of Their Majesties; the fact is, if you do not keep a firm grip upon yourself on the rare occasions when you are with the rich and the great, you notice little and enjoy nothing.

Royal persons are necessarily divorced from the true opinions of people that count, and are almost always obliged to take safe and commonplace views. To them, clever men are 'prigs'; clever women 'too advanced'; Liberals are 'Socialists'; the uninteresting 'pleasant'; the interesting 'intriguers'; and the dreamer 'mad'. But, when all this is said, our King devotes what time he does not spend upon sport and pleasure ungrudgingly to duty. He subscribes to his cripples, rewards his sailors, reviews his soldiers, and opens bridges, bazaars, hospitals and railway tunnels with enviable sweetness. He is fond of Henry, but is not really interested in any man. He is loyal to all his West End friends: female admirers, Jewish financiers and New-market bloods, and adds to fine manners rare prestige, courage and simplicity.

The friend he confides most in is a 'short study' but not a 'great subject'. Esher is a man of infinite curiosity and discretion, what the servants call 'knowing', and has considerable influence at Court. His good spirits, fair judgment and frank address make him plausible and popular, and he has more intelligence than most of the Court pests. Slim with the slim, straight with the straight, the fault I find with him is common to all courtiers, he hardly knows what is important from what is not.

After lunching with the household I retired to my room leaving Henry talking to Morley and Grey.

Our Dane informed me that we were to join Their Majesties in the Castle Courtyard at 4 o'clock to motor first to the gardens and then to Virginia Water, where we were to have tea. On my arrival in

[1] King George, the Prince of Wales and Princess Mary.

the courtyard the King came up to me and said:

'Where is the Prime Minister?'

Curtsying to the ground, I answered:

'I am sorry, Sir, but I have not seen him since lunch: I fear he cannot have got your command and may have gone for a walk with Sir Edward Grey.'

HIS MAJESTY (angrily turning to his gentlemen-in-waiting, Harry Stoner and Seymour Fortescue): 'What have you done? Where have you looked for him? Did you not give him my command?'

The distracted gentlemen flew about, but I could see in a moment that Henry was not likely to turn up, so I begged the King to get into his motor. He answered with indignation:

'Certainly not! I cannot start without the Prime Minister, and it is only 10 minutes past 4.'

He looked first at his watch and then at the Castle clock, and fussed crossly about the yard. Seeing affairs at a standstill I went up to the Queen and said I feared there had been a scandal at Court, and that Henry must have eloped with one of the maids of honour. I begged her to save my blushes by commanding the King to proceed, at which she walked up to him with her amazing grace, and, in her charming way, tapping him firmly on the arm pointed with a sweeping gesture to his motor and invited Gracie Raincliffe[1] and Alice Keppel to accompany him: at which they all drove off.

I waited about anxious to motor with John Morley, and finally followed with him and Lord Gosford. While we were deep in conversation Princess Victoria asked if she could take a kodak of us standing together. (She presented each of us with a copy a few days later.)

When we returned to the Castle we found that Henry had gone for a long walk with the Hon. Violet Vivian, one of the Queen's maids of honour, over which the King was jovial and even eloquent.*

The year 1908 ended in an event which made a deep impression upon me.

The First Lord of the Admiralty asked me if I would launch the latest Dreadnought, and on the 7th of November Henry and I,

[1] The Countess of Londesborough.
* End of diary quotation.

Pamela McKenna and her lord, travelled by a special train to Devonport.

I wore my best garden-party dress; biscuit-coloured cloth with a clinging skirt, string blouse and winged hat of the same colour. Bouquets and addresses of welcome had been presented to us at every station on the journey, and we were met upon our arrival by Admiral Cross and other naval officers. We drove through the decorated streets straight to the dockyard.

It was a brilliant blowing day, and on a dancing sea hundreds of crowded craft were bobbing about between the evil-looking battle-ships. I climbed up red cloth steps to a high platform, where the neighbours of distinction were collected under an awning. Clinging to my hat I kept my skirts down with difficulty. After receiving a bouquet and a water-colour of the ship, and making myself generally affable to the admirals and commanders, I looked up at the vast erection against the sky above me. This was the ship. The lines of her bows were stretched wide as the wings of a bird, and the armour of her plating gleamed and throbbed like diamonds.

The ceremony opened with prayer and the responses were sung by a choir.

I stood away from the people close to the railing that separated me from the ship and looked down upon the dockyard below, which was packed with thousands of enthusiastic people. 'Eternal Father, strong to save' was sung with vigour and supplication; every docker, bluejacket, marine, parson, and admiral singing with all their hearts against the clean sea wind.

After the blessing had been said, the constructor came bustling up to me, and pointing to four little ropes said:

'Come on! Be quick! Don't you see she's straining? Look at the dial!' He pushed a hammer and chisel into my hands.

Oblivious of his meaning and completely flustered I snatched the hammer begging him to let me hold the chisel by myself, but he insisted upon helping me, at which I missed the mark and brought the hammer down upon my own wrist and the constructor's: he instantly let go, and, recovering myself, I raised my hand above my head and said in a slow, loud voice:

'I name you *Collingwood*. God bless you, and all who sail in you', and with a violent blow severed the four ropes that released the galleys and the ship slid splashlessly into the sea.

Every head was strained, and every arm raised to bless her as she struck the water, and we ended the ceremony by singing 'Rule Britannia!' with moist eyes to the massed bands.

While the company buzzed about, I watched the bluejackets below me stuffing small bits of rope into their pockets for luck. A slip of paper was sent up to the Admiral from the yard saying that all the people had heard me, and at the evening party Devonport men told me they had never before heard the name of a battleship at a launch. I said I should indeed have felt inadequate had I muttered as if I had been in front of a mouse-trap.

On Sunday (November the 8th) the McKennas, Henry and I went to morning service on the first-class cruiser *Leviathan*. We sat about 200 of us under a long, low roof below the upper deck. I looked at the faces of the bluejackets; jolly, indifferent, keen men of every type: plain and handsome, tall and short, and thought if they had been women how they would have stared about at the Prime Minister, possibly even at Pamela and myself; but men are uncurious and occupied; they are not whispering, inquisitive busybodies. People may say what they like, but men and women are not what the Suffrage ladies think; they are of a different kind and not a variation of the same species.

I asked Admiral Fawkes, with whom we lunched, if he or any of his sea friends were afraid of the German Fleet. He said he thought the Navy that was copied and did not copy was likely to remain the most powerful, but that the sea scare had done the Service harm, as it kept young men in the home waters when they should have been gaining experience abroad. He added that they knew all about the German Fleet except her target practice at sea.

When I went to bed exhausted and thoughtful, I wondered upon what mission my beautiful *Collingwood* would first sail.

XVIII · *The Veto of the House of Lords*

Our political differences over the House of Lords came to a head in 1909, the year before King Edward died.

They had started in 1908 when after a private meeting in Lansdowne House the Lords rejected the Licensing Bill. For a Democracy to endow two Chambers with equal powers although one represents an elected public and the other the Peers, is, as the Chinese would say, 'distinguishable from true wisdom'.

No one who valued the moral, mental or physical energies of the people in this country could have watched with indifference the paralysing effect that drink and tied houses had upon the public. Except for rare crimes of fraud, our prisons were full of men detained for crimes of violence; and the drink problem, though hampered by teetotallers, became a Crusade.

My husband had taken every care over his Bill, and it needs courage for a Liberal to attack privileges which affect the working man more than the leisured classes. The Unionists, who have always been in sympathy with 'the Trade', counted on the popularity of their cry to cover the clumsiness of their conduct; but in the years of which I am writing there was a public conscience stronger than there is today, and from the moment the Licensing Bill was rejected the powers of the Peers became a question of first-rate importance.

Whatever our Party passed in the House of Commons which was controversial was rejected by the Peers; and it had become a settled policy that every measure a Unionist Government could devise had an easy passage through the Lords. We were being governed by a single Chamber. One danger of allowing this state of things was that, while striking a blow at the Constitution, it must ultimately have succeeded in making the Crown unpopular.

There was no choice before my husband if he were to strengthen the Commons or safeguard the King; but when he undertook to alter the relationship of the two Houses few of his colleagues thought he could succeed. Neither changing our Prison System, providing Old Age Pensions, scotching Protection, or giving the South Africans self-government was as difficult as removing the veto of the House of Lords.

The opportunity came in 1909 over the Finance Bill.

The famous Budget of that year was largely the creation of Sir Robert Chalmers, a clever man and a friend of ours. Its somewhat oriental method of asking for more than it intended to take did not appeal to me. But nothing we did was comparable to the classical behaviour of the Upper Opposition. The Dukes' speeches gave us an unfair advantage, backed as they were by the lesser lights – Earls, Marquises and Barons.

It was hardly to be believed that men who could read and write would have written or spoken in the manner they did. One noble Marquis wrote that if the Budget were passed he would be compelled to reduce his annual subscription to the London Hospital from five pounds to three a year; and in the same paper it was announced that he had bought a yacht 'rumoured to cost £1,000 a month'.

Another noble Earl, speaking in a different vein, said:

'If we Peers are obliged to, we will do our duty; and from what we hear in the country we have nothing to fear'.

I never understood anything about Finance, but gathered from the discussions which took place over the Budget that it was an ingenious, complicated, perfectly sound measure, with a touch of 'art nouvel' and an inquisitorial flavour, which was deeply resented.

* * *

On 4th November 1909, we drove down to the House of Commons to hear the final debate upon the Budget, and found it crowded from the ceiling to the floor.

Henry and Arthur Balfour wound up, and the Division was taken at midnight.

When the figures were announced that our majority (independent of the Irish) was 230, the uproarious cheering and counter-cheering betrayed the mixture of hate and enthusiasm with which the Bill was regarded.

The remarkable thing about the passing of this Budget was the unanimity with which people of different views backed it. Even the men who act according to their humour, which in party politics may make you fancy yourself a leader, but seldom gets you followers – voted for the Bill.

Non-party men do not succeed in this country because we are a political race and understand the rules of the game. Cabinet government is a corporate conscience, and concerted action is more valuable than individual opinion. Men subordinate their opinions on small matters for the sake of larger issues, and only part from one another when those issues are at stake. It is more from vanity than reflection that men of a certain sort always vote against their own Party; and in my judgment the non-party politician is well named when he is called 'a moderate man'. The alternative to the Party System is Coalition, which ends by being all things to all men and scrapping principles for promotion. To sell your faith for your advancement can never succeed, and Politics conducted by Coalition must ultimately lead to disaster.

The House adjourned for nineteen days after a dinner given by the Chancellor of the Exchequer to celebrate the passing of the Budget, which my husband attended.

* * *

On 15th November 1909, we went to stay at Windsor Castle, and, upon our arrival, Henry had a long interview with the King. When he came back I asked him if they had talked about politics, and he said:

'Yes; we discussed freely the folly of the peers. I told him that Queen Elizabeth had sometimes refused to sign her assent to Bills, but that this has not been done since her reign, and had become obsolete for 200 years. He is much vexed with the Lords, and said to me: "Not a line of any sort have I received as to their intentions, and I know no more than the man in the street what they are doing!"'

'Surely it is not at all nice of them!' I said; to which Henry replied:

'Oh! they aren't bound to tell the King what they are doing.

H.M. thinks party politics have never been more bitter, but I told him I was not so sure of that; I thought they were bitterer in the days of Home Rule.'

I asked him if the King had agreed about this, and he replied:

'Perhaps he did, I am not sure; he is not at all argumentative, and understands everything that is properly put to him. He is a clever man and a good listener, if you aren't too long. He has an excellent head and is most observant about people; he said some surprisingly shrewd things to me about Lansdowne and Balfour. The situation really distresses him and he told Knollys today he thought the Peers were mad.'

The Lord Chamberlain[1] at that moment interrupted us to tell Henry that the King wished Ministers to wear white breeches at the Investiture of the Garter for the King of Portugal, which was to take place on the following day.

Henry said: 'I think I am quite safe, my dear Bobby, in my Trinity House dress.'

To which Mr Spencer, looking a little nettled, replied: 'No one must dictate to the Prime Minister, of course!'

The next day we opened the papers and read that Lord Lansdowne had given notice in the House of Lords that, on the motion for the second reading of the Finance Bill, he would move:

'That this House is not justified in giving its consent to this Bill until it has been submitted to the judgment of the country'.

This was a declaration of war which made the General Election in January of the following year, inevitable.*

*　　　*　　　*

The assembly of the House of Lords to discuss the rejection of the Budget was the largest ever known. Aged Peers came from remote regions of the country side who could not even find their way to the Houses of Parliament. The galleries were packed with all the great ladies of England, and the debate extended over ten days.

The best speeches were made by those who, while hating the Bill, realized that its rejection would raise a bigger question than that of the Budget. Lord Rosebery, Lord Cromer, Lord Balfour of Burleigh,

---

[1] The Earl Spencer.　　　　* End of diary quotation.

and the Archbishop of York appealed in words of great eloquence to their fellow-peers not to raise this question. But the Lords acted as if demented. What blindness could have fallen upon Lord Lansdowne and others to urge the Peers down these slippery slopes to the sea will always remain a mystery. It is said that the Whips had promised an immense majority in the country over Tariff Reform. But even if they had won that election their doom could only be a question of time, for it was evident that in future no Liberal Government could take Office without guarantees for the destruction of the Veto.

Obdurate to all these considerations, and influenced by the speeches of Lord Milner and Lord Willoughby de Broke, the Lords by an overwhelming majority on 30th November, rejected the Budget, and on the following Saturday an immense multitude filled Trafalgar Square to demonstrate not so much in the interests of the Budget as against the action of the Lords.

The position which Henry had foreseen had come to pass, and he instantly asked for and obtained sanction for the dissolution of Parliament.

The controversy which raged up and down the country between the Peers and the People was an issue which could have but one result.

The Lords had committed suicide.

The last weeks of the year 1909 we spent in touring all over the country making speeches, and after an unsatisfactory but predictable General Election we were returned in January 1910, by a reduced majority. The general public showed an enlightened interest in the question of Protection, which, considering the ignorance on all financial matters of the majority of people, surprised us. We received many and amusing letters; among the best is the following from Lord Hugh Cecil:

'HATFIELD HOUSE,
'FEBRUARY 18TH, 1910

'Dear Mrs Asquith,
'Lloyd George has got you into a nice mess: nothing left for you but to try and create 500 peers and perish miserably attacking the

King. That's what comes of making an irresponsible demagogue Chancellor of the Exchequer.

'Yours ever,

'HUGH CECIL.'

When we returned to Downing Street, successful and defeated candidates poured in to give us their experiences of the elections. Among others I saw Mr. John Burns,[1] an old and valued friend of ours, whose career, if he would write it, would be among the great and interesting autobiographies of the world.

Among other adventures he served a short sentence in prison for a riot in Trafalgar Square and was defended in the Law Courts by my husband before he became Home Secretary. In protesting against the long hours of the railway men when he was standing in the witness box he said:

'You should always give a man an opportunity of telling his wife he is still her sweetheart.'

I did not meet any of the Conservatives whose opinions were worth recording till a few days later, when Mr Chamberlain asked me to go and see him in his house at Prince's Gate.

Although I had not met him since his health had broken down we had always remained friends.

Mr Chamberlain was essentially loyal – neither mean nor sly – and saw with great clearness a very short distance. He thoroughly understood the view that the average elector was likely to hold, and predicted from the beginning the antipathy there would be to Chinese Labour in this country.

Like many successful organizers he was an interesting man with an uninteresting mind. His intelligence was superior to his intellect, and his sense of drama, love of action, and lack of moods, freed him from complications, which made him an easy man to deal with. Affectionate and faithful to his friends, he was a bad enemy. Though never a knight in the arena, he was too great an artist to be described as a bruiser. He started his political career as an advanced Radical and became the hero of the Tory Party.

History repeats itself in strange ways, and I continue to wonder

[1] The Right Hon. John Burns.

why the Conservatives, who are so easily tamed, should be as leader-less today as they were then.

I was welcomed on my arrival by the lovely Mrs Chamberlain and found her husband sitting erect in his armchair near the tea table; his hair was black and brushed, and he had an orchid in his tightly buttoned frock coat.

The room we were shown into was furnished in early Pullman-car or late North-German-Lloyd style and struck me as singularly undistinguished.

My host's speech was indistinct but his mind was alert. After greeting him with a deep inside pity and much affection, I asked him if he had been pleased with the results of the General Election. I added that I myself had been disappointed with the South, but that the North had gone well for us; to which he answered that he had expected to beat us, and wondered why Scotland was always so Liberal. I amused him by saying that we were an uninfluenceable race with an advanced middle class, superior to the aristocracy and too clever to be taken in by Tariff Reform, and added:

'You know, Mr Chamberlain, I would not much care to be a Unionist today!'

Mistaking my tone for one of triumph, he said:

'But you also have great difficulties ahead of you.'

I explained that I meant that the Protectionist party could not feel any satisfaction at being led by Arthur Balfour, as he had never been one of them. To which he replied:

'He is coming on a little, but the truth is he never understood anything at all about the question.'

Continuing upon our Cabinet, he said of one of them, pointing to his heart:

'He is a vulgar man in the worst sense of the word and will dis-appear; give him enough rope and he will hang himself; I admire nothing in a man like that. Winston is the cleverest of all the young men, and the mistake Arthur made was letting him go.'

I indicated that, however true this might be, he was hated by his old party; to which he replied:

'They would welcome him today with open arms if he were to return to them.'

We ended our talk by his telling me that he had always been a Home Ruler, and that nothing could be done till the difficulties in Ireland were settled.

Wanting to show some of the compassion I felt for him, I told him before leaving that I also had had a nervous break-down, and added:

'You know, Mr Chamberlain, I was *so* ill that I thought I was *done*': to which he answered:

'Better to *think* it Mrs Asquith, than to *know* it as I do.'

I never saw him again.

*   *   *

Mr Chamberlain was right; our party had great difficulties ahead of them; and I began to realize of how little value brains can be; I was tired of cleverness and thanked God that Henry had more than this. In the great moments of life; in times of love, or of birth, or of death, brains count for nothing. The clever among Henry's colleagues were not always loyal, and the loyal, with notable exceptions, were not too clever.

*I sit in No. 10 and wonder how long we shall stay here. Our Lords Resolutions will be over on the 14th and on the 28th April we take the third reading. For the moment we do not know how the Irish will vote, but if they join the Tories against us we shall resign.

Henry wants a complete change of scene. He dines with Lloyd George on the 28th, at the Savoy, to celebrate the passing of the Budget, and motors to Portsmouth after dinner with the McKennas, who take him on the Admiralty Yacht to inspect our fortifications at Gibraltar. He had to say good-bye to the King, and, fearing he might not get back before dinner, left me the following letter:

'DOWNING STREET,
'APRIL 28TH, 1910

'As you know I am dining with Lloyd George to-night, at the Savoy, to celebrate the Budget and go on after dinner with the McKennas to Portsmouth. If I can, I will look in on the chance of seeing you. Send all letters through the Admiralty. I am glad to get

* From my diary, 10 Downing Street, April 1910.

away but sorry to leave you. All through these trying weeks you have been more than anyone sympathetic, understanding, loyal and loving. I have felt it much.

'I had a good talk with the King this evening and found him most reasonable.

'Ever your own'.

Left alone in Downing Street, I dined with the Charles Hamiltons on the 5th of May. I saw no posters in the streets on my return to Downing Street, but was told afterwards that the news of King Edward's illness had been advertised in the Strand and Piccadilly.

*Frances Horner telephoned to me early on the morning of the 6th, and asked me if I was anxious, as she feared the King was seriously ill. I seized *The Times* and read the bulletin of the King's bronchitis signed by the Drs Powell and Reid. Realizing that this was grave, I dressed quickly and hurried round to the Palace. I read in silence the latest bulletin hanging on the wall, while several of my friends were signing the King's book:

'No progress: condition causes grave anxiety.'

I felt full of apprehension, and wondered if the Admiralty Yacht would be in reach of news. I found Charles Hardinge[1] on my return to Downing Street, who told me he had left Lord Knollys in tears and suggested my sending Henry a telegram: I sat down and wrote:

'Advise your returning immediately. The King seriously ill: all London in state of well-founded alarm: Margot.'

This was sent from the Admiralty in cypher. I felt shattered, and received my lunch party with a silent heart.

Lord Kitchener, Lady Frances Balfour, John Burns, Nathalie Ridley, Lucy, Elizabeth and I sat down to lunch. K. of K. walked up to the window and broke the silence by saying the flag was still flying at the Palace, a remark which jarred upon me profoundly; but excepting Frances Balfour none of the company seemed at all able to realize the gravity of the situation.

While we were eating our lunch, messages came from the Palace: 'No improvement.'

* From my diary, 10 Downing Street, 6th May 1910.
[1] Lord Hardinge of Penshurst.

I sent a note to Lord Knollys begging him to send for Kingston Fowler, as Court Doctors are not always the best. He answered with his unfailing courtesy:

'Many thanks for your letter. I will at once tell the Doctors what you say. I am afraid I can give you no better news.'

Our Secretary, Roderick Meiklejohn, came in after lunch and reassured me by saying he was certain the Admiralty Yacht would be in reach of the news of the King's illness, and while he was talking I received the following note from John Burns:

'MAY 6TH, 1910

'*Private.*

'Dear Mrs Asquith,

'I hear and I hope it is true that you have sent to the Prime Minister to come home. The Admiralty will code it on to Spain at once.

'News serious and confirms your view of today.

'Yours sincerely,

'JOHN BURNS.'

In the afternoon I went to see Anne Poynder[1]; she told me that her husband had had an audience of the King upon his appointment as Governor to New Zealand the day before; and that, although H.M. had been up and dressed, he looked alarmingly ill. On his return he had said to her:

'I don't know what other people feel, but *I* think I have been with a dying man today!'

All London is standing still with anxiety and I can hardly refrain from crying.

That night saying my prayers with Elizabeth and Puffin we prayed out loud that God might save the King.

At 10.30 p.m. after dining along with the Islingtons I went round to see the Hardinges. Edward Grey came into the room with Sir Charles and I noticed they both looked white with sorrow. We did not shake hands: I asked for the latest news. One of them answered:

'It is practically over; he is unconscious. He sent for Sir Ernest

[1] Lady Islington.

Cassel this morning and insisted on sitting up in his clothes although breathless and unable to speak; his courage is amazing.'

None of us spoke.

Sir Edward Grey drove me away from the Hardinges and said when we were alone in the taxi:

'This is a very big moment; these things have to be, but it has come as a terrible shock in its suddenness.'

He dropped me at Anne Islington's, where my motor was waiting for me. Our footman had copied the latest bulletin stuck up for the crowd to see outside the Palace and gave it to me as I got into the car. It said:

'The King's symptoms have become worse today and His Majesty's condition is now serious.'

I motored Anne to Buckingham Palace on my way home at 11 p.m., and there we found large silent groups of people reading this same bulletin. On my return to 10 Downing Street I went to bed.

The head messenger[1], followed by his wife in her nightgown, came down to see me, and standing in the doorway of my bedroom asked for the latest news; I said it was practically all over, and they left the room shutting the door noiselessly behind them.

I lay awake with the lights turned on, sleepless, stunned, and cold.

At midnight there was a knock at my door. Mr Lindsay walked in, and, stopping at the foot of the bed, said:

'His Majesty passed away at 11.45.'

'So the King is dead!!' I said out loud and burst into tears.

I slept from 2 till 5 a.m. and then wrote my diary. I sent letters to the Queen and Lord Knollys.

After the Privy Council the next morning Sir Ernest Cassel came to see me and we cried together on the sofa.

I dined that night at Mrs George West's, and met Winston Churchill, the Crewes and the Harcourts. At the end of dinner Winston said:

'Let us drink to the health of the new King.'

To which Lord Crewe answered:

[1] Mr Lindsay.

'Rather to the memory of the old.'

*Henry[1] returned from his cruise on the 9th of May, 1910, and on the 10th he paid his first visit to the new King. He came away deeply moved by his modesty and common sense.

On the 20th of May, 1910, I dressed at 6.30 a.m., and walked into the streets to see the crowd. It was the day of the funeral and people from all parts of the globe were thronging the town. I had sent the children the night before to Lady Lewis' house in Portland Place, as the police had warned me it would be easier for them to go from thence to Lady Wernher's, from whose balcony they were to see the Procession. Henry and I breakfasted alone, and at 9 a.m. we walked to Westminster Hall to see the coffin start and the cortège collect for Paddington station.

We walked slowly down the middle of the soldiered street under a grilling sun, and joined the small official group which consisted of the Speaker, John Burns, Lord Carrington and the Crewes. We stood upon a red carpet outside Westminster Hall awaiting the arrival of the nine Kings who had come from various parts of Europe for the funeral. As most people wanted to see the procession from a balcony and some were motoring or going by train to Windsor, Peggy Crewe and I were the only women among the officials.

We all stood in silence and watched the forming up of the Procession.

The gun-carriage led, followed by the charger with the military boots reversed; then came the King's kilted loader leading his wire-haired terrier[2] by a strap.

---

* From my diary, May 1910.

[1] He wrote the following account for my diary on his return: 'The "Enchantress" after visiting Lisbon was making her way from Cadiz to Gibraltar when we received a wireless message that the King was ill. This was confirmed when we reached Gibraltar, and I directed that we should at once return home, though there was nothing in the message that seemed to call for immediate alarm. We started at once, and about three in the morning of the 7th of May, 1910, I was awakened with the news that a wireless had just arrived announcing the King's death. I went up on deck, in the twilight before dawn, and my gaze was arrested by the sight of Halley's Comet blazing in the sky. It was the first and last time that any of us saw it.'

[2] Cæsar.

Crewe and I patted the little dog, who was most friendly – but the beautiful charger, which I had approached with confidence, stretched out his fine neck and showed me all his teeth.

At 10 a.m. the Kings clattered into the quadrangle followed by two coaches. The Queen, Princess Victoria and the Wales children were in one and Queen Alexandra and the King sat alone in the other. They were closely followed by the Kaiser and the Duke of Connaught, who were mounted upon horseback. They all pulled up a few yards from where we were standing and the Kaiser opened the carriage door with conscious promptness for Queen Alexandra, who stepped out, a vision of beauty, dressed entirely in crêpe with a long black veil floating away behind her. We curtsied to the ground with bowed heads as she passed us. The Archbishop of Canterbury received the King and his mother in the open doorway and they followed him back into Westminster Hall. The only others who went with them were the Kaiser and the Duke of Connaught.

We were told that the horsemanship of the seven Kings might, if they dismounted, lead to complications, so they remained seated while we made a study of their faces. These were not impressive. I like the Crown Prince of Austria's the least, and the King of Spain's the best; but the Kaiser's cut features, observant eyes and immobile carriage, as he swung a short leg across a grey hunter, made him the most interesting figure of them all.

I could not help thinking what a terrifying result a bomb thrown from Big Ben would have had upon that assemblage, and blessed this country for its freedom.

The Kings, the soldiers, and the retinue held the salute like bronzes when the coffin came out upon the shoulders of Guardsmen and was placed upon the gun-carriage; and continued holding it while the white pall, Union Jack, the Crown and the Insignia were placed upon the bier. The Earl Marshal[1], heavily decked in gold, sat uneasily upon his horse and the procession moved slowly away.

We crawled to the station in the motor and found Paddington like the Ascot enclosure. It was closely packed with famous and dazzling people, their uniforms glittering with decorations, and all the fashionable ladies veiled and in black. We travelled down to

[1] The Duke of Norfolk.

Windsor in the same carriage as the Crewes, Edward Grey and John Morley.

On arriving at the Cloisters we looked at the flowers piled up in stacks to the roof. With the curiosity that makes most of us try and pick out our own faces in a photographic group I tried to find the wreath we had sent. It was large and made of sweet briar with a bunch of eglantine roses at the stem, but I never saw it. I do not suppose that there were ever collected in one place so many lovely flowers, or with such moving inscriptions written upon them as we saw that day.

When we went into the Chapel I was interested to see how many times the pew-openers would change their victims' places. The Opposition, the Queen's Pages, the Knights of the Garter, and their foreign equivalents were ruthlessly shoved about, while every new pew-opener of greater prestige than the last rolled and unrolled his list till the seating became a mosaic of indecision and confusion. Luckily, Henry, as the King's chief male, and the Duchess of Buccleuch as his chief female servant, occupied the best seats in the choir, and I was placed next to him.

Gazing opposite at the Corps Diplomatique I caught a friendly recognition from Countess Benckendorff,[1] but the long musicless wait had a stupefying effect, and what with short nights and an excess of emotion I fell into a deep, short and unobserved sleep.

I was awakened by the music of the massed bands playing Chopin's Funeral March in the street. The choir came up the aisle followed by the Bishops and Archbishop, and stood upon the altar steps.

The King walking with Queen Alexandra followed the coffin closely. At some distance behind them came the Dowager Czarina, the Duke of Connaught and the Kaiser; and these were followed by the other seven Kings. A prie-dieu was placed behind the Coffin for the Queen, and when she took her place in front of it the King and the others all fell back and she was left standing erect and alone.

When the Coffin was lowered, and slowly disappearing into the ground she knelt suddenly down and covered her face with both her hands.

That single mourning figure, kneeling under the faded banners

[1] The wife of the Russian Ambassador.

and coloured light, will always remain among the beautiful memories of my life.*

*   *   *

With the accession to the Throne of King George – whom my husband and I had known and loved since boyhood – the Constitutional question dealing with the House of Lords became much more difficult. Rather than embarrass the new King, my husband decided to refer the subject to a round-table Conference, over which he held hopes; but after six months of deliberation the negotiations broke down; and on 10th November, I received a telegram while I was staying with the children in Scotland, in which he wrote:

'Tout est fini.'

It was clear to me that there was nothing for it but for us to have another General Election and as quickly as possible before the discontent of our party could become vocal. I sent our Chief Whip – the Master of Elibank – a telegram to this effect, and another to Henry, who had gone to Sandringham to see the King.

The patience and resolution that the Prime Minister had shown over the Budget had made an impression upon the country, and as the Unionists had no programme I felt no fears as to the result of the Elections. Our opponents were fiercely divided over several questions, and neither lauding the peers nor taxing food was likely to attract the public.

Knowing what my husband would feel at the breakdown of the Conference, I started for London in the evening of the day I received his telegram.

The Cabinet drew up a State Paper of first-rate importance, and on 15th November 1910, Henry took it to Buckingham Palace. He spent two hours with Lord Knollys explaining its various points before he had his audience with the King.

On his return to Downing Street I asked him which of his colleagues had contributed most to this Document. Had Winston?

'No,' he answered, 'all Winston's suggestions were discounted.'

'What about X——?' I said.

Henry answered it was not his 'genre' as he was useless upon

* End of diary quotation.

paper. Lord Crewe had been wise; John Morley had made valuable verbal alterations; but Grey and he had contributed the bulk. He ended by saying:

'If the King refuses to exercise his prerogative, I resign at once and explain the reasons for my resignation by reading this paper in the House of Commons. If we are beaten at the General Election the question will never arise, and if we get in by a working majority the Lords will give way, so the King won't be involved.'

I asked him if he thought we should get in; to which he answered:

'Yes, I think we shall, though the future has a nasty way of turning up surprises.'

Lady Frances Balfour said to me that she had written to her brother-in-law, Arthur, and told him she had travelled all over the country, and that unless he could controvert dear food we should be returned by an overwhelming majority.

On 17th November Henry went to see the King and at seven o'clock of the same evening he walked into my bedroom.

After a pause he sat down and told me that Lord Crewe and he had had a remarkable talk with His Majesty: that they had found him without obstinacy, both plucky and reasonable. He read him the State Paper, and pointed out the impossibility of allowing affairs to drift on as they were doing. He said that, after six months of Conference and doing all that lay in his power to find a solution of this difficult problem, no one could ever accuse him of undue haste. His Majesty listened attentively to him and ultimately agreed.

The audience was over.

Putting an end to the rival powers of the two Houses of Parliament was a political act of supreme courage, but my husband is as convinced today as he was then that it was the only way in which he could safeguard both the Commons or the King.

In telling me of this interview he was deeply moved and ended a memorable conversation by saying:

'You can only make changes in this country Constitutionally: any other method leads to Revolution.'

Lord Knollys told us that when Henry had left the Palace the King had said to him:

'Is this the advice that you would have given my father?'

He replied:

'Yes Sir; and your father would have taken it.'

*   *   *

Between 17th November and 20th December, 1910, the General Election was over and we were returned by a majority of 124 (one seat to the good).

It was a purely personal Election and could not have been won without my husband. I must also add that our Chief Whip had organized the country from top to toe.

Alec Murray – better known as the Master of Elibank – was a rare combination of grit and honey, with a perfect understanding of men and their motives. Having a sunny temper – never taciturn, sudden or contentious – he could 'get into touch' to use his favourite expression with Liberal, Labour or Tory with equal ease. Although at times rusé, he was trustworthy, and Lord FitzAlan told me that, during all the time they were rival whips of the Unionist and Liberal Parties in the House, they had worked together in perfect loyalty.

I loved the Master and have never known anyone at all like him. He was a mixture of slim and simple that no country but my own could have produced, with a devotion to schemes and persons only equalled by an Italian servant of the fifteenth century.

When I am disgusted by lack of heart, candour or character in the people I meet, I do not want to see them; but the Master had no such recoil; I feel it a waste of time being in mean company, but no one wasted the Master's time; he was plump and laughed, and, though an indefatigable worker, was ready to see anyone at any time and in any place. He found a fish in every net, caught some and let others go, and his thinking powers were entirely concentrated upon people. I never knew what his political convictions were but he devoted the best part of his life to Liberalism. He had a real affection for Mr Lloyd George, and did his utmost to make him work loyally with my husband. His flair for stage-management amounted to genius and he was familiar with every form of advertisement.

Working daily with a man like Henry, whose modesty amounts to deformity, and whose independence of character baffles the prophets and irritates the Press, our Chief Whip's ingenuity and resource were invaluable to us in 10 Downing Street, and when he left us we did not find his successor. His pleasure in this world, as well as his duty, was concerned in making men live harmoniously together, and Lord Murray of Elibank should have a high place in the next, if the Almighty keeps His promise to the Peace-makers.

After the final figures of the Elections were known he came to see my husband. He told us that the Unionists, being wrong in their calculations, were raising an outcry over the results of the Election, giving every reason but the right one to account for our success.

He ended his talk by saying:

'I met Acland Hood, who is suffering from all the abuse and recrimination of a defeated Party; he said to me: "Our people want to know how it was we didn't win." I told them frankly that, wherever I went all over the country, I heard the same thing; no one fancied the Lords or dear food.'

Suspicions and divisions in the ranks of our Opponents obscured our difficulties, but nevertheless they were accumulating.

The Parliament Bill went forward from February till July, but, in spite of large majorities in the House of Commons, the Lords reduced it to impotence.

On 21st July 1911, my husband informed the Press that the House of Commons would not accept the Lords' amendments and the King had agreed to exercise his Prerogative of creating sufficient Peers to enable the Bill to pass into law.

This declaration caused an uproar.

Conscious of their follies and smarting under their defeat the more short-sighted of the rank and fashion determined to have their revenge.

I will here quote from my diary:

*On Monday, the 24th of July, 1911, we drove in an open motor to the House of Commons and were cheered through the streets.

The Speaker's Gallery was closely packed, and excited ladies were standing up on their chairs. My husband got a deafening reception as he walked up the floor of the House; but I saw in a moment that

* From my diary, July 1911.

the Opposition was furious and between the counter-cheers I could hear the occasional shout of 'Traitor!'

When the hubbub had subsided he rose to move the rejection of the Lords' amendments; at this Lord Hugh Cecil and Mr F. E. Smith[1] led an organized and continuous uproar which kept him on his feet for over thirty minutes.

'Divide! Divide! 'Vide! 'Vide!!!' was shouted by the Opposition in an orgy of stupidity and ruffianism every time he opened his mouth. The Speaker tried in vain to make them listen, but the House was out of hand and the uproar continued.

Looking at the frenzied faces from above, I realised slowly that Henry was being howled down. Edward Grey got up from his place four off from where my husband was standing, and sat down again close beside him. His face was set.

I scrawled a hasty line from our stifling gallery and sent it down to him, 'They will listen to you – so for God's sake defend him from the cats and the cads!'

Arthur Balfour followed, and when Grey rose to speak the stillness was formidable.

Always the most distinguished figure in the House, he stood for a moment white and silent, and looked at the enemy:

'If arguments are not to be listened to from the Prime Minister there is not one of us who will attempt to take his place,' he said, and sat down in an echo of cheers.

Mr F. E. Smith rose to reply, but the Liberals would not listen to him and the Speaker adjourned the House on the ground of grave disorder.

I met Edward Grey for a moment afterwards alone, and, when I pressed my lips to his hand, his eyes filled with tears.

Sir Alfred Cripps[2] and Colonel Lockwood[3], with the fine feeling that has often differentiated them from the rest of their Party, called a private meeting to draft a letter of apology to the Prime Minster for what had taken place. Among many letters, I received the following from my dear friend, Lord Henry Bentinck:

[1] Lord Birkenhead.
[2] Lord Parmoor.
[3] Lord Lambourne.

'JULY 25TH

'Dearest Margot,

'I have been away from London and have only just returned, consequently have had no opportunity of signing the letter of regret for the hooligan business, which I understand Sir Alfred Cripps has forwarded to Mr Asquith. I should be very grateful if you would tell him how deeply I deplore the ungentlemanlike behaviour of a section of our party and how gladly I would have signed the letter had I been in London—

'I fear we [are] very deeply in the mire, which by the way is one certainly of our own creation.

'This is private please.

'Yours,

HENRY BENTINCK.'

On the 25th of July, *The Times* and other papers published the full text of the speech that my husband had been prevented from making in the House the day before.

After giving a complete history of the Veto Bill and the principle upon which it was founded, and which had been approved by the House of Commons in 1907, and endorsed at two subsequent General Elections, he ended by saying:

'We have, therefore, come to the conclusion – and thought it courteous and right to communicate that conclusion in advance to leaders of the Opposition – that, unless the House of Commons is prepared to concede these essential points, there is only one constitutional way of escape from what would otherwise be a deadlock. It is the method of resort to the Prerogative which is recognized by the most authoritative exponents of Constitutional law and practice, when, as is here the case, the House of Commons must be presumed to represent on the matter in dispute the deliberate decision of the nation.'

He wound up with:

'I need hardly add that we do not desire to see the Prerogative exercised. There is nothing humiliating to a great party in admitting defeat. No one asks them to accept that defeat as final. They have only to convince their fellow-countrymen that they are right and we are wrong, and they can repeal our Bill.'

For a fortnight the excitement continued and the Tories moved a vote of censure on the Government. Ashamed of their action of two weeks before, they listened to my husband in silence. In this vindication of the action he had taken throughout the controversy and the manner in which he had kept the King's name out of the dispute, Henry made one of the most moving appeals ever addressed to the Commons. It was a speech which will live in history, and, as he built up his case in orderly sequence, the ranks of the Conservatives looked shattered and broken. Even *The Times* had to admit that 'Dexterity was a special characteristic of the speech: as it has been of his conduct throughout the whole controversy'.

He ended:

'I am accustomed, as Lord Grey was accustomed, to be accused of breach of the Constitution, and even of treachery to the Crown. I confess that I am not in the least sensitive to this cheap and ill-informed form of vituperation. It has been my privilege, now I think unique, to serve, in close and confidential relations, three successive British Sovereigns. My conscience tells me that in that capacity, many and great as have been my failings and shortcomings, I have consistently striven to uphold the dignity and just privileges of the Crown. *But I hold my office, not only by favour of the Crown, but by the confidence of the whole people. And I should be guilty indeed of treason if, in this supreme moment of a great struggle, I were to betray their trust.*'

When he sat down the whole Liberal Party rose and applauded him, and it seemed as if the cheers would never cease.*

The end is soon told. The Bill reached the House of Lords in a state of confusion. There were Diehards and other Peers who were fighting each other; friend attacked friend, and the issue remained uncertain until the last moment. Some of Lord Murray's possible Peers watched from the gallery, hoping for rejection, the Archbishop of Canterbury was cursed and blessed, as he moved from group to group, persuading and pleading with each to abstain.

Amid passionate excitement the Bill was finally passed by a majority of 17. Most of the Peers abstained from voting.

* End of diary quotation.

XIX · *War*

It is not my purpose to write a history of the war; or of any of the campaign, either in its successes or failures. These have been fully dealt with by most of the great Generals and many competent amateurs. But from my diaries and notes taken often on the same day I shall give a true and simple account of what I saw and heard from August 4th 1914, until we left Downing Street in December 1916.

*   *   *

The London season of 1914 had been a disappointing one for me, and not an amusing one for Elizabeth, and as I was anxious that she should have a little fun I sent her alone on 25th July to stay with Mrs George Keppel, who had taken a house in Holland.

Alice Keppel is a woman of almost historical interest, not only from her friendship with King Edward, but from her happy personality, and her knowledge of society and of the men of the day. She is a plucky woman of fashion; human, adventurous, and gay, who in spite of doing what she liked all her life, has never made an enemy. Her native wit and wits cover a certain lack of culture, but her desire to please has never diminished her sincerity.

When we had to leave Downing Street without a roof over our heads in 1916 – as our house in Cavendish Square was let to Lady Cunard – she put her own bedroom and sitting-room at my disposal and insisted upon living on an upper storey herself.

To be a Liberal in high society is rare: indeed I often wonder in what society they are to be found. I do not meet them among golfers, soldiers, sailors, or servants; nor have I seen much Liberalism in the Church, the Court, or the City; but Alice Keppel was born in Scotland and has remained a true Liberal.

King Edward asked me once if I had ever known a woman of kinder or sweeter nature than hers, and I could truthfully answer that I had not.

When Elizabeth went to Holland on the 25th Foreign affairs were not causing uneasiness to any of the people that I had seen. But a feeling of apprehension made me telegraph to her a few days after her departure to tell her to return.

The apprehension I felt was shared by no one in London society, and as late as the 29th, when the Archbishop of Canterbury and Lord D'Abernon were lunching in Downing Street, they were amazed when I told them I had stopped my sister Lucy going to paint in France, and had telegraphed for Elizabeth to return from Holland.

What had frightened me was that, on Monday the 27th, Sir Edward Grey announced in the House that he had made a proposal to Germany, France, and Italy, to hold a Conference with Great Britain, but that, although France and Italy had accepted, no reply[1] had been received from Germany.

The strain of waiting for foreign telegrams with the fear of war haunting my brain had taken away all my vitality, and on Wednesday the 29th I went to rest before dinner earlier than usual; but I could not sleep. I lay awake listening to the hooting of horns, screams of trains, the cries of street traffic, as if they had been muffled drums heard through thick muslin.

At 7.30 p.m. the door opened and Henry came into my bedroom. I saw at once by the gravity of his face that something had happened: he generally walks up and down when talking, but he stood quite still.

I sat up and we looked at each other.

'I have sent the precautionary telegram to every part of the Empire,' he said, 'informing all the Government Offices – Naval, Military, Trade and Foreign – that they must prepare for war. We have been considering this for the last two years at the Committee of Defence, and it has never been done before; for over an hour and a half we worked, and the last telegram was sent off at 3.30 this afternoon. We have arranged to see the representatives of the Press

[1] This is a complete answer to the Kaiser's contention that Germany did not want war.

daily, so as to tell them what they may, and what they may not publish.'

Deeply moved, and thrilled with excitement, I observed the emotion in his face and said:

'Has it come to this!' At which he nodded without speaking, and after kissing me left the room.

The next day I went to the Speaker's Gallery, full of apprehension.

The House of Commons seemed unfamiliar; yet how well I knew it! The smiling policemen and rapid lift; the courteous servants, noiseless doors; and the ugly, pretty, stupid, clever, West End ladies' faces. The suppressed chatter, dingy air, frugal teas, and cheerless light of the Speaker's Gallery – all these I knew and loved, but they seemed changed for me that afternoon.

The position of affairs following on the Austrian note to Serbia had developed with alarming rapidity. Mr Bonar Law and Sir Edward Carson had seen my husband in the morning, and they had parted in complete agreement over the gravity of the situation.

It was impossible for Henry to move his Irish Amending Bill, which had been awaited with passionate excitement and was to have taken place that day.

I went to the Prime Minister's room on my arrival at the House, but, seeing Dillon and Redmond waiting outside his door, I remained in the passage.

Before going into the Gallery, Henry and I met for a moment alone, and I asked him if things were really so alarming. To which he replied:

'Yes, I'm afraid they are: our fellows don't all agree with me about the situation, but times are too serious for any personal consideration and whether X—— or Z—— do or do not resign matters little to me, as long as Crewe and Grey are there: I don't intend to be caught napping.'

I remember vaguely the frigid acknowledgments of some of the Ulster aristocracy and a withdrawal of skirts as I took my seat in the closely packed Gallery and watched my husband with throbbing pulses as he rose to his feet.

'I do not propose to make the motion which stands in my name,' he said, 'but by the indulgence of the House I should like to give the reason. We meet today under conditions of gravity which are almost unparalleled in the experience of every one of us. The issues of peace and war are hanging in the balance, and with them the risk of a catastrophe of which it is impossible to measure either the dimensions or the effects. In these circumstances it is of vital importance in the interests of the whole world that this country, which has no interest of its own directly at stake, should present a united front, and be able to speak and act with the authority of an undivided nation. If we were to proceed today with the first Order on the paper, we should inevitably, unless the Debate was conducted in an artificial tone, be involved in acute controversy in regard to domestic differences whose importance to ourselves no one in any quarter of the House is disposed to disparage. I need not say more than that such a use of our time at such a moment might have injurious effects on the international situation. I have had the advantage of consultation with the Leader of the Opposition, who, I know, shares to the full the view which I have expressed. We therefore propose to put off for the present the consideration of the Second Reading of the Amending Bill – of course without prejudice to its future – in the hope that, by a postponement of the discussion, the patriotism of all parties will contribute what lies in our power, if not to avert, at least to circumscribe the calamities which threaten the world.'

When he sat down there was a look of bewilderment amounting to awe upon every member's face. I got up to go, but the fashionable females crowded round me, pressing close and asking questions.

'Good Heavens! Margot!' they said, 'what can this mean? Don't you realize the Irish will be fighting each other this very night? How fearfully dangerous! What does it mean?'

The Orange aristocracy, who had been engaged in strenuous preparations for their civil war and had neither bowed nor spoken to me for months past, joined in the questioning. Looking at them without listening and answering as if in a dream, I said:

'We are on the verge of a European War.'

* * *

The next day, Friday the 31st, while I was breakfasting in bed, my husband came to see me. Having heard in a general way that things were going a little better, I looked anxiously at his face; but he said that he himself had given up all hope, and left the room.

After a long Cabinet he lunched at the Admiralty, and went to Buckingham Palace, where he remained for over an hour with the King.

He arrived late at the House, having been kept by an interview with business men in the city.

'They are the greatest ninnies I have ever had to tackle,' he said. 'I found them all in a state of funk, like old women chattering over tea cups in a Cathedral town.'

He left me and hurried into the House to make the following statement:

'We have heard, not from St Petersburg, but from Germany, that Russia has proclaimed a general mobilization of her army and her fleet; and that, in consequence of this, martial law was to be proclaimed for Germany. We understand this to mean that mobilization will follow in Germany, if the Russian mobilization is general and is proceeded with. In these circumstances I should prefer not to answer any questions until Monday.'

I could see that, in spite of Henry's marvellously calm temper and even spirits, he was deeply anxious.

There are certain sorts of men who in times of crisis wonder what they themselves can get out of the situation; and could I but write frankly of the conduct of, not only one or two of the Colleagues, but of other men in the early days of the war, it would be interesting, in view of the stories current at the time, and the nonsense that has been invented since. But the sorrows of those early days, and the tragic events which led up to the war are too fresh in my heart for me to chronicle gossip.

Conversation at dinner in Downing Street that night was difficult, and whatever topic was started was immediately dropped. When we had finished, Henry went down to the Cabinet room and Sir Edward Grey joined us in the drawing-room. We sat and talked in a disjointed way, all sitting in a circle.

I watched Grey's handsome face and felt the healing freshness of his simple and convinced personality. He is a man who 'thinks to scale', as Lord Moulton once said to me of Rufus Reading, and obliges one to reconstruct the meaning of the word Genius.

In the middle of our languid talk, messengers came in with piles of Foreign Office boxes and he jumped up and left the room.

Mr Montagu (Financial Secretary to the Treasury) came in, and, after exchanging a few words, he seized me by the arm and said in a violent whisper:

'We ought to mobilize to-morrow and declare it! I wish X—— and Z—— could be crushed for ever! their influence is most pernicious: would you believe it, they are all against any form of action!'

'How about McKenna?' I asked; to which he replied:

'Oh! he's all right, and in perfect agreement with the Prime Minister. X—— is mad not to see that we must mobilize at once!'

'Don't fret!' I said calmly, 'neither X—— nor Z—— will have the smallest influence over Henry; his mind has been made up from the first and no one will be able to change it now.'

On Saturday the 1st we read in the papers that Germany had declared war upon Russia.

The Benckendorffs[1] dined with us that night and we had a lively altercation. He said that it was not the Kaiser but his War Party that had prompted the Germans to make this move. I disagreed, as I could not but think that the Kaiser, being the big figure in Germany, was unlikely to be influenced by his son or by any person or Party. I added impulsively that I was glad that we could act together as a nation independent of every other country, which was not very tactful, but I could not help thinking how much I would have disliked any alliance with a country as misgoverned as Russia, and remembered in that connection the saying that 'Britons never, *never* will be Slavs!'

We were still worried over the Irish question, and after dinner I wrote a line to Mr Redmond telling him that he had the opportunity of his life of setting an unforgettable example to the Carsonites if he would go to the House of Commons on the Monday and in a great speech offer all his soldiers to the Government; or, if he preferred it, write and offer them to the King. It appeared to me that it would be a dramatic thing to do at such a moment, and might

[1] Count Benckendorff the Russian Ambassador, and his wife.

strengthen the claim of Ireland upon the gratitude of the British people.

On Sunday morning, August the 2nd, he replied to me in the following letter:

'Dear Mrs Asquith,

'I received your letter late last night. I am very grateful to you for it. I hope to see the Prime Minister tomorrow before the House meets if only for a few moments and I hope I *may be able* to follow your advice. With sincere sympathy,

'I am very truly yours,

'J. REDMOND.'

'*Sunday 2nd August* 1914.'

After reading this I went with Elizabeth to the Communion Service at St Paul's. It was a relief to see children sitting as usual on the steps playing with the strutting pigeons, and as I walked out of the baking sunlight into the cool Cathedral my mind felt at rest.

I dropped Elizabeth at 10 Downing Street on my return and went across the Horse Guards to Carlton House Terrace to ask if I could see the Lichnowskys.[1]

It was the habit of the Germans to choose men of honour for their Ambassadors in London, and to appoint as first secretaries men versed in political intrigue capable of keeping the Kaiser informed of every facet of our domestic policy.

Prince Lichnowsky followed the footsteps of his predecessor, Count Metternich, and was a sincere and honest man. He had a pointed head, a peevish voice, and bad manners with servants. He combined in his personal appearance a look of race and a Goya picture. His wife was a handsome woman of talents and character, who from perversity, lack of vanity, and love of caprice, had allowed her figure to get fat; a condition that always prejudices me. But in Princess Lichnowsky I found so much nature, affection and enterprise that, in spite of black socks, white boots and crazy tiaras, I could not but admire her. She detested the influence of the Prussian Court; and the Kaiser – to whom her husband had always been loyal – was a forbidden subject between them.

[1] The German Ambassador, and his wife.

When the Prince first arrived in London, he told me that, on the occasion of his appointment as British Ambassador, he had said to the Kaiser that if he intended making trouble in England he had got hold of the wrong man. On hearing this, I asked if he thought there was much feeling against us in Germany; at which he assured me with perfect sincerity that the relations between the two countries were excellent; that there was a great deal of exaggeration in the talk, and that he himself had never observed any ill-feeling, but added with an innocent smile:

'Our Kaiser is a man of impulse.'

That Sunday morning I found Princess Lichnowsky lying on a green sofa with a Dachshund by her side; her eyes starved and swollen from crying, and her husband, walking up and down the room, was wringing his hands. On seeing me he caught me by the arm and said in a hoarse, high voice:

'Oh! say there is surely not going to be war!' (he pronounced war as if it rhymed with far). 'Dear Mrs Asquith, can *nothing* be done to prevent it!'

I sat down on the sofa and putting my arms round Mechtilde Lichnowsky we burst into tears. She got up and pointing out of the window to the sky and green trees said with impulse:

'To think that we should bring such sorrow on innocent happy people! Have I not always loathed the Kaiser and his brutes of friends! One thousand times I have said the same, and I will never cross his threshold again.'

Prince Lichnowsky sat down beside us in great agitation:

'But I do not understand what has happened! What is it all about?' he asked.

To which I replied:

'I can only imagine the evil genius of your Kaiser . . .' at this the Prince interrupted me:

'He is ill-informed – impulsive, and must be *mad*! He never listens, or believes one word of what I say; he answers none of my telegrams.'

I told him that Count Metternich had been treated in precisely the same manner; Mechtilde Lichnowsky adding with bitterness:

'Ah! that brutal hard war-party of ours makes men fiends!'

I remained for a few moments doing what I could to console them but felt powerless, and when I said goodbye to the Ambassador tears were running down his cheeks.

Mr Montagu dined with us that night. Though gloomy and depressed he was less excited than he had been on the previous Friday.

'Till last night,' he said, 'I had hoped against hope that we might have been able to keep out of this war, but my hopes have vanished. All the men I've seen feel like me except X——, who is intriguing with that scoundrel Z——. I asked the Attorney General yesterday what was going to be said upon specie in the House tomorrow, and he answered:

'"Don't worry! none of us can say at this moment what resignations the Prime Minister may or may not have in his hands at tomorrow's Cabinet." '

Feeling profoundly indignant I thought of saying:

'All right! You can warn these men that nothing will affect my husband; he will form a Coalition with the other side and then they will be done for'; but, as there was no one whose judgment I particularly valued on the Opposition benches, I refrained, and contented myself by asking if he really thought X—— and Z—— would resign at the next day's Cabinet. We were interrupted by O—— coming into the room, and, not having seen him for some days, and, knowing that he knew the inner workings of X——'s mind, I asked him if it was really true that X—— was intriguing with the Pacifists, to which O—— replied:

'He has always loathed militarism, as you know, since the days of the Boer War, and has an inferior crowd round him, but, until he knows how much backing he will have in the country, I doubt if he will commit himself.'

After what Mr Montagu and others had told me I felt full of anxiety when I woke up on the Monday morning and, thinking over the two Ministers most likely to resign, I wondered what line Henry would take in the Cabinet.

I had no opportunity of asking my husband on the morning of the 3rd about the resignations as I never saw him before I went to the House of Commons.

Our Foreign Minister was to make his historic speech, and when I arrived the House was crowded.

Sir Edward Grey rose and said:

[1]'Last week I stated that we were working for peace not only for this country, but to preserve the peace of Europe. To-day's events move so rapidly that it is exceedingly difficult to state with accuracy the actual state of affairs, but it is clear that the peace of Europe cannot be preserved.

'Before I proceed to state the position of His Majesty's Government, I would like to clear the ground so that the House may know exactly under what obligations the Government can be said to be in coming to a decision on the matter. First of all, let me say that we have consistently worked with a single mind, and all the earnestness in our power, to preserve peace. But we have failed because there has been little time, and a disposition – at any rate in some quarters – to force things to an issue, the result of which is that the policy of peace, as far as the Great Powers are concerned, is in danger. I do not want to dwell on that, or say where the blame seems to us to lie, because I would like the House to approach the crisis in which we now are from the point of view of British interests, British honour and British obligations, free from all passion. The French Fleet is now in the Mediterranean, and the Northern and Western coasts of France undefended. It has been concentrated there because of the confidence and friendship which has existed between our two countries. My own feeling is that if a foreign fleet engaged in a war which France had not sought, and in which she had not been the aggressor, came down the English Channel and bombarded and battered the undefended coasts of France, we could not stand aside and see this going on practically within our sight, with folded arms!

'I want to look at the matter without sentiment, and from the point of view of British interests, and it is on that that I am going to justify what I say to the House. If we say nothing at this moment, what is France to do with her Fleet in the Mediterranean? If she leaves it there, with no statement from us, she leaves her Northern and Western coasts at the mercy of a German fleet coming down the Channel, to do as it pleases in a war which is a war of life and

[1] I have only had space for a short transcript of this great speech.

death between them. If we say nothing, it may be that the French fleet is withdrawn from the Mediterranean. We are in the presence of a European conflagration; can anybody set limits to the consequences that may arise out of it? Let us assume that we stand aside in an attitude of neutrality, saying: "No, we cannot undertake and engage to help either party in this conflict." Let us suppose the French Fleet is withdrawn from the Mediterranean, and let us assume that the consequences make it necessary at a sudden moment, in defence of vital British interests, we should go to war:

'Nobody can say that in the course of the next few weeks there is any particular trade route, the keeping open of which may not be vital to this country. We feel strongly that France was entitled to know – and to know at once – whether or not, in the event of attack upon her unprotected Northern and Western Coasts, she could depend upon British support. In these compelling circumstances, yesterday afternoon, I gave the French Ambassador the following statement:

' " I am authorised to give an assurance that, if the German Fleet comes into the Channel or through the North Sea to undertake hostile operations against the French coasts, the British Fleet will give all the protection in its power. This assurance is, of course, subject to the policy of His Majesty's Government receiving the support of Parliament, and must not be taken as binding His Majesty's Government to take any action until the above contingency of action by the German Fleet takes place."

'I read that to the House, not as a declaration of war on our part, but as binding us to take aggressive action should that contingency arise.

'Things move hurriedly from hour to hour. French news comes in, which I cannot give in any formal way, but I understand that the German Government would be prepared, if we would pledge ourselves to neutrality, to agree that its fleet would not attack the Northern coast of France. I have only heard that shortly before I came to the House, but it is too narrow an engagement for us. And, Sir, there is the more serious consideration – the question of the neutrality of Belgium.

'Before I reached the House I was informed that the following telegram had been received from the King of the Belgians by our King George:

' "Remembering the numerous proofs of Your Majesty's friendship and that of your predecessors, and the friendly attitude of England in 1870, and the proof of friendship she has just given us again, I make a supreme appeal to the Diplomatic intervention of Your Majesty's Government to safeguard the integrity of Belgium."

'We have vital interests in the independence of Belgium. If she is compelled to submit to her neutrality being violated, the situation is clear. Even if by agreement she admitted the violation of her neutrality, she could only do so under duress. The one desire of the Smaller States is that they should be left alone and independent. The one thing they fear is, I think, not so much that their integrity but that their independence should be interfered with. If, in this war which is before Europe, the neutrality of one of those countries is violated, and no action be taken to resent it, at the end of the war, whatsoever the integrity may be, the independence will be gone. It may be said, I suppose, that we might stand aside, husband our strength, and, whatever happened in the course of this war, at the end of it intervene with effect to put things right; but for us, with a powerful Fleet, which we believe able to protect our commerce, our shores, and our interests, we shall suffer but little more if we engage in war than if we stand aside.

'We are going to suffer terribly in either case. Foreign trade is going to stop, not because the routes are closed, but because there is no trade at the other end. Continental nations with all their populations, energies, and wealth, engaged in a desperate struggle, cannot carry on the trade with us that they are carrying on in times of peace. I do not believe for a moment that at the end of this war, even if we stood aside, we should be in a position to use our force decisively to undo what had happened, or prevent the whole of the West of Europe falling under the domination of a single Power, and I am quite sure that our moral position would be such as to have lost us all respect.

'There is but one way in which we could make certain at the present moment of keeping outside this War, and that would be to issue a proclamation of unconditional neutrality. We cannot do that.

'The most awful responsibility is resting upon the Government in deciding what to advise. We have disclosed the issue and made clear to the House, I trust, that should the situation develop we will face it. How hard, how persistently, and how earnestly we strove for peace last week, the House will see from the papers that will be put before it; but that is over. If, as seems probable, we are forced to take our stand upon the issues that I have put before the House, then I believe when the country realizes what is at stake, and the magnitude of the impending dangers, we shall be supported throughout, not only by the House of Commons, but by the determination, the courage, and the endurance of the whole country.'

Sir Edward Grey sat down in a hurricane of applause and the news of his statement instantly spread all over London.

When we returned to Downing Street the crowd was so great that extra police had to be brought from Scotland Yard to clear the way for our motor. I looked at the excited cheerers, and from the happy expression on their faces you might have supposed that they welcomed the war.

I have met with men who loved stamps, and stones, and snakes, but I could not imagine any man loving war.

Too exhausted to think I lay sleepless in bed.

Bursts of cheering broke like rockets in a silent sky, and I listened to snatches of 'God Save the King' shouted in front of the Palace all through the night.

*   *   *

DECLARATION OF WAR
Tuesday, August 4th, 1914

Downing Street was full of anxious and excited people as we motored to the House of Commons the next day: some stared, some cheered, and some lifted their hats in silence.

I sat breathless with my face glued to the grille of the gallery when my husband rose to announce that an ultimatum had been sent to Germany. He said:

'In conformity with the statement of policy made here by my right hon. friend the Foreign Secretary, yesterday, a telegram was early this morning sent by him to our Ambassador in Berlin. It was to this effect:

' "The King of the Belgians has made an appeal to His Majesty the King for diplomatic intervention on behalf of Belgium. His Majesty's Government are also informed that the German Government has delivered to the Belgian Government a Note proposing friendly neutrality entailing free passage through Belgian territory and promising to maintain the independence and integrity of the Kingdom and its possessions, at the conclusion of peace; threatening in case of refusal to treat Belgium as an enemy. We also understand that Belgium has categorically refused this as a flagrant violation of the law of nations. His Majesty's Government are bound to protest against this violation of a Treaty to which Germany is a party in common with themselves, and must request an assurance that the demand made upon Belgium may not be proceeded with, and that her neutrality will be respected by Germany. You should ask for an immediate reply."

'We received this morning from our Minister at Brussels the following telegram:

' "German Minister has this morning addressed Note to the Belgian Minister for Foreign Affairs stating that, as Belgian Government have declined the well-intended proposals submitted to them by the Imperial Government, the latter will, deeply to their regret, be compelled to carry out, if necessary by force of arms, the measures considered indispensable in view of the French menaces."

'Simultaneously – almost immediately afterwards – we received from the Belgian Legation here in London the following telegram:

' "General staff announces that territory has been violated at Gemmenich (near Aix-la-Chapelle)."

'Subsequent information tends to show that the German force has penetrated still further into Belgian territory. We also received this morning from the German Ambassador here the telegram sent to him by the German Foreign Secretary, and communicated by the Ambassador to us. It is in these terms:

' "Please dispel any mistrust that may subsist on the part of the British Government with regard to our intentions by repeating most positively formal assurance that, even in the case of armed conflict

with Belgium, Germany will under no pretence whatever annex
Belgian territory. Sincerity of this declaration is borne out by the
fact that we solemnly pledged our word to Holland strictly to
respect her neutrality. It is obvious that we could not profitably
annex Belgian territory without making, at the same time, territorial
acquisitions at expense of Holland. Please impress upon Sir E. Grey
that German Army could not be exposed to French attack across
Belgium, which was planned according to absolutely unimpeachable
information. Germany had consequently to disregard Belgian neutrality, it being for her a question of life or death to prevent French
advance" '.

Henry paused after this and then said in a slow, loud voice:

'I have to add on behalf of His Majesty's Government: We cannot regard this as in any sense a satisfactory communication. We have,
in reply to it, repeated the request we made last week to the German
Government, that they should give us the same assurance in regard
to Belgian neutrality as was given to us and to Belgium by France
last week. We have asked that a reply to that request, and a satisfactory answer to the telegram of this morning – which I have read
to the House – should be given before midnight.'

I looked at the House, which was packed from gallery to floor
while my husband was speaking, and through misty eyes the heads
of the listening members appeared to me as if bowed in prayer.

. . . *'A satisfactory answer before midnight . . .'*

These fateful and terrible words were greeted by wave upon
wave of cheering, which continued and increased as Henry rose and
walked slowly down the floor of the House.

Few understood why he went down to the Bar, and when he
turned and faced the Speaker, excitement knew no bounds.

I quote from Hansard:

'THE PRIME MINISTER at the Bar acquainted the House that he had
a message from His Majesty, signed by His Majesty's own hand, and
he presented the same to the House, and it was read by Mr Speaker
(all the Members of the House being uncovered), and it is as followeth:

' "GEORGE R.I.—The present state of public affairs in Europe
constituting in the opinion of His Majesty a case of great emergency
within the meaning of the Acts of Parliament in that behalf, His

Majesty deems it proper to provide additional means for the Military Service, and therefore, in pursuance of these Acts, His Majesty has thought it right to communicate to the House of Commons that His Majesty is, by proclamation, about to order that the Army Reserve shall be called out on permanent service, that soldiers who would otherwise be entitled, in pursuance of the terms of their enlistment, to be transferred to the Reserve shall continue in Army Service for such period not exceeding the period for which they might be required to serve if they were transferred to the Reserve and called out for permanent service as to His Majesty may seem expedient, and that such directions as may seem necessary may be given for embodying the Territorial Force and for making such special arrangements as may be proper with regard to units or individuals whose services may be required in other than a military capacity." '

When the Speaker had finished reading the King's message all the members poured out of the House, and I went down to the Prime Minister's room.

Henry looked grave and gave me John Morley's letter of resignation, saying:

'I shall miss him very much; he is one of the most distinguished men living.'

For some time we did not speak. I left the window and stood behind his chair:

'So it is all up?' I said.

He answered without looking at me:

'Yes, it's all up.'

I sat down beside him with a feeling of numbness in my limbs and absently watched through the half-open door the backs of moving men. A secretary came in with Foreign Office boxes, he put them down and went out of the room.

I looked at the children asleep after dinner before joining Henry in the Cabinet room. Lord Crewe and Sir Edward Grey were already there and we sat smoking cigarettes in silence; some went out, others came in; nothing was said.

The clock on the mantelpiece hammered out the hour, and when the last beat of midnight[1] struck it was as silent as dawn.

[1] The ultimatum in fact expired at 11 p.m. G.M.T.

We were at War.

I left to go to bed, and, as I was pausing at the foot of the staircase, I saw Winston Churchill with a happy face striding towards
the double doors of the Cabinet room.

*　　　*　　　*

On the morning of 6th August, my husband had it announced
in the papers that Lord Kitchener had become Secretary of State
for War, and in the afternoon I went to the House of Commons to
hear him move his Motion for a vote of credit of £100,000,000.
I will quote some of his speech.

'I do not propose to traverse the ground which was covered by
my right hon. friend the Foreign Secretary. He stated the ground
upon which with the utmost reluctance His Majesty's Government
have been compelled to put this country in a state of war with what
for many years and indeed in generations past has been a friendly
Power. If I am asked what we are fighting for I reply in two sentences. In the first place to fulfil a solemn international obligation,
which no self-respecting man could possibly have repudiated.
Secondly, we are fighting to vindicate the principle which, in these
days, when force seems to be the dominant influence in the development of mankind, we are not to be crushed, by the arbitrary will of
an overmastering Power. I do not believe any nation ever entered
into a great controversy with a clearer conscience. With a full
conviction, not only of the wisdom and justice, but of the obligations
which lay upon us to challenge this great issue, we are entering into
the struggle. Let us now make sure that all the resources, not only
of this United Kingdom, but of the vast Empire of which it is the
centre, shall be thrown into the scale, and it is with that object that
I am now about to ask this Committee to give the Government a
Vote of Credit of £100,000,000. I am asking also in my character of
Secretary of State for War – a position which I held until this
morning – for a Supplementary Estimate for men for the Army.
Glad as I should have been to continue the work of that Office, it
would not be fair to the Army, or just to the country, that any
Minister should divide his attention between that department and
another, still less that the First Minister of the Crown, who is

ultimately responsible for the whole policy of the Cabinet, should give perfunctory attention to the affairs of our Army in a great war. I am glad to say that a distinguished soldier has at my request stepped into the breach, and I am certain he will have with him the complete confidence of all parties and all opinions.

'I am asking on his behalf for the Army power to increase the number of men of all ranks, in addition to the number already voted, by no less than 500,000. I am certain the Committee will not refuse its sanction, for we are encouraged to ask for it not only by our own sense of the gravity and the necessities of the case, but by the knowledge that India is prepared to send us certainly two divisions, and that every one of our self-governing Dominions spontaneously, and unasked, has already tendered every help they can afford to the Empire in a moment of need. The Mother Country must set the example, while she responds with gratitude and affection to those filial overtures from the outlying members of her family.

'Sir, I will say no more. This is not an occasion for controversial discussion. In all that I have said I have not gone beyond the strict bounds of truth. It is not my purpose to inflame feeling, to indulge in rhetoric or to excite international animosities. The occasion is far too grave for that. We have a great duty to perform, a great trust to fulfil, and confidently we believe that Parliament and the country will enable us to do it.'

When Henry resumed his seat the whole House roared with applause and everyone was moved. I found myself speculating on when he could have prepared any of this speech (of which I have given but a short transcript). I knew he had been working most of the night as I had found him writing at two that morning. He told me afterwards that he had neither written nor prepared a single line of it.

On the 9th the King's Message to the Army and Lord Kitchener's Advice were published:

'LORD KITCHENER'S ADVICE
'The True Character of a British Soldier

'The following instructions have been issued by Lord Kitchener to every soldier in the Expeditionary Army, to be kept in his Active Service Pay Book:

'You are ordered abroad as a soldier of the King to help our French comrades against the invasion of a common enemy. You have to perform a task which will need your courage, your energy, your patience. Remember that the honour of the British Army depends on your individual conduct.

'It will be your duty not only to set an example of discipline and perfect steadiness under fire, but also to maintain the most friendly relations with those whom you are helping in this struggle. The operations in which you are engaged will, for the most part, take place in a friendly country, and you can do your own country no better service than in showing yourself in France and Belgium in the true character of a British soldier.

'Be invariably courteous, considerate and kind. Never do anything likely to injure or destroy property, and always look upon looting as a disgraceful act. You are sure to meet with a welcome and to be trusted; your conduct must justify that welcome and that trust.

'Your duty cannot be done unless your health is sound. So keep constantly on your guard against any excesses. In this new experience you may find temptations both in wine and women. You must entirely resist both temptations, and, while treating all women with perfect courtesy, you should avoid any intimacy.

'Do your duty bravely,
'Fear God,
'Honour the King.

'KITCHENER,
'Field-Marshal.'

I might have been reading an old Memoir of some great soldier had this appeared on any printed page a week before, but, in the short five days since the Declaration of War, one's mind had got attuned, and whatever you read or heard could not affect it.

In the course of that afternoon, I was summoned to Buckingham Palace to see the Queen; she asked me to sit with her upon a Committee to settle what needlework should be done to help our soldiers, and I went to our first meeting on the 10th.

A fine room was crowded with ladies of every shade of opinion, sitting round a large table; Peeresses and Commoners, journalists' wives and Ministers' wives, and an animated discussion took place on what form of needlework we should start all over the country. I suggested it would not be popular to do anything that would compete with the shops, and said I would undertake to make surgical shirts.

Lady Lansdowne sat on my right, and Princess Mary on my left, and next to her sat the Queen. Everyone was brave and cheerful but I felt horribly depressed, and after listening to a great many suggestions, some trivial, and some important, I returned to Downing Street where I had an appointment to say goodbye to Sir John French.

I found him waiting for me on my arrival and we had a long and memorable conversation. I asked him to give me any trifle that would remind me to pray for him, and I gave him a small silver-gilt saint which he put in his pocket.

I travelled north that night to join my little son on the Moray Firth. Before leaving for the train I talked to Henry in his dressing room.

I found him reading *Our Mutual Friend*. He told me he was going to read all the Dickens novels, as they removed his thoughts if only for a short time from Colleagues and Allies, and we went on to discuss his Cabinet.

In reading my diary today, in which I record the whole of this conversation, I am struck by the insight he shewed upon that occasion about the men who were working both for and against us, in and out of the Cabinet, and could almost wish he had been less patient with some of the Colleagues he criticized. When I alluded to the recognized brilliance of two of them, he said:

'I could do with less cleverness: and should feel no anxiety if I had a few more Crewes and Greys. In public politics as in private life, character is better than brains, and loyalty more valuable than either; but,' he added, 'I shall have to work with the material that has been given to me! Dictatorships generally end in disaster.'

I received the following letter forwarded from 10 Downing Street, when I was in Scotland:

'94 LANCASTER GATE, W.,
'AUGUST 10TH, 1914

'My Dear Mrs Asquith,

I have cut the *A.D.C. General* badges off my horsecloth and enclose them. It is the sort of thing you said – in your great kindness
of heart – you would like. I am not going to say "Good-bye" but
"Au revoir". Thank you a thousand times for your kind and
affectionate friendship.

'Yours,

'J. D. P. FRENCH.'

I will end this chapter by quoting an account out of my diary of
the only visit I paid to the Front in the Great War.

*   *   *

*Henry and I went to Hackwood to stay with Lord Curzon to
meet the Queen of the Belgians and her children.

After dinner when I told her I thought the war would certainly
last over two years she was amazed and I could see she did not think
it would be half as long.

She asked me to go and stay with her in Belgium and see the
fighting Front.

There was a handsome Scotchman staying in the house, Major
Gordon, secretary to the Duke of Wellington, with whom I made
friends, and on hearing of Her Majesty's invitation he said he would
accompany me; so on the 10th of December, 1914, we started off
together.

I spent an uncomfortable night at the Lord Warden, and at
7 a.m. the next day Major Gordon and I crossed over to Dunkirk
in the Admiralty ship, Princess Victoria. I was too sick to see anything on the journey; but the captain told me that floating mines
and fear of German submarines accounted for our serpentine route
and our arrival being delayed by over an hour.

It was Arctic cold when we arrived, but I wore sensible clothes:
leather breeches and coat, a jersey over my blouse, a short serge
skirt, a Belgian soldier's black forage-cap and a spotted fur overcoat.
All very ugly but businesslike.

* From my diary, December 1914.

We took untold time to pass through the locks into Dunkirk Harbour. There we were met by a private chauffeur and the best Benz motor I have ever driven in, both smooth and powerful. Our Belgian drove us at a shattering pace on sheer and slippery roads.

Major Gordon was more than resourceful and kind: quite unfussy, and thinking of everything beforehand.

We drove straight from the Harbour to Milly Sutherland's[1] Hospital.

There among the wounded I saw Arab, Indian and Moor soldiers lying in silence side by side. The distant expression of their mysterious eyes filled me with a profound pity, nor could they speak any understandable language to their nurses or their doctors.

After leaving the Hospital we went on to the Headquarters of the Belgian Army where we were met by General Tom Bridges, "the heart and soul" as we were told of the Belgian Army and in many ways a remarkable man.

He gave us our passwords and passports for the next two days. "Antoine" from 6 p.m. to 6 a.m., and "Cassel" from 6 a.m. to 6 p.m.

We had a repelling meal in a dirty restaurant at Furnes before arriving at King Albert's Headquarters.

It was 4 o'clock and in drenching rain when we reached La Panne. The King's household received me with courtesy and cordiality in a brick and wooden house built on the sand dunes by the sea. The villa was like a lodging-house at Littlestone – pegs for hats and coats in a tiny hall, with a straight short wooden stair and no carpets. It was bald, and low and could only put up seven people – two men-servants, one housemaid, a cook and ourselves.

Comtesse Caraman-Chimay, the Queen's lady-in-waiting, is a delightful woman with fine manners and a great deal of nature and kindness. The Master of the Horse, M. Davreux – a cavalry officer in the Household – helped the servants to bring my things upstairs into a hideous bedroom, where I was glad enough to retire.

We messed in the kitchen. The only other sitting-room in the house was a warm, open-fired smoking-room where we sat after dinner. I was relieved not to have to walk in the rain 200 yards to

[1] Lady Millicent Hawes.

dine with the King on the night of my arrival, as I was too tired to move.

We dined early in fur coats, skirts and shirts; and all went to bed at 9.15 after an interesting general conversation upon the war and various other topics.

My bald bedroom had neither curtains, blinds, nor shutters, and I put on a jersey over my nightgown. On one side the windows looked on to a sort of sand railway, covered with trucks and scattered villas, and the other on to the sea. Telephone and telegraph wires connected all the villas together and glass doors opened out on to brick paths; the whole place was sunny but bleak, and exposed to every gale.

Luckily for me it was a glorious day when I woke; and I shall not easily forget the beauty of the beach in the early morning. I saw nothing but stretches of yellow sand, and shallow ice-white lines of flat waves, so far out that no tide looked as if it could ever bring them any closer.

Detachments of mounted soldiers of every nationality and every colour were coming and going on the beach, and an occasional aeroplane floated like a gull upon the air. Troops of Moors (Goumiers, as they call them) rode past in twos and twos, mounted on white and grey arabs, tattooing odd instruments with long brown fingers. Though picturesque on the beach, they looked as if they might be ineffectual in battle.

At 1.30 on December the 12th, the Belgian Commander accompanied me across the brick paths through the sand dunes to the King's villa. My coat was taken off by two footmen in black, and I was shown into the sitting-room, where I found a tall fair man studying a map, and leaning over a low mantelpiece. He turned round and shook hands, and we sat down and began to talk. I thought to myself:

"You are extraordinarily like your King", but I have often observed that Court people take on the look of their Kings and Queens, imitation being the sincerest form of flattery.

It was not till he congratulated me on having a remarkable husband, and alluded in touching terms to Henry's speech on him and the sorrows of Belgium that I suspected who he was. I instantly got up and curtsied to the ground, at which he smiled rather sadly, and, the Queen interrupting us, we all went into the dining-room.

We had an excellent lunch of soup, roast beef, potatoes, and a sweet flavoured with coffee.

I found the King easy and delightful; both wise, uncomplaining, and real. He has no swagger, and is keen and interested in many things. I told him I had bought several photographs of him to sign for me to take back to England, but they all had dark hair. He said it was clever of the photographer to give him any hair at all, as he was getting balder daily, and felt that everything about him was both dark and bald.

He told me, among other things, that the Germans had trained off to Germany all his wife's clothes and under-clothes, and all his own wine, adding:

"As I drink nothing, this is no loss to me, but it is strange for any soldier to steal a woman's clothes."

After lunch M. Davreux, Major Gordon and I motored to the Belgian trenches and on to Pervyse Station. We passed a dead horse lying in a pool of blood and heard the first big guns I have ever heard in my life; the sound of which excited and moved me to the heart. Aeroplanes hovered like birds overhead in a pale and streaky sky.

We passed a convoy of men with straggling winter trees upon their bent backs going to hide the artillery. For miles round the country was inundated with sea-water; and the roads, where they were not *pavé*, were swamps of deep and clinging mud. The fields were full of holes, and looked like solitaire boards. The houses had been smashed and gutted and were without inhabitants; only a few soldiers could be seen smoking or cooking in the deserted doorways. Every church was littered with bits of bombs, and *débris* of stained glass, twisted ribbons of molten lead, and broken arms of the outstretched Christ.

Major Gordon had brought a wooden cross with him to put on the grave of the Duke of Richmond's son, and I had taken one out at the request of Lord and Lady Lansdowne to put on their boy's grave at Ypres, where we ultimately arrived.

The Ypres cemetery will haunt me for ever. No hospital of wounded or dying men could have given me a greater insight into the waste of War than that dripping, gaunt and crowded churchyard. There were broken bits of wood stuck in the grass at the head of hundreds of huddled graves, with English names scrawled upon them in pencil. Where the names had been washed off, forage-caps were hanging, and they were all placed one against the other as closely as possible. I saw a Tommy digging, and said:

"Who is that grave for?" He answered without stopping or looking at me:

"For the next . . ."

Two English officers, holding their caps in their hands, were standing talking by the side of an open grave, and single soldiers were dotted about all over the cemetery.

Major Gordon, who had borrowed a spade, asked me if I would help him by holding the cross upright, which I was only too glad to do till we had finished.

All the time I was standing in the high wet grass I thought of the Lansdownes and my heart went out to them.

Suddenly a fusillade of guns burst upon our ears. It seemed as if some of the shells might hit us at any moment, they were so near and loud. Aeroplanes circled over our heads, and every soldier in the cemetery put on his cap and rushed away.

An excited Belgian officer, with a few other men, ran up to me and pointing to a high mound, said would I not like to see the German guns, as one could only die *once*.

As Major Gordon had left me to go to a further cemetery, I was glad enough to accompany them.

Frightfully excited and almost deafened by the Crack! Crack!! Crack!!! Boom!! Boom!!! I tore up to the top of the hill with the officer holding my elbow.

Had it not been for a faint haze over the landscape I could have seen everything distinctly. Thin white lines of smoke, like poplars in a row, stood out against the horizon, and I saw the flash of every German gun. My companion said that if the shells had been coming our way they would have gone over our heads; the German troops, he explained, must have come on unknown to them in the night, and he added he did not think that either the Belgians, the British, or the French knew at all what they were up to.

A French officer, looking furious, arrived panting up the hill and coming up to me said I was to go down and remain under the shelter of the Hospital walls immediately. Two Belgian soldiers who had joined us asked me if I was not afraid to stand in the open, so close to the German guns. I said not more than they were, at which we all smiled and shrugged our shoulders; and the French officer took me down the hill to the Hospital quadrangle, where I waited for Major Gordon.

The clatter of the guns was making every pane in every window shiver and rattle till I thought they must all break, and sitting in our motor, writing my diary, I felt how much I should have hated fighting.

A French sentry after eyeing me for some time came up and presented me with his stomach-belt of blue cashmere. I thanked him warmly and gave him six boxes of Woodbine cigarettes, of which I had brought an enormous quantity. A Belgian Tommy, on seeing this, took off his white belt and presented it to me with a salute which moved me very much.

I began to think Major Gordon must be killed, as he had been away for over an hour. The sun was high and when he returned his face was bathed in perspiration. He told me he had put the Duke of Richmond's cross on his son's grave in a cemetery so close to the German lines that he thought every moment would have been his last, and after munching a few biscuits we started off on our journey south.

On our way to Merville we stopped at Major Gordon's brother-in-law's house, a cottage at the side of the road. It was pitch dark and we had tea with him in the kitchen, lit by one dim oil lamp.

We had not been at the table more than a few minutes when a loud sound, like the hissing of an engine, made the whole cottage rock and sway.

I felt genuinely frightened and wondered what the children were doing at home.

'An aide-de-camp dashed out of the room and came back scarlet in the face.

"If you please, sir," he said, saluting: "four Jack Johnsons have dropped thirty yards from the door."'

General Nicholson jumped up white as a sheet and said to his brother-in-law:

"Great God, what will the Prime Minister say? I've let you in, my dear Gordon! . . . but I assure you, Mrs Asquith, we've not had a shell or a shot here for weeks past. . . ."

I reassured him as to his fears of my personal safety and asked him why the Germans wasted ammunition on such a desolate, inundated spot, to which he replied:

"Pure accident! But let me tell you, if there had been no water, not a brick in this cottage would have remained above ground, and neither you nor I would have had an eyelash left! . . . Now, Dopp, give us the tea."

After leaving our host we pursued our journey and arrived at Merville, where I was the only woman among 20 men who sat down to dinner that night with General Sir Henry Rawlinson.

It is always a surprise to an amateur why Generals and Ministers have such large staffs, and I have often wondered if they are kept for ornament, companionship, or use; but expect it is an unconscious form of vanity. All the time my husband was Prime Minister he never took a secretary away with him either at home or abroad, but in old days I have known idle and rich young men travel with a loader, a valet, a secretary, a coiffeur and a chiropodist.

Sir Henry and I knew each other hunting in Leicestershire and he received us with cordial hospitality. He not only gave us an excellent dinner – which was very welcome, as, except for tea and biscuits, we had had nothing to eat since the early morning – but he gave up his own bedroom and bath to me, an act of courtesy for which I shall ever be grateful.

I was glad to observe how popular my chaperon, Major Gordon, was wherever we went – nor was I surprised, as a better looking, better hearted, more capable and devoted person I have seldom met.

We left Merville on December the 14th, at 7.30 in the morning, and arrived at Havre that night.

On looking at the boisterous, choppy sea I made up my mind that nothing would induce me to spend twelve hours upon it, so after a peaceful night we motored back to Boulogne, starting at 7 a.m. and got back the same night to London.*

* End of diary quotation.

XX · *The Coalition*
and Mr Asquith's Resignation

━━━━◦◦⊙◦◦━━━━

I cannot avoid writing, however perfunctorily, of some of the
events which led not only to the resignation of my husband but to
the downfall of a Party which had smashed the Unionists in 1906
by the biggest majority ever known, which had won three successive
General Elections, and which had been led for a longer period than
any in our political history by the same Prime Minister.

This is a matter of such delicacy that for obvious reasons I shall
not always be able to give the names of those chiefly concerned, nor
shall I deal in any great detail with the matter.

In times of great physical and moral strain, or intense mental
excitement, trifles become portents.

In the year 1915 the recurring failures of our Offensive, and want
of proper co-ordination in the General Staff, provoked adverse
criticism of the conduct of the war. The silence so conspicuous in
1914 had disappeared, and the patience of the public was ebbing.

It was at this moment that the lie that sinketh was spread.

'Wait and see' – a phrase originally uttered as a threat by my
husband in the House of Commons – was taken up by a group of
influential newspapers, and quoted upon every occasion as meaning
apathy and delay. It is not difficult to preceive the prejudice this
created in the minds of men and women whose brothers, sons and
lovers were being killed in a conflict that touched our shores; and
it gave a great opening to self-seeking men who fancied that if they
were in the position of Prime Minister things would be very different.

In years of War the Press if it desires to inflame the rabble-rousers
has powers which it possesses at no other time, and, in criticizing
the patriotism, one must make allowances for the disappointment

of Correspondents who were not only severely censored at home but were forbidden to go to the Front. The irritation this produced was shown by a stream of abuse, and a deliberate desire to alarm the public at the expense of the Prime Minister.

It is an easy matter to frighten people. By gazing at a chimney pot you can collect a crowd in a street; by shouting 'Fire!' you can kill people in a theatre; and if twenty or thirty papers write daily that the War Office is incompetent, the Foreign Office misled, and the Prime Minister asleep, they will be believed.

A certain air of authority was given to this abuse, as these papers having received private information of Cabinet decisions before the decisions could reach any of the Allies, were able to announce that they had forestalled the Prime Minister and to congratulate themselves on hastening up his 'wait and see' methods. So persistently was this campaign pursued that several donkeys wrote signed letters to *The Times* praising it for its God-like prescience. I also had my social and political enemies, and will quote what I wrote in my diary at that time:

*'The D——ss of W—— and others continue spreading amazing lies about me and mine: they would be grotesque if they were not so vile.

'Elizabeth is in turn engaged to a German Admiral or a German General; Henry has shares in Krupps; I "feed Prussian prisoners with every dainty and comestible", and play lawn tennis with them at Donnington Hall – a place whose very whereabouts is unknown to me.

'These private fabrications are not only circulated but believed, and, had it not been for my receiving £1,000 for a libel action which I took in the Law Courts against the Globe Newspaper, the whole of our thoughtful Press would have published them. As it is, they mutter incantations about the "Hidden Hand," "Apathy in high places," etc., and, like Pilate "willing to content the people," Barabbas is released.

'I am told by John Morley and other students of History that no greater campaign of calumny was ever conducted against one man than that which has been, and is being, conducted against my hus-

* From my diary, 1915.

band today. When I point out with indignation that someone in the Cabinet is betraying secrets, I am counselled to keep calm. Henry is as indifferent to the Press as St Paul's Cathedral is to midges, but I confess that I am not! and I only hope the man responsible for giving information to Lord N—— will be heavily punished: God may forgive him; I never can.'*

As Lord Kitchener, Sir Edward Grey and my husband were the most powerful men in the Government, they were the chief victims of this abuse. Had they been as sensitive to the papers as Lord Rosebery, Lord Derby, or Lord Curzon, some effort might have been made to stop the divulgence of Cabinet secrets, but they were harassed with work, and only thinking of how to keep the Allies together and win the war.

We should never have been told to love our neighbours in the Bible had it not been a matter of difficulty: and, although it is probable that if we could have given more information and with greater rapidity of what was happening at the Front we should have satisfied people at home, it was impossible to let the public into our confidence when working with Allies as different from ourselves as the French, the Russians, and the Italians. Violent quarrels in what is called 'the Silent Service', intrigue in the Army, and disloyalty at home, obliged us to form the Coalition of 1915.

Men's minds were distraught, their nerves shattered, and their hearts broken by the tragic events that were taking place close to our shores, rumours of which were received on the same day, and the patriotism and reserve shown at the outbreak of war were gradually evaporating.

A Coalition may suit other nations but it does not suit Great Britain. The Parliamentary groups which govern France and other countries do not lend themselves to stability, and we have lived to see the failure of trying to govern men either by Autocracy or Bureaucracy.

In England we have evolved for ourselves from long political experience the system of Party Government by a corporate conscience which we not only understand but which has been the envy of the world. The *esprit de corps* which is essential in a Cabinet

* End of diary quotation.

presents no attractions to a Coalition, and ours was conspicuously lacking in it.

Intrigue of every kind arose, due to the impatience of the frightened, the credulity of the fools, and the ambition of our friends.

Some men and women not only like but live upon Gossip. With a smile of welcome they proffer you one hand while concealing a stiletto in the other, and, without knowing it, the whole tenor of their talk is bearing false witness against their neighbours. These are they who sin against the Holy Ghost.

My husband, although an excellent judge of men and events, despised suspicion, and abhorred intrigue.

I read the following sentence somewhere:

'Suspicions are like bats amongst birds, they ever fly by twilight'; and it was not until the 1st July 1915, that I realized there was a deliberate attempt being made by the Press and certain persons to entangle the Prime Minister in a mischievous personal controversy.

On the 1st July 1915, a friend of Mr Lloyd George's and a Member of Parliament moved a resolution in the House that it would be expedient that all powers exercised by the Ordnance Department of the War Office – under the control of General von Donop – in respect of the supply of munitions of war should be transferred to the new Ministry of Munitions then under the command of Mr Lloyd George.

In the course of a violent attack upon the Government he said that:

'By its scandalous neglect of the most elementary considerations of warfare and its innumerable blunders it had seriously endangered the security of the country'; and wound up a virulent speech with:

'The history of the Ordnance Department is failure in the past, chaos in the present and hopelessness for the future. We demand that the new Ministry should assume all the power of this Department in regard to the supply of munitions and that the Ordnance Department should be robbed of every vestige of its authority.'

The Times, being the only paper to publish a verbatim report the next morning, must have been given that speech before it was delivered, and the author dined with Mr Lloyd George on the night of the attack.

Private Members being commissioned to defame the Prime

Minister, in conjunction with a group of hostile papers, was not only a new form of propaganda in our political history, but if sufficiently indulged in would bring all Parliamentary Government to an end.

A few days later (on the 5th July) Lord Haldane made a speech warmly defending General von Donop from the inaccurate and unjustifiable abuse which had been showered upon him. He observed that it is not in accordance with British ideas of fair play to attack a Civil Servant who from the nature of his position is unable to defend himself; and pointed out that the Committee appointed as recently as October to look into the matter of shells had not only gone thoroughly into the matter, but included Mr Lloyd George himself, and ended by saying:

'Had the order for shells then given by the Government been carried out, we should have had a very large surplus today'.

This speech nettled the pioneers and was promptly answered. On the 8th, Mr Lloyd George issued a statement to the papers in which he said:

'Lord Haldane's version of what took place some months ago at a Committee of the Cabinet on Arms is incomplete and in some material respects inaccurate. At the proper time it will be necessary to go more fully into the matter, though Mr Lloyd George hopes that he will not be driven to do so at this stage. But he would like to point out that the very fact of this conflict of memory having arisen shows the unwisdom of these partial and unauthorized disclosures of the decisions of highly confidential Committees of the Cabinet.'

Here Mr Lloyd George was right. Nothing of a confidential nature should ever be disclosed, either in public or in private, and whoever flattered the Press by giving away Cabinet Secrets at that time showed personal treachery of a kind fortunately rare in British politics; but he was wrong about Lord Haldane's memory.

I wrote to congratulate Haldane on his courage, and in his answer, which I received the same day (the 8th July 1915), he ended:

'So long as I have breath in my body officers who are misrepresented in public and are unable to defend themselves shall not be attacked with impunity.'

On the 10th he came to see me and said:

'X—— and Co. are out to smash the Prime Minister, but Grey and I intend to stand on each side of him to protect him from such baseness.'

A few days before this Lord French had sent a message to ask if he could see me. We had not met since the formation of the Coalition, and, as the whole cruel campaign about the shells had arisen from someone at his Headquarters falsifying the truth by supplying the Press with misleading information, I was not at all anxious to meet him; but it takes me longer than most people either to suspect or to drop old friends, so I gave way.

Confronted by my questions, Lord French blandly denied all knowledge of the shell affair, but he appeared dejected and confused, and after a painful interview we parted.

Haunted by his look of misery and knowing what he must be suffering over the war, I wrote him a letter to wish him 'God-speed', and this is his answer:

> 'HEADQUARTERS,
> 'BRITISH ARMY,
> 'FRANCE
> 'JULY 13TH, 1915

'My Dear Mrs Asquith,

'I am sending one line by F. Guest to thank you for the very kind letter I got from you before I left England the other day. It was so nice and kind of you to let me see you, and I loved having a talk with you although you gave me a terrible "Damning!" We were delighted to have the Prime Minister with us again. Please write me a line when you have time.

> 'Yours always sincerely,
> 'J. D. P. FRENCH.'

This was followed up by several letters of such gratitude and affection to my husband and myself that, although I was puzzled, my suspicions were allayed.

It needs a mean nature to think of yourself when events of such tragic importance were taking place all over the world, and none of us were allowed to know at the time what Henry felt about the daily attacks upon himself. Through all those silent nights and waiting mornings, news of failure, and the anxiety as to the fate of his own sons, he showed an evenness of mind and sweetness of nature rare even in the most courageous. (Lord Kitchener said in his farewell interview with the King: 'I have never seen Asquith rattled: he is the best of the lot.')

My husband shook himself like a dog getting out of dirty water over the X—— episode, and the papers continued, adding to their personal abuse, glowing praises of Mr Lloyd George. This was so noticeable that even the *Morning Post* – a paper that has never concealed its loathing of the name of 'Asquith', wrote in the last week of July 1915:

'There are certain political intrigues directed to the replacing of Mr Asquith by some other politician, the origin and purpose of which are obscure; we will frankly confess that, while we are not numbered among the admirers of the Prime Minister, we would not think it any gain to see King Stork in the place of King Log.'

In quoting this I do not mean to imply that Henry was popular with the Unionist Party, but – difficult as it is to believe today – nor was Mr Lloyd George.

Col. Lockwood,[1] a genuine Conservative of the highest type, wrote in answer to a letter of mine:

'Did I not tell you how all would some day recognize how great a man your P.M. was? While I listened to his speech in the House of Commons the other day I wondered if some saw the light at last.

'Yours ever, dear kind friend,

'MARK LOCKWOOD.'

*   *   *

The night before the first anniversary of the war – the 3rd August 1915 – Lord Kitchener, Mr Bonar Law, Mr Winston Churchill, my sister Lucy and Lord D'Abernon dined with me: my husband and Elizabeth were to arrive the next day from the country.

Having heard of the death of Billy Grenfell,[2] I felt like cancelling all engagements, but fearing this would inconvenience my guests I went down to dinner with a heavy heart.

[1] Lord Lambourne.   [2] The Hon. William Grenfell.

In less than six months Lord and Lady Desborough had lost their two sons; young men of 25 and 28, who combined all that life can give of courage, brains and good feeling, and I could hardly think of them without tears.

I would like to write of these and others that I loved who were killed in the war: Charles Lister, John Manners, Edward Horner, George Vernon, Eustace Crawley and Rupert Brooke, but the list of the dead that I cared for and the parents I mourned with would be too long to put in any single volume.

While discussing the Grenfell brothers with Lord Kitchener at dinner that night, I said with impulse that I thought faith should be rewarded in this world by more knowledge, and that I longed for one glimpse of God's purpose – if only a gleam of hope as to our sure immortality. The expression on Lord Kitchener's face was one of puzzled kindness, and he handed me the port. To hide my emotion he turned abruptly to the table and, changing the subject, said we had only ourselves to thank for the failures in the war.

'The Germans attack us and we wait to counter-attack them. This is madness', he said: 'you must do it at once, while your enemy is exhausted, or, if you *can't*, you should reform your plans with deliberation and slowly; but to wait, and then counter-attack impulsively, is to court disaster.'

Mr Churchill asked him which he would rather have under his command, English, French or German troops: he said that after the English he thought the Germans were the best soldiers: Winston said he thought the French were superior; to this Lord Kitchener – who had fought in the Franco-Prussian War – demurred, but both he and the whole company were agreed that in attack the French Army had not a rival in the world.

We went on to discuss what form the Memorial Service for the anniversary of the war at St Paul's Cathedral should take on the next day. Lord Kitchener said:

'The clergy are the most conservative, tiresome, unimaginative men to deal with that I have ever come across; I suggested all sorts of things to them: proper hymns like "Eternal Father Strong to Save", and "Onward Christian Soldiers", but they would not listen to me: I want this service to be a great recruiting occasion. The

Archbishop could, in a short sermon, stir up the whole congregation, which would be a far better way of doing things than all this intrigue about Conscription.'

I was surprised to find that Lord Kitchener not only disliked intrigue but was averse to Conscription.

I am not going to write about the difficulties with the Colleagues and the Country over Conscription, but in this connection I would like to say that Mr Walter Long,[1] although a strong Tory, showed us a loyalty all that time which neither my husband nor I will ever forget.

The next day (August 4th) my husband, my sister Lucy, my son Anthony and I went to St Paul's Cathedral. In spite of soldiers, sailors, Ministers, Ambassadors, the crowd and the King, it was a disappointing service, and a great occasion missed. 'Rock of Ages' was taken at different paces by the choir and the congregation, the prayers were long, and the music meagre.

My thoughts scattered as I listened to the sermon, and I wondered if the ways of man were not as mysterious as those of God.

We were watching little States bargaining over land and begging for money. Labour quarrels and employers' profits; an English-speaking nation 'Too proud to fight'; and the only contribution of a great Church, the canonization of Charles the 1st – I thought of the Fighting and the Dead; of Julian and Billy Grenfell; of Lord Kitchener handing me the port; and came to the conclusion that, if it is hard to believe in God, it is no easier to believe in man.

*   *   *

Before I left London for Scotland in the late autumn of 1915, and after a painful political Session, I received a charming letter, dated 20th August 1915, from Mr Bonar Law in answer to one from me in which I asked him if nothing could be done to prevent Cabinet secrets being published in the Press, which I said was not only doing my husband and the Cabinet incalculable mischief, but hampering the conduct of the war.

'I am strongly of opinion', he wrote, 'that The Times should not be allowed to go on day by day discrediting the Government in a

[1] Lord Long of Trowbridge.

way which most certainly is damaging the country in the prosecution
of the war. There was an opportunity of raising the question in the
Cabinet today and I pressed it as much as I could. It was decided
that Carson and the Lord Chancellor should look into the question,
and I hope that it will be dealt with.'

The matter, however, never was dealt with.

On 5th July, I received a letter from Raymond Asquith,[1] written
from outside the Ypres salient, that curious strategic position that –
whether from British obstinacy or foreign pressure I do not know –
our Army occupied at such tragic cost and for so long a time:

'JULY 5TH, 1916

'Dearest Margot,

'I was delighted to get your excellent letter with its capital news
that Puff has got his scholarship; he will enjoy Winchester much
more than Summerfields. What you say of the snobbery of some
soldiers is appallingly true! If you look at any list of honours, it's
always the same story. The Dukes are proved to be the bravest
men of all, and after them the Marquesses. We've been having stirring
times these last months. We were rushed up in motor-buses in the
middle of our rest as an emergency measure to relieve the Canadians
after their counter-attack at Hooge. We took over what was in
effect a battlefield and an untidy one at that. Mined trenches, con-
fluent craters, bodies and bits of bodies, woods turned into a wilder-
ness of stubby blackened stumps and a stink of death and corrup-
tion which was supernaturally beastly. The Canadians fought extremely well and are brave and enterprizing, but they are deficient
in system and routine. No troops can be first rate unless they are
punished for small faults and get their meals with regularity. The
Canadians are frequently famished and never rebuked, whereas the
Brigade of Guards are gorged and d——d the whole time. We
stayed among the smells for a week.

'I had a narrow escape one night. I had taken a man with me to
inspect the barbed wire in front of our trench and when we were
40 yards out we found ourselves suddenly illuminated by a glare of
½ dozen German rockets. We bobbed down behind a lump of earth

[1] Raymond Asquith, 3rd Grenadier Guards.

and the next moment a bomb burst a yard away; I was spattered all over but not hurt.

'We have 10 more days to get through these two lines before we can change our linen or take our boots off; sixteen days without undressing is excessive in my opinion, but I suppose P—— S—— knows best.

'Love to you and Father.'

This was the last letter I had from him.

I will here quote from my diary.

*'On Sunday, September the 17th, we were entertaining a week-end party, which included General and Florry Bridges, Lady Tree, Nan Tennant, Bogie Harris, Arnold Ward, and Sir John Cowans. While we were playing tennis in the afternoon my husband went for a drive with my cousin, Nan Tennant. He looked well, and had been delighted with his visit to the front and all he saw of the improvement in our organization there: the tanks and the troops as well as the guns. Our Offensive for the time being was going amazingly well. The French were fighting magnificently, the House of Commons was shut, the Cabinet more united, and from what we heard on good authority the Germans more discouraged. Henry told us about Raymond, whom he had seen as recently as the 6th at Fricourt.

'As it was my little son's last Sunday before going back to Winchester I told him he might run across from the Barn in his pyjamas after dinner and sit with us while the men were in the dining-room.

'While we were playing games Clouder, our servant – of whom Elizabeth said, "He makes perfect ladies of us all" – came in to say that I was wanted.

'I left the room, and the moment I took up the telephone I said to myself, "Raymond is killed".

'With the receiver in my hand, I asked what it was, and if the news was bad.

'Our secretary, Davies, answered, "Terrible, terrible news. Raymond was shot dead on the 15th. Haig writes full of sympathy, but no details. The Guards were in and he was shot leading his men the moment he had gone over the parapet."

* From my diary, The Wharf, September 1916.

'I put back the receiver and sat down. I heard Elizabeth's delicious laugh, and a hum of talk and smell of cigars came down the passage from the dining-room.

'I went back into the sitting-room.

' "Raymond is dead," I said, "he was shot leading his men over the top on Friday."

'Puffin got up from his game and hanging his head took my hand; Elizabeth burst into tears, for though she had not seen Raymond since her return from Munich she was devoted to him. Maud Tree and Florry Bridges suggested I should put off telling Henry the terrible news as he was happy. I walked away with the two children and rang the bell:

' "Tell the Prime Minister to come and speak to me", I said to the servant.

'Leaving the children, I paused at the end of the dining-room passage; Henry opened the door and we stood facing each other. He saw my thin, wet face, and while he put his arm round me I said:

' "Terrible, terrible news."

'At this he stopped me and said:

' "I know. . . . I've known it. . . . Raymond is dead."

'He put his hands over his face and we walked into an empty room and sat down in silence.'*

*   *   *

I have outlined the beginning of the intrigue which led to my husband's resignation; but although I have kept a careful and precise record of all that happened in the last months and weeks of the year 1916 it is not my purpose to quote the conversations or correspondence either public or private that led up to the final event. Had it not been that we are threatened with the publication of several memoirs upon the subject I would not have referred to it at all. The anonymous volumes which have already appeared are negligible; as it is safe to assume, when an author is ashamed to reveal his name, the book is written either by a servant, a self-starter, or by prejudiced and confused eavesdroppers.

* End of diary quotation.

After Lord Kitchener's death in June a reconstruction of the Cabinet became inevitable, and when I heard who had succeeded him at the War Office I wrote in my Diary:

'We are out: it can only be a question of time now when we shall have to leave Downing Street.'

My opinion was shared by none of Henry's secretaries, and some of his family abjured me for them.

The trackless progress of intrigue interests people of different characters in varying degrees. To men like my husband, Lord Grey, Lord Buckmaster, or Lord Crewe, no one but the boldest or silliest would mention the subject, and the confidential few to whom I spoke met my fears with surprise tempered by disagreement. I felt a sense of acute isolation in those last months in Downing Street, while I observed what was going on as clearly as you see fish in a bowl.

In a book, entitled *The Pomp of Power*, which I have just received, I find a wholly erroneous account of what occurred in December 1916. On page 155, I read:

'Asquith came back on Sunday; and that afternoon the Unionist members of the Government wrote him that they resigned if Lloyd George did. In fact, they did send in their resignations, but withdrew them when Asquith replied that the matter raised by Lloyd George was not settled.'

None of Mr Asquith's colleagues resigned; nor did a single member of them write to him. No one was more surprised than his Unionist colleagues when they were summoned to a meeting suddenly and unexpectedly called on Sunday, the 3rd December – to which Lord Lansdowne was not invited. We were subsequently told that the written decision taken at that meeting was torn up on its way to 10 Downing Street, and all that we received was a verbal message to the effect that some of the Colleagues wished the Prime Minister to resign.

Given sufficient reason you will always find a high standard of honour among certain kinds of thieves, and personal ambition – after Love – is the strongest motive in life.

To bring off a big thing with success, you must not only be highly prepared and choose your moment, but you must be certain of your men, and nothing interested me more in those Autumn manœuvres than speculating upon the rewards promised, and the motives that moved the men who were engaged upon them.

Today I can write with calm of these events, but at the time of their occurrence I was shocked and wounded by the meanness, ingratitude and lack of loyalty shown to a man who in all the years he had been Prime Minister had disproved these qualities in a high degree.

Mr Lloyd George could never have formed his Government in the December of 1916, had Mr Balfour or the Labour leaders refused to join it. It is at least probable that neither Lord Curzon, Lord Robert Cecil, Mr Walter Long nor Mr Austen Chamberlain would have served under the present Prime Minister if their old chief had stood out at that moment, and I doubt if Mr Bonar Law or Lord Carson, even with the assistance of a large body of the Press, could have succeeded in the task.

To transfer the allegiance of the majority of the Parliamentary Labour Party from one combination to another was easier of achievement after the promises made than I had supposed, and Mr Balfour acquiesced. After this defection it would have been difficult, if not impossible, for my husband to carry on the Government.

The situation of our soldiers fighting abroad was too anxious to contemplate fighting for himself at home, and on the 5th, after consultation with other colleagues, he sent in his resignation to the King.

To a man of Henry's type, the knowledge of what others were suffering would always preclude him from thinking of himself, nor is it a topic he can ever be accused of dwelling upon. It is certain that one Prime Minister could not have retained office throughout the whole period of the War, and, as long as a war is won, it matters little to the right sort of Commander who claims the credit for it.

My husband fell on the battle-field surrounded by civilians and soldiers whom he had fought for, and saved; some of whom owed him not only their reputations and careers, but their very existence. Only a handful of faithful men remained by his side to see whether he was killed or wounded, and on the 7th December, Mr Lloyd George became Prime Minister.

XXI · *The Armistice*

When my daughter Elizabeth ran into my bedroom at midnight in her nightgown on the 10th November 1918 to tell me that the war was over, I felt as numb as an old piano with broken notes in it. The strain of four years – waiting and watching, opening and reading telegrams upon matters of life and death, and the recurring news of failure at the Front had blunted all my receptive powers, and what she said did not seem to penetrate me.

A young man from the War Office had rung her up to tell her that the Germans had signed the Armistice. I put on my dressing-gown and took her into her father's room, where we found him reading. Being far too excited to go to bed, we sat together talking over the probable terms of Peace till far into the morning.

After drinking my tea at 6 o'clock the next day and feeling too tired to write my diary, I lay awake reviewing the past and chronicling in my mind the many events that had taken place since we had left Downing Street.

The door suddenly opened and my husband came into the room to say that what we had heard and discussed in the middle of the night was inaccurate, as the Germans had not signed after all. I felt no surprise, but he had hardly shut the door before the bell of my telephone started ringing, and taking up the receiver I recognized the voice of my American friend, Mr Paul Cravath:

'The Germans signed the Armistice at 5.30 this morning and the War is over', he said.

I ran downstairs and gave orders for as many flags as could be bought, for the house, the roof, and the motor; and wrote three telegrams. The first was to the King, the second to Queen Alexandra, and the third to General Sir John Cowans; I took them into my husband's room and we signed them: 'Henry Margot Asquith'.

While reading the newspapers, odd noises from the streets broke upon my ears. Faint sounds of unfinished music; a medley of guns, maroons, cheering, and voices shouting 'The British Grenadiers', and 'God Save the King'. I looked out of the window and saw elderly nurses in uniform, and stray men and women clasping each other round the waist, laughing and dancing in the centre of the street.

It was a brilliant day and the sky was light.

Henry and I felt it our duty to attend the cremation of a relative, and motored to Golders Green immediately after breakfast. I had never been there before, and was struck by the bleakness of the ceremony.

Just as Railway Stations are man without God, so is the Cremation a funeral without a landscape. A button is pressed and an elaborate kind of casket – if less clumsy quite as costly as a coffin – disappears upon runners through the wall, and your mind, which should be bowed over the silence and inevitability of Death – as interpreted by the fine Burial Service – is alive and quickened by curiosity over the mechanism of the folding doors, and the subsequent consignment of the casket.

Nothing, however, could affect us seriously that morning. The whole thoughts of the scanty congregation were either circulating round the signatories of the Armistice, or centred on some nameless grave in France.

When we returned from Hampstead we could see the progress that the great news had made. Flags, big and little, of every colour and nationality were flying from roofs, balconies and windows. The men who were putting them up were waving their caps at each other from the top of high ladders, and conventional pedestrians were whistling or dancing breakdowns on the pavement; a more spontaneous outbreak of simple gaiety could hardly have been imagined, and I have sometimes wondered if any of the Allies on that day gave way to such harmless explosions of innocent joy.

We arrived at No. 20 and found that our thoughtful butler, with praiseworthy patriotism, had smothered the house in flags; even the Welsh harp could be seen fluttering greenly from the window of Henry's library.

I was told that in a short time it would be impossible to move in the streets except upon foot, as they were already jammed with wagons, trollies, motor-cars and coster-carts; and that the queues outside the shops which sold flags were of such a length as to block the passage of any passers-by. On hearing this I jumped into the motor and told our chauffeur to drive down the main streets so that I might see the crowd. It was a wonderful sight, and more like a foreign carnival than what we are accustomed to in this country. Heavy motor-lorries were flying backwards and forwards stacked with munition workers; males and females in brilliant colours were standing on each other's shoulders yelling and waving flags or shaking tambourines at one another. Everyone was nailing up some sort of decoration, or quizzing their neighbour. No one intended to work that day, nor could they be expected to when the whole world was rejoicing.

After lunch we motored to the House of Commons to hear the terms of the Armistice read by Mr Lloyd George.

Thinking the Speaker's Gallery would be crowded I went alone, but to my surprise it was almost empty and I wished profoundly that I had taken Elizabeth, as I enjoy nothing to the same degree without her or Anthony, and on such an occasion could have wished they had both been with me.

The grille of the Gallery having been removed I was able to put my elbows on the rail and watch excited members rushing through the glass doors into the House.

The Prime Minister and my husband received a great ovation upon their entry, and every man was moved when Mr Lloyd George rose to read the terms of the Armistice.

The French Army, led by their victorious Generals, was to march into Germany and occupy both the banks of the Rhine, while our soldiers were to guard over Berlin and other towns of importance. The entire German Navy was to sail into Rosyth between the lines of our men-of-war ranged up upon either side. We would watch from decks cleared for action battleships that had seldom left the Kiel Canal, thick with barnacles, and stripped of paint, slowly sail into harbour with all our guns pointing at them; and every soldier was to surrender his sword upon every Front.

I pressed my forehead into my hands and a wave of emotion moved across my heart. To the average individual the Terms that we had listened to were what had been expected; but I could only conjecture with compassion what they must mean to a proud race who, until 1914, had everything that industry and science could achieve, and had maintained a conflict for four years, in which they expected not only to beat France, but half Europe; and not for the first time I felt I was in a position to obey the High Command that tells us to extend mercy with judgment.

A thanksgiving service in Westminster had been improvised by the Archbishop of Canterbury, and when the Prime Minister finished speaking we all walked across Parliament Square to St Margaret's.

As I was alone I had to fight my way through the crowd, and, had it not been for a policeman who recognized me, I could never have got into the church.

After taking my seat, I observed that all the Peers and the Commons were placed in the centre of St Margaret's, and the women in the side aisles.

The Archbishop read a simple service in moving tones, and the whole congregation joined in singing 'O God our help in ages past'.

I thought of the chapter in Isaiah where it says:

'And strangers shall stand and feed your flocks, and the sons of the alien shall be your plowmen and your vine-dressers.

'For I the Lord love judgment, I hate robbery for burnt offering; and I will direct their work in truth, and I will make an everlasting covenant with them.'

I found my mind straying to the terms of the Armistice, and wondered whether the Germans also were saying their prayers; and if so to what God; the God of Peace, or the God of War?

When I returned to 20 Cavendish Square, my beautiful nieces, Laura Lovat and Diana Capel, were waiting to have tea with me. They described how they had spent several hours of the morning outside Buckingham Palace, where a crowd had collected the moment the maroons informed the people that the war was over. They said that everyone in London, rich and poor, fashionable and obscure, were standing and shouting for the King, and many of the spectators had tears in their eyes; that, when they left, the crowd was greater than when they arrived, and was accumulating every minute.

I told them that as I was engaged to go and see Lord Stamfordham I would have to leave them, and we parted after tea.

It was dark and wet when I arrived at the Palace, and the court-yard so packed with people that I had to get out of the motor and walk.

The King and Queen were sitting on a balcony exposed to the rain, and two dazzling stage reflectors illuminated their faces. The people below were shouting hymns or patriotic songs, and 'God Save the King' was being played on every kind of instrument. The W.A.A.C's and the W.R.N's were parading in close formation in the outer yard, and, when I stopped to look up at the King, their Commander-in-Chief, with the rudeness habitual to women in authority, hustled me unceremoniously out of the way.

The King was in khaki, a uniform which he had worn since the first day of the War – and the Queen was dressed in pretty light colours with diamonds and pearls round her neck. She has at all times a lively, lovely smile, and the public were cheering two very happy people that day.

Finding myself pushed about by female agriculturists, female soldiers and female police, I took refuge from the rain with the King of Portugal, who was standing in the Palace doorway.

After a little conversation with him, a servant showed me into Lord Stamfordham's room.

The knowledge that, to many, and very specially to him, the end of the War could not mean the end of mourning. I embraced him on both cheeks and after congratulating him on the love and service he had rendered to his King, we sat down unable to speak for emotion.

After a pause he told me that during Their Majesties' drive in the afternoon the poorest of the poor had clung to their carriage and by special request of the King had not been interfered with by the police. He said that nothing could have exceeded the enthusiasm of all His Majesty's subjects.

As boxes, telegrams and people came in and out while we were talking, and my friend looked exhausted, I left him.

The rain had not stopped when I walked out of the Palace, and the King and Queen were still bowing on the balcony (I was informed afterwards that they did not leave it till after midnight, except for their meals and their drive).

On the following day we went to the General Thanksgiving Service in St Paul's Cathedral.

Thoroughly exhausted, my thoughts strayed, and I was reminded of the American Ambassador's conversation with Elizabeth when, after a similar service had taken place the year before, upon the entry of America into the war (20th April 1917), my daughter had called at the American Embassy.

Mr Page was not only one of the wisest but one of the best of men. His lanky, dislocated figure was easily recognized, and the pathos, humour, and gestures of his face had gained him the confidence and delight of us all.

He will ever remain a hero in the minds of my countrymen, as we cannot but connect the illness which ended with his death as having been brought about by the continued efforts he made to bring his President and his people into the war.

Being a very great friend of ours, a few days after we heard that America had come in, my daughter Elizabeth went to see him. She was shocked by his appearance. Excitement and apprehension had protected him like a scaffolding, but when the strain was removed, the shakiness of the structure was revealed, and she saw without knowing it a doomed man standing in front of her.

'Dearest Mr Page,' she said, 'you look ill; you can see me any day, but send me away now, as I love you far too much to tire you.' To which he answered:

'My dear, it isn't talking to you that tires me; but I have received the Representatives of ten American Associations today, each of which has asked for a speech to be delivered in the Albert Hall. I said to them:

' "Gentlemen, we're under the very serious temptation of making fools of ourselves. It is a temptation that we shall probably not resist, therefore it appears to me that a service in St Paul's Cathedral would give us less opportunity than any other form of public ceremony." '

While my memory was straying upon this and other matters the service came to an end and we all hustled out of the Cathedral.

We had been invited to lunch with the King, an order we were proud to accept as we wanted to thank him in person for his telegram of the day before, and after leaving St Paul's we motored straight to the Palace.

There was no sign of fatigue in Their Majesties' faces when they greeted us, and the devotion shown by their subjects the day before had put them both in the highest spirits.

After kissing the Queen's hand, I said to her:

'You ought to be a very proud woman today, Ma'am, when all over Europe such sorrows are happening to Monarchs and Rulers, to feel how much you and His Majesty are loved by a free and happy people.'

I was touched to see her eyes fill with tears. The King took my hand in both of his, and said with that directness and simplicity which are peculiarly his own:

'No man, Mrs Asquith, ever had a better or wiser friend than I had, and *have* in your husband.'

A few days later, Henry seconded the address of congratulation to the King, which was moved by Mr Lloyd George in the House of Commons.

It was a great occasion, and one which he took advantage of in a noble speech. Rising after Mr George had sat down, he said:

'I am sure that the whole House will desire to associate itself with the admirable words in which my right hon. friend has moved this address, and with the terms of the address itself. When history comes to tell the tale of these four years, it will recount a story the like of which is not to be found in any epic in any literature. It is and will remain by itself as a record of everything Humanity can dare or endure – of the extremes of possible heroism and, we must add, of possible baseness, and, above and beyond all, the slow moving but in the end irresistible power of a great Ideal.

'The old world has been laid waste. Principalities and Powers, to all appearances inviolable and invincible, which seem to dominate a large part of the families of mankind, lie in the dust. All things have become new.

'In this great and cleansing purging it has been the privilege of our country to play her part – a part worthy of a people who have learned themselves beforehand the lesson to practise the example of ordered Freedom. The time has not come to distribute praise between those who, in civil life and naval and military action, have won this great victory, but, as my right honourable friend has well said, we can anticipate that task by rendering at once a heartfelt, unstinted tribute to the occupant of the Throne.

'I had the privilege to be Prime Minister when His Majesty ascended the Throne, and I continued to hold that office until more than two years had passed of the progress of the War. There is no one who can bear testimony – first-hand testimony – more authentic or more heartfelt than I do to the splendid example which His Majesty has set in time of peace, as well as in time of war, in the discharge of every one, day by day, of the responsible duties which fall to the Sovereign of this Empire. In the crash of thrones, built, some of them, on unrighteousness, propped up in other cases by a brittle framework of convention, the Throne of this country stands unshaken, broad-based on the people's will. It has been reinforced to a degree which it is impossible to measure, a living example of our Sovereign and his gracious Consort, who have always felt and shown by their life and by their conduct that they are there not to be ministered unto, but to minister.

'As the right hon. gentleman said, monarchies in these days are held, if they continue to be held, not by the shadowy claim of any so-called Divine Right, not, as has been the case with the Hapsburgs and Hohenzollerns, by any power of dividing and dominating popular forces and popular will, not by pedigree and not by traditions; they are held, and can only be held, by the highest form of public service; by understanding, by sympathy with the common lot and by devotion to the common weal. There are some lines of one of our old poets which are perhaps worth recalling, as they sum up and express the feelings of many of us today:

> ' "*The glories of our blood and State*
> *Are shadows, not substantial things.*
> *There is no armour against fate,*
> *Death lays his icy hand on kings.*" '

'And at the end of these fine lines he adds, what we in these testing times in Great Britain have seen and proved to be the secret and the safeguard of our Monarchy:

' *"Only the actions of the just*
Smell sweet and blossom in the dust." '

XXII · *The General Election of 1918*

⟶∘☉∘⟵

After the signing of the Armistice it seemed a strange moment for anyone to think of themselves, and, when I heard it rumoured that there was to be an Election, I did not believe it.

The defeated Party is apt to describe the General Election as an outrage; but I do not think anyone today would say the Khaki Elections of December 1918 had been other than a great political crime.

The chief blame of the 'Coupon' Election will be ascribed in history to Mr Lloyd George. It broke the historic Liberal Party to pieces at the moment when Liberalism – and especially British Liberalism – was most needed at Versailles. To this assassination, and the Coalition Government which followed, most of the disastrous mistakes of the succeeding four years can be attributed. The drowsiest summer owl might have observed that both the strength and the weakness of Mr Lloyd George lay in his having no policy. Neither his personal charm, infinite persuasiveness, the quick changes of an agile mind nor his eloquent speeches on the British aristocracy had captivated the confidence of the Conservative Party, and the Leader[1] of the Diehards, in a spasm of courage, wrote a fine letter to the *Morning Post*, saying there was something wrong with *their* Augean Stables and he thought that they should be purified. But the spasm passed, and a few days later, at a time when every moment was vital, and Peace was the Prayer of an exhausted Europe, he and the whole of his Party acquiesced in the *coup* of the coupon and we did what no other Ally thought of doing, we had a General Election within two months of the Armistice, *when men's hearts were tired, their minds confused, and the flower of the nation was still abroad.*

[1] The Marquis of Salisbury.

The French and British people encouraged by the patriotic cries of 'Hang the Kaiser! and make the Germans pay' – modestly followed by 'the man who won the war' – were convinced that Germany was to be crushed, and it was not until afterwards that they discovered the enemy was the Liberal Party.

I will quote from my diary what I wrote of the last day of the 1918 Elections.

*'This fateful day for us, opened by Henry, Gilbert Murray and Edward Grey going on a Deputation to convey to President Wilson the admiration they felt for his great Idea involved in the League of Nations.

'They started at 10.30 in the morning, and, when their interview was over, my husband and I motored through the decorated streets to attend the Guildhall, where a great company had been invited to see the Freedom of the City of London conferred upon the American President.

'We received a warm reception as we walked through the aisle of people up to the platform, and watched a ceremony with which we were all familiar.

'I sat next to Lord Cave, a kind and sensible man who had been strong enough when he was Home Secretary to oppose the meanest and most cowardly of all the Government stunts – turning men and women of German name out of this country, even when their sons had fought and died for us.

'In a short talk before the company was seated, he spoke with contempt of the methods of the Government, but in this he is not peculiar, as I never met a Tory who praised them. Every eye was upon President Wilson – a figure of world-wide reputation – who was seated next to his wife on a vast gold chair in the centre of the platform.

'I examined his lanky face, egotistical, slightly sensual mouth, and charming if too frequent smile, and noted the refinement of his brow and nostrils.

'He made an excellent though rather uninspiring speech, but, disliking oratory of the rose and sky type and the long pauses of the highly prepared, I admired the President's penetrating calm.

* From my diary, Saturday, 28th December 1918.

Each sentence was perfect in structure, and he might have sat down after any one of them. He spoke in a voice which everyone could hear, nor did he indulge in a quotable peroration.

'When I was praising this speech, in the interval between the Freedom of the City and the Mansion House luncheon, Mr Davis[1] said to me:

' "Yes, Mrs Asquith, I agree; Wilson doesn't pull many feathers out of the Eagle's tail."

'At this moment Henry came up and introduced me to the President, with whom I had a short but memorable conversation. I found him easy to talk to and much quicker than most of the famous Americans I have met.

'He told me that he had only got to express a sound opinion in a common-sense manner, and he was at once accused of being both unpractical and a dreamer; that obviously to prepare for another war was less practical than to prepare for Peace.

'When I was talking to him I wondered why he was so much disliked, and if he would not have had a larger following in his own country had he made a moral protest or pronouncement of some sort over Belgium in the early days of the war. The League of Nations, in which lie our best hopes, might have been less hated if it had been proposed by a man of indignation; whereas now it jars on America, infuriates France, confuses Italy, and is suspected in England.

'People say: "It's all very well, Wilson hasn't suffered in the War! *He* can dictate with his cool head and colder heart that a League of Nations, which includes Germany, will give us a Peace that we all want, or *ought* to want. But we'll never stand that! Germany must be made to suffer *all* and *more* than she has made others suffer. We must bring this home to her in *every* way, from generation to generation. We won't let America save Germany from the consequences of her defeat, or deprive us and the Allies of the consequences of our victory."

'The mistaken part of this reasoning is that there is no "Victory"; and the revengeful Peace for which men clamour means a return to old rivalries, and the subsequent preparation for War. As the Germans are the most orderly, scientific, and hard-working of the

[1] Mr Davis succeeded Mr Page as American Ambassador.

European races, Germany will ultimately suffer less than the Allies, and to what good purpose can be the perpetuation of Hate?

'I am only interested in the President inasmuch as he wants to rebuild a dying world instead of inflicting fresh wounds, and it matters little what instrument is used if it can fulfil this purpose.

'President Wilson is trying to emulate the famous saying of the eighteenth century:

' "Christianity has been tried and failed, the Religion of Christ remains to be tried."

'The Republican Party in America stand for many things with which I am out of sympathy, but I cannot believe their dislike of the President is entirely political. From what I hear he is an Egotist; uncertain in his personal relations because he is not grateful; and a man who trusts few and those mostly his inferiors.

'This last is what really counts: men who like their inferiors seldom achieve high purposes. Nevertheless, President Wilson will go down to History as having produced the only Great Idea in the War, and, after listening to one of the finest speeches that I ever heard in my life at the Mansion House lunch, I said to myself:

' "What is there that this man could not do, if his moral stature was comparable to his intellectual expression?"

'When he had finished speaking – knowing as I did that the Election returns might be out at any moment – I felt an apprehensive but burning curiosity to hear what had happened. I was about to ask a waiter behind me if he could find out some of the figures, when I heard a man say:

' "Herbert Samuel, McKinnon Wood, and Runciman are out."

'We left the dining-room and made our way down to the crowded front door. People waiting for their motors were standing in groups discussing the Election returns.

' "McKenna is beat: Montagu is in by over 9,000," was whispered from mouth to mouth, while the men thrust their arms into their coat sleeves changing their cigars from hand to hand in the process, and asking for their motors.

'The news spread; man after man of ours was out.

' Were we all *beaten?* . . . who *could* I ask? . . . who would tell me? Henry crushed up against me and said calmly:

' "I see our footman."

'Lady Cave pushed up and took my arm; I suppose I looked pale as she said:

' "You are a brave woman, don't turn a hair, the thing *can't* last, it's a disgrace, a fraud, and a sham."

'Among the crush in the large open doorway, waiting for his motor, I perceived Rufus Reading, looking snow-white. Did he or did he not know if Henry was beaten? . . . perhaps they all knew.

'I was jammed up against my husband and had no idea what he had heard.

'I looked at him out of the corner of my eyelids; he was standing a little in front of me, but not a sign of any kind could be seen on his face. A man pushed up to us and said:

' "Never you mind! the Elections have been fought on gigantic *lies*; no one could tell the truth, but it will come out some day, and I hope they will all be severely punished!"

' "Who are you?" I asked vaguely.

' "I've written on the *Morning Post* for 15 years," the man answered. "I'm a hot Liberal and believe in Asquith. He's the only man who ought to be on the Peace Conference. You stick to it! *and make him stick*, for if he is not put on the Conference this country is lost. God bless you."

'He slipped away – and after two kind squeezes from the Caves, and a lift of the hat from Rufus, we drove away in our motor, leaning back silent and exhausted.

'I saw as if in a trance the cheering crowds, eager faces, mounted police, and swaying people, while we shot down the streets with our minds set and stunned. Not one word did we say till we got near home; then Henry broke the silence:

' "I only hope," he said, "that *I* have not got in; with all the others out this would be the last straw."

' "I expect we're all out," I said: "they are sure to have sent us the figures to Cavendish Square from the Whip's Office, aren't they? or do you suppose they've sent them to The Wharf?"

' "We're certain to get the figures," Henry answered.

'The motor slowed down; we had arrived. I jumped out and ran through the open door in front of Henry; I found the odd man labelling our luggage piled up in the hall. Not a note or a message of any kind was to be seen.

'Henry went into his library, and I rang up 21 Abingdon Street on the telephone in my boudoir.

' "Not got in all the returns yet? . . . Yes? . . . All our Whips out? . . . *Yes?* . . . East Fife? *Yes?* . . . Asquith beat! *What??* BEAT?? Thank God. Thank God!!" I said and looking up I saw Maud Tree standing behind me. Covering her face with her hands she burst into tears and said:

' "Oh! I can't bear it!! darling, darling Margot!! it's NOT true!!"

'Still holding the receiver, I said:

' "Yes? Go on – Yes . . .Yes . . ."

'Henry came in and Maud left the room.

' "I'm out, am I?" said he; "ask by how much; tell them to give us the figures, will you?"

' "Give me the East Fife figures," I said, and taking a pencil wrote:

'Asquith 6994 – Sprott 8996.'*

THE END

MARGOT ASQUITH
1922

---

* End of diary quotation.

Index

INDEX